Knowing God's Ways

A user's guide to the Old Testament

Knowing God's
Ways

A user's guide
to the Old Testament

Patton Taylor

Scripture Union, 207–209 Queensway, Bletchley, MK2 2EB, England.
Email: info@scriptureunion.org.uk
Web site: www.scriptureunion.org.uk

ISBN 1 85999 349 4

Except where otherwise stated, Scriptures are quoted from the
New Revised Standard Version, Anglicized Edition © *1989, 1995* by the Division of
Christian Education of the National Council of Christ in the USA, 475
Riverside Drive, New York, NY 10115-0050 USA

British Library Cataloguing-in-Publication Data
A catalogue record for this book is available from the British Library.

Cover design by D'ART Design
Printed and bound in Great Britain by Creative Print and Design (Wales)
Ebbw Vale.

Contents

Preface

was Spring Harvest in 1996 at Minehead. I had been asked to lead
series of seminars on Old Testament hermeneutics. 'Herman Who?'
ked the Spring Harvest steward when he was told the title of the
minar!

The thinking behind this book began with those seminars. I
lieve there are many people who would love to spend more time
ith the Old Testament scriptures, but who are not sure how they
ould read and interpret the Old Testament books in the light of
le New Testament message.

I should like to thank the students at Union College, Belfast
vhere much of the material of this book has been 'tried out' in
asses and seminars) for their helpful comments and insights.

I would like to thank my wife and five children for their support
nd encouragement. My daughter, Victoria, typed much of the
anuscript. My wife, Marlene, is herself a gifted preacher and
acher – and she inspired many of the illustrations in the book! The
ook is dedicated to Marlene and the family.

I hope that all those who read this book will come to share some-
ing of my excitement and enthusiasm for the Old Testament
criptures.

James P Taylor
Union College, Belfast
October 2000

Introduction

The Old Testament: a fascinating world

The Old Testament contains some of the most powerful stories every told and some of the most profound literature ever written – and all the more wonderful because it is also the Word of God! It includes stories of war and conquest, love and passion, spies and intrigue, success and empire, danger and suspense, loyalty and betrayal – all the ingredients which make for exciting reading for people of any age or culture. We read of kings and rulers and also of ordinary women and men like ourselves whose lives have been used by God to change the course of history.

The Ten Commandments and the other laws in the early books of the Old Testament have become the foundation on which most of the legal systems of western civilisation have been built. The prophets challenge us on issues of social and political justice, as well as foretelling events far into the future. The Old Testament contains stirring poetry. In Psalms we find the cry of the faithful believer, sometimes out of tragedy and despair, sometimes in thanksgiving and praise – words which have proved a treasure house of assurance and hope for Jews and Christians across the centuries. The Song of Songs contains some of the most moving love poetry ever written. In the book of Job we discover a profound discussion of the purpose of suffering; it raises questions which have taxed the minds of philosophers since time began. No reader can fail to be moved by the tragic outpouring of human grief in Lamentations.

the Old Testament is anything but dull!

Bible books are not always thought of as something you can pick up and read and enjoy! But in fact the Old Testament is anything but dull! It has something for people of all ages and backgrounds. It contains stories often told to young children. It also presents material which theologians and scholars have grappled with across the generations.

The purpose of present book is to encourage you to read and to enjoy the books of the Old Testament for yourself and to help you to appreciate their relevance for life in the twenty-first century. In particular, I want to encourage you to read each Old Testament book as a *book* – right through from beginning to end – and not just to dip into them for a story here or a proof text there! Hopefully this book will help you to understand, interpret, and apply what you read, not just to your own life as a Christian but also to the major issues which we face in the church and world of today.

he Old Testament - a vital part of the Christian ible

he Old Testament is of immense importance for Christians; it lays ıe foundation for the gospel message. God communicates with us ırough the Old Testament on a whole variety of issues which are mazingly up to date. These include issues of economics, social ıstice, and political structures, as well as matters of personal faith ıd morality.

The Old Testament has sometimes been neglected by Christians r relegated to a 'second-division' status. Many people are familiar ith only a limited number of well-known passages. Preachers some- mes use the Old Testament as little more than a storehouse of lustrations for New Testament teaching. The result of this is that e miss out on much of what God has to say to us. It is important to emember that the Old Testament was the only Bible of the earliest hristians – and indeed of Jesus himself.

Right from the earliest days of the church, there have been those ho have wanted to jettison the Old Testament, rejecting it as sub- hristian or pre-Christian. This kind of thinking is sometimes called *1arcionism* after a man called Marcion who held such views in the ery early days of the church. From the outset Marcionism was ejected by the church as heresy, but it is sometimes said that 1arcionism is as alive and well in the church as it ever was! Certainly here are many Christians who in practice regard the Old Testament s secondary to the New.

Part of the reason for this is the time-gap of thousands of years etween us and the events of the Old Testament story as well as the ap of geography and of culture. As a result, parts of the Old 'estament can be difficult to understand without background :nowledge. I hope that this book will help you become familiar with he Old Testament world.

One issue that has undermined the Old Testament in the modern vestern world is the 'Bible and science debate', particularly with egard to creation. We will discuss this in the chapter on Genesis. Another difficulty arises from those passages where God demands .ctions which seem abhorrent from a modern western perspective, uch as the slaughter of the Canaanites in the book of Joshua. These ınd similar issues will also be discussed in later chapters, and hope- ully it will become clear that the mercy, love, and grace of God are as mportant in the Old Testament as they are in the New.

Jesus interpreted his whole ministry as the fulfilment of the Law, meaning the whole of the Old Testament message; and he emphatically said on one occasion: 'For truly I tell you, until heaven and earth pass away, not one letter, not one stroke of a letter, will pass from the Law until all is accomplished (Matt 5:18). Paul also says of the Old Testament: 'All scripture is inspired by God and is useful for teaching, for reproof, for correction, and for training in righteousness' (2 Tim 3:16).

The Old Testament – a library of different books

Sometimes we speak of the Old Testament as if it were a single book. In actual fact it is a collection, a library of thirty-nine different books. The word *Bible* comes from a Greek word *biblia,* which is a plural, meaning *books.* The Bible that we are accustomed to, with all sixty-six books bound together in one single volume, is in fact a very recent development – only possible since the invention of printing. Before then, the different books of the Bible would have been hand copied separately. In our English Bibles, the Old Testament books can be divided into several groups.

The first group consists of the first five books, from Genesis to Deuteronomy. These five books form what we call the *pentateuch* (meaning 'the five volumes'). The pentateuch begins with the creation of the world and other early events such as the flood. The beginnings of the Israelite people is then described, from Abraham down to the escape from slavery in Egypt and the wilderness years. The pentateuch also contains the Ten Commandments and Israel's other God-given laws.

Next come the history books, which carry on the story of Israel from the invasion of Canaan under Joshua, through the era of the kings of Israel and Judah, down to the devastating destruction of Jerusalem and the Temple by the Babylonians in 586 BC. The books of Ezra and Nehemiah record the eventual return of the Jewish exiles to Jerusalem. The book of Esther focuses on one famous episode in the history of the Jewish exiles under the Persian empire.

The poetic books form another group: Psalms, Song of Solomon and Lamentations. The wisdom books (also in poetic form) are Proverbs, Job, and Ecclesiastes. The final group consists of the books of prophecy, from Isaiah to Malachi, which record the lives, the preaching, and the writings of prophets across the generations.

The canon of the Old Testament

Out of all the books that must have been written across the years of Israel's history, some were chosen to be part of the Bible and others not. We actually know very little about the process by which books came to be accepted into what we call the *canon* (the list of Bible books).

When the Babylonians destroyed Jerusalem in 586 BC, most of the leading citizens were taken into exile. Seventy or so years later, a small number of Jews were allowed to return to Jerusalem, to reconstruct the city, and to rebuild the temple. It seems that it was in this late period, when the Jews were seeking to revive and preserve the faith of their ancestors, that the canon of Scripture was established. Some books which had survived from before the destruction of Jerusalem may have re-edited or expanded at this stage. Other books were not written until this late period, such as 1 and 2 Chronicles.

Indeed it was not until the Jewish Council of Jamnia, seventy or so years after the birth of Christ, that the Jews finally settled on the books that were to be regarded as Scripture. We believe, of course, that God inspired not just the original writing of the books but also this whole long process by which the canon was determined.

> It's not about finding coded or secret meanings hidden in the text.

Old Testament interpretation (or *hermeneutics*)

Part of the purpose of this book is to introduce Old Testament *hermeneutics*. This word comes from an ancient Greek word meaning 'interpretation'. Hermeneutics is about developing a *systematic* and *consistent* approach to interpreting the Bible and *applying* what we learn to the real-life situations we face in the world in which we live.

Hermeneutics is certainly *not* about finding coded or secret meanings hidden beneath the surface of the text. However, much of the message of the Old Testament is complex. Misunderstandings can easily result from the fact that it was written in an age and culture very different from our own. And with effort and study there is always the opportunity to discover yet more of God's message which is much deeper and richer than most of us have realised.

It has been said that you can prove anything from the Bible and indeed across the centuries people have used Old Testament texts to justify horrendous things – such as slavery and apartheid. Those who

did this were using a false hermeneutic. Many of the so-called 'sect
base their beliefs on texts which come from the Bible but which a
taken out of context and misinterpreted. So you can see how impo
tant it is that we should give careful thought to *how* the Bible shoul
be interpreted.

There are many laws in the Old Testament that we instinctivel
feel must apply to Christians such as the Ten Commandments an
the laws on sexual morality. But other Old Testament laws may see
of little relevance today such as the requirement to cancel debts ever
seven years (Deut 15:1), or the commandment not to mix tw
different kinds of cloth in the one garment (Lev 19:19). How do w
decide which laws are binding on us and which are not? This is
question of hermeneutics. Our interpretation has to b
systematic and *consistent* otherwise we just end up pickin
and choosing those biblical laws that suit us! If we adopt
pick-and-choose approach, then we actually rob the Bibl
of any real authority.

If we adopt a pick-and-choose approach, then we rob the Bible of any real authority.

Inconsistency can easily arise in discussion of mora
issues. Take, for example, the issue of homosexuality
Probably the majority of evangelical Christians believe tha
homosexual practice (as distinct from homosexual orienta
tion) is contrary to biblical teaching. One verse that is ofte
quoted on the matter is Leviticus 20:13, which prescribe
the death penalty for homosexual acts. This may sugges
that we should have laws against homosexual behaviour. But vers
10 of the same chapter prescribes exactly the same penalty for hetero
sexual adultery! Why is it that in the past we made laws for th
punishment of homosexual practice but did not also make simila
laws for the punishment of adultery? Why the inconsistency of inter
pretation?

I hope I have now said enough to illustrate why we need to giv
careful thought to hermeneutics – to a systematic and consisten
approach to interpreting and applying the Word of God to our lives
and to the world in which we live. One of the most fundamenta
principles of hermeneutics is that we use *Scripture to interpret Scripture*
We must always be prepared to rethink traditional interpretations
Remember how Jesus criticised the scribes and Pharisees because
they put their traditional *interpretations* of the Bible on the same leve
as the Bible itself!

The Old Testament as 'literature'

Each of the books in the Old Testament is a work of literature. Each had its own human author or authors. Each was written in a specific set of historical circumstances and with a particular message and purpose. Some of the books record events of the author's own time. Other books record events that took place long before the writer's time. Like any author, ancient or modern, the Bible writers would have had research to do before setting pen to parchment.

They would have listened to the ancient stories of triumph and tragedy that had been handed down by word of mouth from one generation to the next. We know from many cultures around the world of the great ability of master story-tellers to retell stories of amazing length with word-for-word accuracy. No doubt this was true also of the story-tellers of ancient Israel. Similarly, the book of Proverbs may contain proverbs which had been handed done for generations by the wise men of the towns and villages of Israel and Judah.

Eventually, of course, such material was written down. Archaeologists have shown that the ability to read and write was much more widespread at an early stage in Israel's history than was once thought. Religious centres were places where material was written down and collected. At a later stage, careful records of events would have been maintained by the scribes at the Jerusalem temple and by government officials. Many of these official archives would have been available to the writers of the Bible books.

In some cases we know very little of the particular circumstances in which individual Bible books were written or of the original audience for whom they were intended. I say *audience* because we can be certain that the Bible books were originally intended to be read aloud. The concept of buying a book (or borrowing it from the library), and taking it home to read, is a very modern one! In the ancient world, books were read aloud to groups of people. There may have been public readings at the village gates or in the town square or in the temple courtyard.

It is always important with any book to consider the *purpose* for which it was written. A great work of literature is written to communicate a message, to challenge and to inspire. A book may be written to preserve the memory of significant events that must never be forgotten and to draw out the lessons of the past. Books may also be written to challenge and undermine a corrupt religious or political establishment.

The books of Chronicles, Samuel and Kings largely cover the same period of history. Chronicles were written several centuries later than the others, when the circumstances and issues faced by the people were very different. The historical period which they described was the same; but the later author put a different 'spin' on the events, because he was writing for a different generation, who faced a quite distinct set of questions, problems, challenges, and controversies.

The writers of the Old Testament books were probably quite unaware that they were being used by God to write books that would one day form part of the Bible! They had a more immediate purpose in view. Seeking to understand that original purpose is one very important dimension of hermeneutics. If we have not made the effort to understand what the original writer sought to convey to the original audience, we will not fully understand what the books have to say to us in our contemporary situation.

Different types of literature

It will already be clear that the Old Testament contains many different types of writing. A basic distinction is that between prose and poetry. As you will probably remember from school, poetry requires a different style of interpretation from prose.

The word *genre* is the term used for a specific type and style of writing which is customary for a particular purpose. In our modern context, a newspaper is written in quite a different style from that of a school textbook, which in turn is quite different from a novel. These are different *genres*. Each genre has its own distinctive features. If a story begins with the words 'once upon a time', then we know that it belongs to the genre of fairy tale. A headline is a clear distinguishing feature of a newspaper.

The Old Testament world had its own genres. Indeed, if we misunderstand the genre of a particular book, then we may seriously misunderstand what the book is all about. As with modern literature, Hebrew genres have specific features which help us to distinguish them. For example, historical literature in Hebrew regularly began each main episode with the expression 'and it came to pass'[1].

Sometimes, the precise genre of a particular Old Testament book is not certain. An example would be the book of Jonah. Some people view this book as straightforward historical narrative. Others suggest that it may be more like an extended parable, a story with a message like the parables of Jesus, not necessarily describing real events. A parable is not 'untrue' even though the events it describes are not real. A parable seeks to communicate a moral or theological truth by means of a 'what if' story. Parable is a different genre from history. Those who take the parable view of Jonah are not necessarily people who disbelieve the Bible. The difference of opinion is about genre, about the intention and purpose of the writer. Did he intend to write history or was he telling a parable with a moral?

I should emphasise that only in a small minority of cases is there disagreement of this kind, and it is important that we do not become so pre-occupied with these questions that we actually miss the message of the book! Whether it is history or parable, Jonah has a great deal to challenge us with, for example, regarding our attitudes to people of other religions and nationalities.

Reading Old Testament books 'as books'

One of the commendable features of recent Bible scholarship has been to emphasise that the Bible books are great works of literature. Of course, as Christians we believe that the Bible books are far more than *just* works of literature. However, we should feel no need to apologise for them as regards their literary worth for they are composed with tremendous skill and artistry, just like any great work of art. They can take their place beside Shakespeare or any other great author you care to name.

It follows from this that we should read the Bible books *as books*. Most of us rarely sit down with a Bible book and read it through from beginning to end as we would do with a novel! The way the author begins the book, the way the themes are developed, the way episodes and characters are contrasted and interwoven, the emotions that are aroused in the reader, the final impression that the reader is left with at the end of the book are essential to discovering the overall message of a book.

In the college where I teach, the students training for ministry learn to read the Old Testament in Hebrew. In their message end-of-year examination it is difficult to find suitable Bible passages for them to translate from Hebrew. It has to be a relatively easy passage for beginners – but not so familiar that the students will know the English by heart! One year we set the story from the opening verses of Judges, about a Canaanite king called Adoni-bezek who had his thumbs and big toes cut off! As the students came out of the exam room, many of them said to me, 'Where on earth did you get that story from?' I replied, 'Do you mean to say that you have preached sermons from Judges but you have never read the book through from beginning to end?' Even preachers can fall into the trap of using episodes from a book without considering the book as a whole!

Part of the greatness of the Bible stories is that they can be told in a form which even young children can understand and enjoy. But they are much more than this. The well-known story of David and Goliath comes from 1 Samuel, which is one of the most profound tragic dramas ever written. The story of Daniel in the lions' den comes from a complex type of literature (called *apocalyptic*) which offers a prophetic interpretation of history.

By using words like literature or story, I do not mean that the events did not actually take place. Nor would I wish to take away from their significance as the Word of God. However, I am sure that there are many people outside of the church who have never considered reading Old Testament books but who might well be encouraged to read them as works of literature. If people can be encouraged to read the Bible for whatever reason that can only be good. Hopefully they will then be led by God's Holy Spirit to appreciate also the God-given message of the Bible.

Old Testament books are multi-dimensional

If you think of a gifted writer as someone who paints pictures with words, then the Bible books are full colour not just black and white; they are multi-dimensional, with breadth and depth. We can learn more of what a Bible author is seeking to communicate if we pay careful attention to things like how the book is structured and arranged, and to features such as the author's use of conversation, of repetition, of irony, and even of humour. We will also want to consider the way in which certain events are developed in detail while others merit only a passing reference.

Often it is important to note the way in which one character is skilfully contrasted with another (for example Saul and David whose careers are intertwined in 1 Samuel). The description of different episodes often follows a pattern, which is one of the ways by which an author can draw our attention to what is important, to what is the core or climax of the story.

If you and I were both to look at a painting, it is quite possible that what you would see as the most striking feature in the painting may not be what strikes me, because perhaps we would be looking from different angles or in a different light. It could be that the painting strikes a chord with some experience I have had which you do not share. So it is with Old Testament literature. When we look back from our New Testament standpoint, we may well see things in Old Testament books that the original writer was not aware of. God often used Old Testament writers to communicate a message that was for *our* time as well as for their own. It may also be that what strikes you as the main message of a book will be different from what strikes me. We are looking from different angles, we are facing different issues in our lives, and therefore the Bible literature strikes and interacts with us in different ways.

In one sense, the Bible message is unchanging. However, the application of that message may differ, not only from one person to another, but also from one generation to the next, and from one culture to another. This is one of the most marvellous things about the Bible. God's Holy Spirit uses the Scriptures to speak to a whole variety of different people in different ways. This does not mean that we can each make the Bible mean whatever we want it to mean! Our interpretation must be strictly controlled by what the text actually says. This is why *consistent* hermeneutics is all-important. However, hermeneutics is not a once-for-all thing, it is an ongoing process. It is not enough to have the classic commentaries on the Bible from the reformation era, or the 'sound' books of a previous generation. We constantly need to come afresh to the Scriptures and to be open to new dimensions of what God is saying to us.

> **The Bible message is unchanging... the application of that message may differ**

We live in a changing world. The world-view of our western culture (sometimes called *post-modernism*) is very different from the world-view of a generation ago. The social issues we face, the ideas that are taught in our schools, the perspectives presented on our TV screens, the prevailing moral outlook, all of these have changed. Whether we like it or not, this affects the way people approach the Bible. That is why our interpretation must constantly be rethought and refined, so that the Scriptures can be relevantly applied in our ever-changing situations.

The way in which a different world-view can influence how we interact with the Scriptures can be illustrated by contrasting the traditional approach to the Bible in western Europe with the recent liberation theology of South America. In Europe, much of our Bible

interpretation has been done in the 'ivory towers' of universities an
theological colleges; and discussion has often focussed on thos
points of doctrine that divide our different denominations and trad
tions. There has been an emphasis on personal faith and moralit
with little interest in what the Bible has to say about social justice
Indeed social justice matters have often been neglected as periphera
to the real 'spiritual' message of the Bible.

In South America, however, a very different approach to the Bibl
has arisen among people for whom poverty, hunger, suffering, an
oppression by government are very much features of their daily live
They have looked to the Bible for answers to very different question
from those of us in the comfortable west. What the Old Testamen
has to say about social justice has seemed central to them. They wan
to know why God allows the suffering and oppression they experi
ence daily. Our debates about details of doctrine, and ou
discussions about church structures and worship styles, are wha
seem peripheral or irrelevant to them!

Evangelical Christians are generally not happy with the emphase
of liberation theologians since they may seem to focus on earthl
liberation rather than on eternal salvation. However, our evangelica
tradition may also have been unbalanced if we have failed to give du
weight and attention to the many parts of the Bible that call fo
social justice here on earth.

Bible literature is probably broader, deeper, and richer than mos
of us have realised. We must not allow interpretation to be frozen i
the past without room for the Holy Spirit to speak to us afresh an
to challenge us in new ways.

The value of Old Testament scholarship

I have referred several times to Old Testament scholarship. Scholar
are sometimes called *critics*. When *criticism* is used in this sense it i
not a negative word. Bible *criticism* is about careful study and analysi
in order to deepen our understanding. Part of criticism is to question
and to probe in order to re-evaluate traditional interpretations.

Of course not all scholars view the Bible as God's inspired Word
The result of this is that many evangelical Christians are suspiciou
of scholarship. There may be some grounds for this suspicion
However, we must be careful not to 'throw out the baby with th
bath water' or to reject the positive contribution that much scholar
ship has undoubtedly made to our understanding of the Bible.

elieve firmly in the Bible as God-given and God-inspired. However,
1 this book I will try to make full use of those insights from recent
ible scholarship which are positive and useful. Sometimes this will
1ean probing and questioning – for not even the most cherished
raditional interpretations are infallible!

he authority of the Old Testament [2]

he story is told of a murder trial at the Old Bailey. The accused
ffered a plea of self-defence. His counsel was summing up his case
ɔ the jury with all the eloquence at his command. He concluded
vith the words: 'Members of the jury, we have it on the highest
uthority, for the Bible says, "Skin for skin, yea, all that a man hath
vill he give for his life."'

The elderly judge, who knew his Bible better than most, leaned
cross the bench and observed, 'I am interested to note whom
-arned counsel takes as his highest authority!' For the words which
ad been quoted were none other than Satan's (Job 2:4)!

This story illustrates how easy it is to quote a Bible verse as if it
vere an authoritative word from God directly into our particular
ituation when in fact it may be nothing of the kind. To quote the
vords of Satan as 'the highest authority' is an extreme example but it
lustrates a danger that we always need to be aware of. In fact, an
xpression like 'the Bible says' can be misleading. It makes much
etter sense to say, 'Jesus says' or 'Job says' or 'God says'.

The point can be further illustrated from Job. In the book, Job
1akes a number of long speeches in which he protests to God about
is suffering. Although Job is essentially God's man, it is clear by the
nd of the book that by no means everything he had said was
•leasing to God. So it will not do simply to quote some of Job's
vords as if they were direct words from God. The authoritative
nessage is in the book as a whole and not necessarily in the words of
ny one character.

For most of us, the word authority suggests orders and
ommands, rules and laws. Legal authority which has to be obeyed is
ertainly one very important kind of authority in the Old Testament,
vhich contains many commandments and laws. However, this is not
he only kind of authority. It is important to draw the distinction
etween a *law* and a *proverb*. The difference can be illustrated from
amily life. When a parent says to a child, 'If you take food from the
ridge you will be punished', that is a *legal* authority – an instruction

to be obeyed. However, when the parent says to the child, 'Do not stand too near the fire in case your clothes catch fire,' that statement is *proverbial*. Proverbs are advice to be followed rather than rules and regulations to be obeyed.

Take a game like football. There are the official rules or laws of the game, as laid down by the FA, and enforced on the pitch by the referee. These rules have a *legal* authority and there is a punishment for breaking them, be it a free-kick, a penalty, or a red card! On the other hand, the team coach will give advice on how to play the game better. Such advice has a proverbial rather than a legal authority: it is guidance to be followed, not instruction to be obeyed.

Now, of course, law and proverb can overlap. For example, the statement, 'Drive carefully because the roads are slippery and there often are police speed-traps', involves both a proverbial warning of the danger of icy roads and also a warning of the legal consequences of speeding.

Proverbs are advice to be followed rather than rules ... to be obeyed

Both of these kinds of authority are found in the Bible and they have often been confused. Proverbs deal with generalities. They may apply in some circumstances and not in others. Throughout the Old Testament (not just in the book of Proverbs) much of the teaching is God-given guidance on how to get the best out of life, which is quite a different thing from commandments and laws. This is also true of Jesus' teaching, much of which belongs to the world of proverb rather than law.

There are other types of authority as well. We sometimes say that someone is an authority on a subject. Theirs is an authority to be believed, rather than to be obeyed, an authority which comes from insight and understanding. We are given the opportunity to learn from the authority of experience of the various Bible characters and of the people of God as a whole. We must not limit the biblical material to only one type of authority.

Which translation?

The Old Testament was originally written in the Hebrew language. We read it in translation. You may well be asking which translation into English is the best one to use.

The classic translation of the Bible into English was the *King James Version* (often called the *Authorised Version*), which was produced almost four hundred years ago. In recent years, however, a variety of odern translations have been produced.

You may ask why new translations are needed if the Bible never changes. The Bible has not changed but English grammar, meaning and even pronunciation has changed very considerably across the centuries since King James's time. The *King James Version* is therefore not a translation into the language we speak today. Keeping the Bible in the language of yesteryear is a considerable barrier to understanding and can be quite misleading. The great Bible translators of old, such as Wycliffe and Tyndale, sought to translate in such a way that ordinary people could hear and understand the Bible in their familiar everyday speech. The various modern translations seek to do the same for our day and age.

But which of the many modern translations is the best? They all have their own particular strengths and weaknesses. Translation is an immensely complex task, since the meanings of words in one language never correspond exactly with the meanings of words in another. The grammar, word order, and idiom of Hebrew differ markedly from English and it is not possible for any one translation to capture fully every aspect of the original. There are many aspects of *meaning* which the translator has to handle, and accuracy is much more complex than just word-for-word correspondence. That is why two translations can be significantly different from one another without one being right and then other wrong.

A translator has to be concerned with the tone and atmosphere of the translation as well as with the literal meanings of the words. Has someone ever quoted something which you said as a joke and caused misunderstanding or upset because they changed the tone of voice? To change the tone can distort the meaning just as much as getting some of the words wrong. So it is with Bible translation. If the original Hebrew sounded normal and natural to the original hearers, then the translation should sound normal and natural in English. This is a very important criterion for deciding which is the best translation.

Different translations focus on different things. I use the word 'focus', because an illustration from the camera may be helpful. When taking a picture, it is not always possible to get both the foreground and the background in full focus at the same time. One type of film may capture the colours better but lose out on definition and sharpness. There is no such thing as a perfect photograph, no matter how good the camera or skilled the photographer. Similarly, there is no such thing as a perfect translation, no matter how skilful the

translator. It is not possible for any one translation to get ever
aspect of the meaning into proper focus. Different translations ma
be 'focussed' for different purposes and different readerships. On
translation may be better for personal reading, a different translatio
may be more suitable for public reading in church, and yet anothe
version may be best for Bible students.

It would not possible here to discuss at length the pros and con
of different translations. However, let me suggest that the *Good Neu
Bible* (GNB) is perhaps the most reader-friendly of the main moder
English translations, and I would encourage you to make it th
version you use for reading Bible books right through from begin
ning to end. I have found the *New Revised Standard Version* (NRSV
particularly good for closer study of individual passages. For tha
reason quotations in this book will mostly be taken from the NRSV
The *New International Version* is also highly thought of by man
people; and the New Jerusalem Bible often gives a fresh perspectiv
that is worth considering.

In the end, it probably does not matter all that much which of th
main translations you use, so long as you find one that is easy fo
you to follow and understand.

Yahweh, God's special name

Throughout the Old Testament, God was regularly referred to by hi
special name *Yahweh* – the name by which he revealed himself t
Moses at the burning bush (Exod 3:13-22). It means something like
'He exists and he brings to pass'. You might be more familiar with
the older pronunciation of this name in English – *Jehovah*. This is th
name which the Old Testament characters used when talking abou
God and when talking to God. It is found on every page of the Bibl
in Hebrew. This may come as a surprise to you because you will no
find the name *Yahweh* in most of our English translations.

The reason for this goes back to Jewish custom. Long after Ol
Testament times, the Jews became very conscious of the thir
commandment, which says: 'You shall not make wrongful use of the
name of the LORD your God, for the LORD will not acquit anyon
who misuses his name' (Exod 20:7).The best way, they thought, t
make sure that God's name was never misused was simply never t
use it! And so when the Bible books were read aloud in the syna
gogue, the Jews would never actually pronounce the name Yahweh
Instead, they substituted *Adonai* – their word for LORD.

When Christians came to translate the Bible into Latin, and then later into modern languages, they too followed this practice. Whenever the name *Yahweh* was used in the Hebrew original, the translators would substitute the word LORD. From a translation point of view this is a very doubtful practice – for a translator ought not to change what is there in the original. But this practice has been customary for so long that most modern translations still follow it[3].

English translations, however, always print the word LORD with four capital letters whenever it represents the name Yahweh. So, wherever in your Bible you see the word LORD, *all* in capitals, remember that the original Hebrew in fact has Yahweh, the special name of God. On the other hand there are some places where in English you will find *Lord* with only one capital letter. In those cases the original Hebrew actually does say *Lord* and not Yahweh.

In this book, I will regularly use the name Yahweh, especially when discussing passages where that is what God is called in the Hebrew original. (However, when quoting from a particular English translation, I will use LORD if that is what the translator has used.)

In the chapters which follow

Literature has been described as a tapestry of words. One way to study a tapestry might be to focus on each small portion, analysing the colour and type of thread and the method employed in the weaving. But it would be pointless doing this if you did not also stand back and look at the tapestry as a whole.

Sometimes we analyse the details of Bible books very closely, verse by verse and chapter by chapter, but don't stand back and survey the book as a whole. It is in fact only possible to understand the detailed teaching of individual parts of a book if we have first considered the overall purpose and message.

In the chapters which follow, we will look at the different groups of Old Testament books in turn. It will not be possible (for reasons of space) to consider all of the books in the same depth. I have deliberately devoted more space to some of the less well-known books. With each book or group of books, there will first be some general explanation of the genre and other background and introductory matters. Then the reader will be invited to read through book (or a major section of it). This will be followed by some commentary and explanation. Links with the New Testament will be highlighted, as will the relevance of the book's message for today.

I hope that through this book you will come to share my excitement and enthusiasm for the Old Testament books, and that through them God will speak to you 'in many and varied ways' (Heb 1:1).

Endnotes

1 This expression is usually left out in modern translations, but it is a key feature of Old Testament history-writing.

2 Much of this section was inspired by a public lecture on 'The Authority of the Old Testament' given by David Payne in the Queen's University of Belfast, in 1974.

3 A major exception is the Jerusalem Bible – which quite properly uses the name Yahweh, wherever that is what then original Hebrew says.

Part One

Creation, covenant and conquest: The pentateuch

1.1 THE BIBLE AS STORY

I am writing this on the day when we have expierenced a total eclips
of the sun. In Northern Ireland, where I live, we only had glimpses
a partial eclipse through the clouds. But by television we were able
share in the full event. A sense of awe and wonder was evident ever
where – especially among those who experienced the 'totality' of th
event. People who would not normally describe themselves as rel
gious spoke of it in interviews as a 'spiritual' experience.

The opening books of the Bible introduce us to the God wh
created this vast and intricate universe. They describe the creation c
the world and of the first human beings. They also depict the begir
nings of sin, the origins of the people of Israel, and the first stages i
God's plan of salvation for humankind as a whole. The God c
creation is all powerful and all knowing. But he is not remote an
unknowable. He is a personal God. He cares about individual peopl
He reveals himself and his nature through his involvement with ind
vidual human beings.

These five books, from Genesis to Deuteronomy, are collectivel
known as the *pentateuch* (meaning a work in five volumes) or the *Tora*
(meaning 'teaching'). Each is complete in itself and very differer
from one another in their presentation and style. Yet together the
form a collection in which themes, stories, characters, and laws ar
woven together into a literary and theological masterpiece[1].

Think of an orchestra playing a great symphony or concertc
There are many different instruments. Each group of instrumen
plays something different; and yet all blend into one tremendou
sound. Only the trained ear can distinguish the different parts. Mos
of us are only conscious of the main melody on the surface.

Interpreting a great work of literature is similar to interpreting
concerto. The pentateuch contains many well-known themes – lik
the melodies of a musical work – such as baby Moses in th
bulrushes or the miraculous crossing of the Red Sea. But there is fa
more to these books than just the surface story-line. They have
depth and a breadth so that every time we read through them there i
some new dimension not noticed before!

The pentateuch belongs to the *genre* of narrative literature: it take
the form of story. When I say *story*, I certainly believe the pentateuc
to be a true story! However, *story* is not the same thing as *history*. Th
modern historian seeks to give a comprehensive overview of a partic

ar period and strives to be as neutral as possible. The storyteller, on
e other hand, selects episodes which will inspire his audience and
mmunicate his message. So the writer of Genesis focuses on
oraham and his descendants, and only in passing does he give us
formation about the wider history and culture of the age. Nor is
e Bible storyteller 'neutral': for he tells the story quite deliberately
om a perspective of faith. The Bible accounts are certainly *historical*,
it they are more than mere *history*.

Who wrote the pentateuch?

ne pentateuch has always been closely associated with Moses. He is
e major character in four of the five books. Traditionally the Jews
ve believed that Moses himself was the author, though the books
emselves do not claim this. The New Testament uses phrases such as
e 'books of Moses' and the 'Law of Moses'; but these phrases do not
cessarily imply that Moses was the author. It may simply be that the
ooks were named after him. A modern parallel might be the way we
lk about the King James translation of the Bible. Even though we call
the *King James Version*, we know that he did not do the translation
ork himself! It was sponsored by him, and dedicated to him.

This whole question of authorship of the pentateuch has been the
bject of a great deal of debate over the years. Some believe that a
umber of authors contributed to the books. Other scholars now
mphasis the unity of the five pentateuch books, the careful literary
ructure which has shaped them, and the skill and craftsmanship
th which they are put together. All of these factors suggest a single
thor rather than a piecemeal amalgamation of different docu-
ents over a long period.

Some conservative scholars still feel strongly that Moses himself
as the author of the whole pentateuch – a view which is certainly
pported by very ancient tradition. Others point out that the Old
stament itself does not claim that Moses was the author and that
e New Testament references are not conclusive.

I certainly believe that there is much in the pentateuch which does
retch back to Moses himself, including the laws which God gave
rough him, and the sermons or addresses preached to the Israelite
ople. However, it may be that a later author composed the books
the form in which we now have them. Whoever the human
thors or compilers may have been, this should not diminish our
derstanding of the books as inspired by God!

1.2 GENESIS
THE BOOK OF BEGINNINGS

Most of us are fascinated by questions to do with origins. The Bib
opens with the words, 'In the beginning God created the heavens an
the earth'. These words set the scene not just for Genesis but also f
the Bible as a whole. The name *Genesis* means 'beginning' or 'origir
The book is named after its first word, *in-the-beginning* (which is a
one word in Hebrew).

The book opens with the creation story. This is followed by
description of other pre-historic events, including the first sin
Adam and Eve, the story of Noah and the flood, and the episode
the tower of Babel. Despite the fact that everything in the origin.
creation was 'good', the first section of the book ends by depicting th
human race as totally sinful and rebellious against God (chapter 11).

In chapter 12 the drama of salvation begins – the story of the lor
process by which God used his chosen people of Israel to prepare f
the coming of Jesus Christ. This salvation-redemption process bega
with Abraham – but it will not be completely finished until th
Second Coming of Jesus.

READ GENESIS 1–11: BEFORE HISTORY

A scientist was once asked how he could believe in the biblical stor
of creation. He took his watch from his pocket, removed the bac
cover, and showed his audience the complex mechanism inside, a
amazing array of little wheels and gears, moving the hands with a
the precision needed for an accurate time-piece. 'The amazing thing
said the scientist, 'is that no one made this watch. It just came abou
by accident! By sheer chance all those tiny cogs, and all the othe
parts of the complex mechanism, fell into exactly the right position
No one designed it, it just happened by sheer chance!'

The scientist had made his point well. Of course the watch mus
have had a designer and maker! So it is with the complex precision c
the universe. There must have been a Creator. Whether we loo
through a telescope at the vastness of outer space, or through
microscope at the intricate detail of the smallest living organism, w
cannot fail to be awe-struck at the wonder of God's intricat
creation. Few parts of the Bible have been surrounded with suc

ntroversy as these opening chapters of Genesis. Until the middle of
e nineteenth century most people took the Genesis story at its face
lue. However two events were to change that.

The first was the publication of Charles Darwin's book, *Origins of
e Species,* in which he put forward his famous theory of evolution.
arwin proposed that all higher forms of life, including human
ings, developed by means of a long and gradual process of evolu-
on from simple, basic life-forms. This theory runs counter to
enesis, in which God separately creates each individual species, and
which human beings are made 'in the image of God'. Controversy
tween *creationists* and *evolutionists* has raged ever since.

The second of the two events was the discovery by archaeologists
the library of King Ashurbanipal of ancient Assyria. It contained a
ide variety of literature from the surrounding nations of the
ncient Near East. From this library it became clear that other great
iltures had their own stories of creation and of the flood, with
any close similarities to the early chapters of Genesis. The initial
action of many scholars was to claim that the Genesis stories were
mply the Israelite version of a mythology which was common to all
the surrounding peoples.

However, scholars soon began to realise that the Genesis narra-
ves are fundamentally different from these other ancient accounts,
espite a certain similarity of language and themes. Indeed, Genesis
-11 may have been written specifically to *challenge* the popular
eliefs of the rest of the Ancient Near East.

In mythology it was commonly believed that the human race
ame about as a result of an illicit union between a male and a female
od. In Genesis there is none of this. There is only one **the Genesis**
od. Human beings are not *begotten* by a god, they are **narratives are**
eated by the one and only true God. In the Ancient **fundamentally**
ear Eastern myths, the gods are constantly struggling **different from**
gainst Chaos, which constantly threatens to over- **other ancient**
helm even the gods themselves. The God of Genesis, **accounts**
y contrast, is not under any threat from forces beyond
is control! The gods of mythology were said to have
ade the world out of already existing materials, which were of poor
uality and difficult to mould and shape. In Genesis, God creates
verything out of nothing.

Heavenly bodies such as the moon, the sun, and the stars were
idely regarded as gods in the Ancient Near East. However, in
enesis 1, these heavenly bodies are simply aspects of God's creation.

Indeed light comes into existence (on day one) before the creation [of the] sun, moon, and stars (on day four). The sun and moon are not eve[n] the ultimate source of light! In ancient mythology human bein[gs] were created to be slaves for the gods, but in Genesis men an[d] women are the pinnacle of God's creation, appointed to rule over t[he] world on God's behalf, and to have companionship with the Creat[or.] And so I could go on. It can be summed up by saying that Genes[is] offered a *theology* as a deliberate counter to the *mythology* of the wid[er] Ancient Near East.

Scholars do, however, sometimes use the word *myth* in connectio[n] with Genesis – and you may come across this usage in books or T[V] documentaries. In ordinary conversation a *myth* is som[e]**the writer of** thing which is not true! However, when scholars use th[e] **Genesis was** word, they mean something different. Baden Powell, f[or] **not writing a** example, spoke of myth as: 'a doctrine expressed in sto[ry] **science** form'. A theologian called Bultmann gives this definitio[n:] **text-book** 'Mythology is the use of imagery to express the othe[r] worldly in terms of this world'. Another commo[n] definition is: 'the pictorial description of those things which cou[ld] not be understood if described with the formal precision of science'[.]

Scholars do not use the word myth to mean *untrue*. Rather the[y] use myth to refer to picture language which expresses a truth th[at] cannot be expressed in any ordinary way. I think that to apply t[he] word myth to the Bible in this way is confusing. But we shoul[d] understand that when scholars use the word they are not necessari[ly] intending to deny the truth of the Bible.

There is always a difficulty when we use human language t[o] describe God, for God is beyond description by means of ordina[ry] words. For example, we call God *Father*. By the logic of ordina[ry] language if there is a father there must also be a mother. But whe[n] the word *Father* is applied to God, this normal logic does not hol[d.] We know what we mean when we call God *Father*, but it is not th[e] ordinary meaning of the word.

In Genesis 2:7, there is a description of God making the fir[st] human being. The Hebrew words suggest a potter modelling a figu[re] out of clay and then breathing life into it. This is picture languag[e] which points us towards a truth that cannot be expressed in an[y] other way. Similarly, in Genesis 7:11 rain falls from 'windows' i[n] heaven. We realise that the writer is using picture language.

The writer of Genesis was not writing a science text-book. He wa[s] inspired by God to paint a picture in words, which ordinary peop[le] uld understand, and which would provide a sufficient basis for elief and faith. He was concerned to communicate a theological essage, not to address issues of physics or chemistry!

Take as another example the six *days* of creation. The sun and ther heavenly bodies are not created until the fourth day, so the ord *day* cannot have its normal meaning of the period between one inset and the next. Many Christians, therefore, do not interpret the ays in Genesis as literal twenty-four hour periods, but think of them stages within God's creation, each of which may have stretched ross a vast period of time. Sometimes these words from 2 Peter 3:8 e quoted: '...with the Lord one day is like a thousand years, and a iousand years are like one day'.

These are not people who disbelieve the Bible! Rather they believe iat the Bible writer was using pictorial language in a specialised way describe the indescribable. Other Christians do feel strongly that ie early chapters of Genesis should be interpreted in a literal way. he important thing to realise is that the difference is not between iose who believe the Bible and those who don't. It's a difference etween two different *interpretations* of what the Bible says.

I firmly believe that the early chapters of Genesis are part of God's ivinely inspired Word. I am not an evolutionist. However, I would ot want to reject everything that scientists say![2] Christians once isisted that the world was flat and that the sun and the ioon revolved around the earth. This belief was based on a teral interpretation of passages such as Psalm 19. When alileo taught the earth revolves round the sun, he was ersecuted for refusing to believe the Bible! The Bible had een interpreted wrongly. Those who are caught up in oday's Bible-versus-science debate must make sure that iey do not make the same kind of mistake as those who nce insisted that the earth must be flat! We have got to llow for the possibility that traditional interpretations iay need to be looked at again.

the early chapters of Genesis are part of God's divinely inspired Word

hapters 1,2: the beginning of it all

hese chapters contain two complementary accounts of the creation. he second account begins at Genesis 2:4. They describe creation om two different perspectives – a description in stereo. In both ccounts, the creation of human beings is the climax. Unlike the different species of animal, human beings are made 'in the image of God' (1:27). There has been much discussion about the precise meaning of this phrase. It certainly means that human beings are spiritual, capable of having a relationship with God. It also implies that we have free will and that we are capable of choosing between right and wrong. Those made in the image of God have the potential for eternal life.

Chapter 2 focuses on the creation of the first two human beings whom we know as Adam and Eve. However, the Hebrew word *adam* was not originally a proper name. It was the ordinary Hebrew word for a human being (whether male or female); and it could also be used as a collective noun to refer to humankind as a whole. Out of this original human being, a second human being was created. It is only after verse 22 that we have *male* and *female*. In marriage, the female and the male are joined to become 'one flesh' again. This verse has been described as the charter for marriage: 'Therefore a man leaves his father and his mother and clings to his wife, and they become one flesh' (2:24).

A great deal of misunderstanding has arisen out of the fact that the first woman is described as a *helper* for the man (2:18). Indeed, this phrase has been used across the centuries as a justification for relegating women to a servile role. Nothing, however, could have been further from the mind of the writer of Genesis. For the Hebrew word used here for helper is never used in the Old Testament of an inferior helping a superior. It is most often used of God as helper for Israel – and God is certainly not to be thought of as an inferior or as a servant! The word is also used in Hebrew for mutual help and support between equals.

Chapters 3, 4: the fall

So far the story has been positive. As one commentator has said, 'God has made an ideal world for a fully rational, relational, functional human race that in turn enjoys work, sex, and spiritual pursuits.'[3] In chapter 3, however, disaster strikes in the story of the fall. By eating the forbidden fruit, the first man and the first woman fall from the state of sinlessness in which they were originally created. Theologians have debated across the centuries as to what the forbidden fruit was. A common view once was that the forbidden fruit was sex, and this has contributed to a very negative view of sex.

Part One: Creation, covenant and conquest

ality among some Christians. In fact, however, sexual relationships between men and women were part of God's purpose from the outset. The forbidden fruit is not about any one kind of sin. It is symbolic of *any* disobedience to God and of the tendency to disobedience that has been in the human heart ever since.

The consequences of this first sin were considerable. Adam and Eve were expelled from the Garden of Eden. Hard labour, pain, suffering, and struggle became the norm for both women and men. Things which had originally been created to be positive and fulfilling (work, sex, childbirth) would now be a source of toil and distress. Human relationships would be characterised by subjection and enmity. Access to the tree of life is now denied to human beings, so from now on death will be the fate of all.

What of the serpent? The serpent is the first appearance of the being who works against God and who seeks to destroy humankind. Later we come to know him as Satan or the devil. Not only does he tempt the first humans to sin, but he does so by casting doubt on God's word. Sin begins with mistrust of God. Punishment is inflicted also on the serpent (3:14,15). These verses may refer to ongoing conflict between the human and reptile worlds. But Christians have always understood them to point towards the ultimate victory over Satan by Jesus[4]. Evil will not triumph in the end.

> **the serpent is the first appearance of the being who works against God**

Chapter 4 speaks of the consequences of sin in the next generation. Why Abel's sacrifice to God was more acceptable than Cain's is not made clear. What is made clear is that the murder resulted from jealousy, pride and resentment which are the 'sin lurking at the door' (4:7) which God had warned Cain against. This story has many echoes in the teaching of Jesus – that internal emotions such as hatred or lust are as sinful as the outward acts of murder or adultery.

Cain's punishment is severe, but notice that Cain is in fact given God's protection (4:15)! Right from this early stage in the Bible it is clear that even the most grievous of sinners is not beyond the possibility of redemption!

Chapters 5–11: judgement and promise

Events in Genesis 1–11 come in pairs. There are two parallel creation accounts. Chapters 3 and 4 record the first sin and then the first murder. Next there are two episodes where God intervenes i judgement – the flood story, and the episode of the tower of Babel.

Chapter 5 is a transitional chapter. The descendants of Adam a listed, showing that even outside of the Garden of Eden there is st the prospect of long life and fulfilment. However, as soon as w move into chapter 6 it becomes clear that sin has spread like a canc throughout the human race. Scholars have long debated who we 'the sons of God' (whose sexual misbehaviour is described here) an the giants descended from them. It may be that they were falle angels. Others think that the Hebrew expression means 'sons of th mighty' and that the word 'giants' was a way of describing notor ously wicked rulers. However, there was one exception to God displeasure: Noah.

Almost every culture across the world has a folk memory of great flood – a fact which points to the truth of the Bible stor Various scientific explanations for the flood have been offered, suc as a meteor striking the earth. In Ancient Near Eastern mytholog the flood was explained as the forces of chaos overwhelming th world, forces which the gods struggled to keep at bay.

almost every culture across the world has a folk memory of a great flood

In Genesis, however, God is completely in contro The flood is his decisive act of judgement against wicked human race. For Noah and his family there wa only one way to be saved and that was to trust in God promise. Christians have always seen the flood story a symbolic of the final judgement, from which also the is only one way to be saved (Matt 24: 27–42). After th flood, God made an everlasting *covenant,* or promis with Noah and his descendants that he would never again destroy th world by a flood. God would find another way of dealing with huma sin.

The end of the flood story leaves the reader with the prospect of fresh start for the human race. But any such hopes are soon sha tered by the closing events of chapter 9, in which even Noah and hi sons behave so irresponsibly. The resulting curse on Noah grandson Canaan (ancestor of the Canaanites), and blessing fo Shem (ancestor of the Israelites), prefigures the later struggle between Canaanites and Israelites.

In the episode of the tower of Babel, the people even attempt t raise themselves up to be on a level with God! God's response is t scatter them across the whole of the earth, each group speaking different language.

By the end of chapter 11, we have a tragic picture of fallen and battered humanity – seemingly irredeemable. What could God do – except for some further act of judgement such as the flood? The stage is now set for the long drama of God's salvation and redemption; a story which begins with the call of Abram in chapter 12 and which runs right through to the end of the book of Revelation.

READ GENESIS 12–50

For Abram (later renamed Abraham)[5], the journey must have been daunting – setting out without map or road signs, with no communication back home, and with little prospect of return. His destination was an unknown country whose inhabitants might well be hostile – and all this when Abraham was already seventy-five years old!

It was at the command of his God, Yahweh, that Abraham undertook this journey from his homeland in Mesopotamia to the land of Canaan. Since the time of the tower of Babel, knowledge of the one true God had virtually disappeared. We do not know if Abraham had always been a worshipper of Yahweh; nor do we know how Yahweh spoke to him or how he recognised who was speaking. What we do know is that Abraham responded to Yahweh's call, he believed Yahweh's promises, and in faith he set out to emigrate to this new land with his wife Sarah, his nephew Lot, and their servants and retainers.

These chapters of Genesis describe how the early forefathers of Israel gradually got to know Yahweh, who had chosen them for a special destiny. They learned that he was not just one among many gods but the only true God. They came to understand more of his nature and of his will and purpose. Though they remained faithful overall to God, they were far from perfect and often behaved badly. They frequently experienced God's forgiveness and his willingness to allow a fresh start. As so often in the Old Testament, God did not use them because they were more righteous than anyone else; he used them *despite* their failings and shortcomings. As the writer to the Hebrews was later to say, it was their *faith* not their deeds that enabled them to win God's approval (Heb 11:1,2).

Yahweh's covenant with Abraham

Yahweh's relationship with Abraham was a *covenant* relationship. Covenant is a very important word in the Old Testament. The Hebrew word could be used in a variety of different contexts, to refer to an agreement, a contract, a binding promise, or a treaty. The word denotes more than just a legal contract. It implies loyalty and commitment. We use the word when we speak about a marriage covenant. Marriage is a legal contract – but it is much more.

The Hebrew word for covenant was often used for a treaty between rulers. Sometimes the treaty or covenant would be between equals; and sometimes it would be between a more powerful king and a lesser ruler. When God entered into a covenant with Abraham it was like a treaty relationship between a great king and a vassal. It was God who took the initiative and gave assurance of protection and blessing. Allegiance and obedience were required of Abraham.

This *covenant* with Abraham is not the first time the word 'covenant' is used. Back in chapter 9, you will recall that God had already entered into a covenant with Noah and the whole of humankind never again to destroy the world by a flood. Now with Abraham, God enters into a covenant with one chosen individual and his descendants, who are singled out to be the means of bringing God's blessing to the world.

In chapter 17, the sign of circumcision is introduced as a perpetual sign of the covenant relationship. Notice that not just Abraham's literal descendants are to be included in the covenant relationship but the whole of his household, including his slaves and their descendants. It was at this point that God changed Abram's name to Abraham[6].

God promised Abraham that his descendants would become a great nation; that they would possess the land of Canaan as their own, and that they would enjoy God's blessing and protection in this land. He also promised that through Abraham's 'seed' (or offspring) God would bring blessing to all the nations. Christians have always understood this promise to be ultimately fulfilled in Jesus Christ, the 'seed' (or descendant) of Abraham. The covenant promises could indeed be summed up in two words – *land* and *seed*.

The long-term promises of the covenant were unconditional. However, the immediate blessings of the covenant were dependent on obedience and faithfulness from Abraham and his descendants. Right from this early stage, it was *faith* that concerned Yahweh more than specific acts of righteousness. A key verse in the theology of the Bible as a whole is chapter 15:6: 'And he believed the LORD; and the LORD reckoned it to him as righteousness'[7].

This covenant with Abraham is the basis for the whole of the rest of the Bible story. When God later hears the cry of the people in

avery in Egypt, we are told that he remembers his covenant with
braham. At Mount Sinai God expands and develops the covenant
ith the Ten Commandments and the other laws and instructions
ven through Moses. When Joshua leads the people to victory over
e Canaanites, this is in fulfilment of God's promise of the land to
braham. A further development of the covenant takes place when
od enters into a special relationship with King David and his
ccessors; making promises which ultimately find their fulfilment
Jesus Christ as the descendant of David.

It was by the standards of Yahweh's covenant that the prophets
dged the kingdoms of Israel and Judah. It was because of the
ilure of the people to keep faith with the covenant that God's
ecial protection was eventually withdrawn – so that first Samaria
d then Jerusalem were destroyed. After the eventual return of the
ws to Jerusalem it was the memory of the covenant that gave them
basis for renewed faith as the people of God. Jeremiah looked
rward to the *new covenant* (or New Testament) that God would one
ay make with his people[8]. In the closing book of the Old Testament,
lalachi similarly looks forward to the future fulfilment of the
ovenant in the New Testament[9].

Chapters 12–23: the life of Abraham

he story of Abraham's life is very much a story of the ups and
owns of faith. Among the high points are his willingness to allow
ot, his nephew, to chose the better pasture land; his prayer on
ehalf of the people of Sodom and Gomorrah, and his faithfulness
ven when he believed that God wanted him to sacrifice his son,
saac. The two occasions on which he passes off Sarah as his sister
re examples of lapses of faith by Abraham. His fathering of Ishmael
y his servant-girl Hagar is another instance of lack of faith in God's
romise; and his differential treatment of Ishmael compared with
saac was bound to lead to trouble.

It may be helpful to understand a little of the cultural and polit-
cal circumstances of Canaan at this time. The area was then part of
he Egyptian Empire – though day-to-day rule was in the hands of the
etty kings of numerous Canaanite city-states. These city-states ruled
he peasant population of the countryside. Often they fought against
ne another. There were also independent tribal groups. Abraham
nd his retinue formed one such group. On one occasion, he was able

to muster over 300 fighting men to rescue Lot (chapter 14). We also see him as a chieftain entering into treaty relationships with local city rulers. Such tribal groups are frequently referred to in Egyptian writings as *Apiru* – an Egyptian word which corresponds to our word *Hebrew*. Often the *Apiru* groups fought as mercenary soldiers for the Egyptians or for one of the city-states. On other occasions they seem to have had a semi-outlaw status. It is probably in this 'outlaw' sense that Abraham is referred to as a *Hebrew* in 14:13.

A very important episode that might easily pass unnoticed by the reader is the meeting between Abraham and Melchizedek (14:17–24). Melchizedek was Priest-King of Salem (Salem is a shortened form of Jerusalem). Melchizedek blesses Abraham and Abraham

Abraham is the first person in the Bible to be called a *prophet*

pays a tenth (or tithe) of all the booty which he had just won in battle. The full significance of this little episode might well be missed if it were not for the fact that it is discussed in the book of Hebrews[10]. Melchizedek, unlike other Canaanite kings, was a worshipper of the one true God – indeed more than just a worshipper, he was 'priest of God Most High', an agent of God's blessing.

The later Israelite priests were descended from Levi, Abraham's great grandson. As the Letter to the Hebrews puts it, when Abraham bowed down to Melchizedek, Levi was present – inside Abraham's body! This implies that Melchizedek's priesthood was of a higher order than that of Levi and his descendants, the later Israelite priests. We do not know anything else about Melchizedek – but his story does make clear that Abraham was not the only one through whom God was working in those ancient times[11].

Abraham is the first person in the Bible to be called a *prophet*. A prophet was God's special representative or spokesman. Often the role of the prophet was to speak to the people on behalf of God. However, it was also part of the role of a prophet to pray to God on behalf of the people – such as when Abraham prays on behalf of Abimelech[12]. The other main episode where Abraham prays to God on behalf of the people is his famous plea on behalf of Sodom and Gomorrah (chapter 19).

All of Yahweh's promises to Abraham are dependent upon a son and heir – and yet Isaac is not born until chapter 21, very near the end of Abraham's career. It took some faith for Abraham to keep on believing in God's promises when Sarah was well beyond normal childbearing age!

The episode in which Yahweh commands Abraham to make a sacrifice of his son, Isaac, is both frightening and puzzling (chapter 22). It is presented to us as the ultimate test of Abraham's faith and allegiance. Yet Yahweh was the God who abhorred the pagan practice of child-sacrifice, which is vigorously condemned elsewhere in the Old Testament. As we read of the son chatting happily with his father as they go together to the place of sacrifice, we are surely left wondering how any parent could even contemplate such a thing (vs 6-8). The clue, I think, is in Abraham's remark in verse 8 – in answer to young Isaac's observation that there was no lamb with them for the sacrifice. Abraham replies, 'God himself will provide the lamb for a burnt offering, my son'. Abraham by now must have got to know Yahweh well enough to realise that he would never actually want a human sacrifice and that he would surely provide a substitute. This episode points forward to God's sacrifice of his own Son as a substitute for our sins.

Chapters 24–36: the next generations: Isaac and Jacob

Though Abraham's death is not recorded until chapter 25, the focus of the story now moves to the next generation – to Isaac, and then to Isaac's sons Jacob and Esau. Once again it is the story of the ups and downs of faith. Abraham takes great care to ensure that a wife is found for Isaac from his own family back in Mesopotamia; but also is at pains to make sure that Isaac does not leave the land of God's covenant promise. In the next generation, Jacob persuades Esau to sell him his birthright and then later he deceives his father and cheats Esau. This is a further demonstration that God does not choose people because of their goodness. He uses people despite their sin and failure.

There are positives as well, of course. Someone remarked to me recently that there is little in the Old Testament on the subject of reconciliation. He had obviously never read Genesis. The reconciliation between Ishmael and Isaac when they came together for Abraham's funeral (25:7–11) and between Jacob and Esau (chapters 32,33) show reconciliation where there had been considerable grounds for hurt and resentment.

The reconciliation effected by Abraham (and later also by Isaac) with King Abimelech is also an example of putting aside differences and learning to live with people of a different culture. Genesis finishes with the famous story of forgiveness between Joseph and his brothers.

On the other hand, the aftermath of the rape of Jacob's daughter, Dinah, is a classic example of failure to cope with breakdown in human relationships (chapter 34). We understand the view expressed by Dinah's brothers that rape could not be passed off as a 'misunderstanding' to be sorted out by a few small gifts among the men-folk. Indeed the brothers' strength of feeling on the matter (if genuine) was strikingly commendable in a society where men often regarded women's rights as of little consequence.

However, the deceit with which the brothers pursued their vengeance (using the religious symbol of circumcision as a cover) could scarcely be justified. Nor could the extent of their revenge, which included murder and robbery on quite a scale – especially since Shechem, the culprit, had shown every evidence of penitence and willingness to make amends.

Could it be that the brothers (the same brothers who were later to sell Joseph into slavery) were simply exploiting the situation for their own aggrandisement, with little real concern for Dinah? Their lack of sincerity is further suggested by Jacob's later comments (49:4–7). It often happens that people who claim the moral high ground are in fact seeking their own advancement or enrichment! This chapter is (understandably) rarely read or preached on and yet it has a great deal to teach us about human nature and about the consequences of allowing breakdown in human relationships to spiral out of control!

Notice how the theme of covenant continues to pervade the narrative. During Jacob's encounter with Yahweh at Bethel (when he sees the famous ladder up to heaven), Yahweh reaffirms the covenant with Abraham (chapter 28). Whatever the precise significance of Jacob's wrestling with God at Peniel (32:22–32), it should be understood as a further strengthening of the covenant relationship. It is at this point that Jacob's name is changed to Israel – the name by which his descendants are to be known.

The era of Abraham, of Isaac, and of Jacob and his twelve sons is known as the age of the patriarchs, the ancestral figures of Israel. It is clear that despite the closeness of the patriarchs to Yahweh, they still had much to learn about his nature and his law. The marriage practices of the patriarchs was one area where they were still falling in line with local culture and had not learned the distinctive teaching on marriage that comes later in the Bible.

It is certainly clear that the patriarchs were no stained-glass saints! Indeed the behaviour of Jacob's sons might make us marvel that they should have been chosen by God to be the ancestors of his covenant people! Levi was one of the culprits in the revenge after the rape of Dinah – and yet he became the ancestor of all of the Israelite priests! Judah, who was to be the ancestor of King David, behaved outrageously in chapter 38.

There is no attempt in this book to gloss over the sins and failures of the patriarchs as most ancient nations tended to do with their ancestral heroes. God chooses and uses the most surprising of people! To this day, God is able to bring good out of evil; and he works out his purposes despite the constant failures of his people.

Chapters 37–50: Joseph and his brothers

Joseph, the teenage dreamer, with his coat of many colours, who constantly annoys his family with his 'big talk', is a figure most of us know well. The story forms a bridge between the books of Genesis and Exodus by explaining how the Israelites came to be in Egypt. Yet it is also a story complete in itself, composed in such a way that the skilled storyteller can hold his audience spellbound with it, even though they may have heard the story many times before. There are exciting and tense moments which move the audience to tears. There is a happy ending. It has a simplicity that young children can enjoy; and yet it raises issues which are profound and thought-provoking. Joseph is sold into slavery in Egypt by his brothers and then falsely accused by Potiphar's wife and imprisoned. His interpretations of the dreams of his fellow prisoners and then of Pharaoh himself, followed by his wise rule over Egypt in the years both of plenty and of famine, demonstrate that he is at the centre of Yahweh's will and purpose.

Yahweh brings good out of the evil of Joseph's brothers' misdeeds. He is the one who controls the affairs of empires, and yet he is concerned about the lives of ordinary people, such as Pharaoh's baker and the butler.

The final penitence of Joseph's brothers is particularly note-worthy. Reuben (who had slept with his father's concubine), Simeon (who had been involved in avenging the rape of Dinah), and Judah (whose outrageous behaviour in chapter 38 is intruded into the middle of the Joseph story) emerge as changed men. Joseph, too, has changed – from the arrogant youth to the magnanimous governor who forgives his brothers with the words:

> And now do not be distressed, or angry with yourselves, because
> you sold me here; for God sent me before you to preserve life. ...
> So it was not you who sent me here, but God[13] .

And so the first major segment of the Old Testament story of
salvation ends with Jacob's sons and their families happily settled in
Egypt under Joseph's governorship and with the blessing and
welcome of Pharaoh and his court.

These twelve sons of Jacob are the ancestor figures of the twelve
tribes of Israel. Do not pass too quickly over the different blessings
which Jacob bestows on these twelve sons in chapter 49 – for the
words of his blessing are important pointers to future episodes in the
story. Notice the reference to future kings who will be descended
from Judah (v 10). Whether or not there should be an earthly
kingship in Israel is later to become a major and controversial issue.
As Christians, we see Jacob's blessing on Judah as ultimately fulfilled
in his eventual descendant, Jesus Christ.

1.3 EXODUS
SALVATION, COVENANT AND LAW

READ EXODUS 1–18

Pharaoh had a problem. A previous administration had recruited foreigners into the country – Asians. In the dark days of the Egyptian economy in the 1950's (BC that is) they had helped out considerably. In fact, without the technological and administrative expertise of one of the earliest immigrants, Joseph, it is doubtful whether Egypt would have pulled through the series of droughts which came right on top of the depression, war years, and the post-war credit squeeze!

The trouble was that, instead of sticking to a bit of land they had been given, east of the river, in Goshen, they had grown in numbers, got themselves together, and begun to demand their rights.

Pharaoh's economic planners were very worried.

'These Israelites are so numerous and strong that they are a threat to us.' 'In case of war they might join our enemies in order to fight against us.'

So Pharaoh made a public announcement: 'We must find some way to keep them from becoming even more numerous'.

Family planning (of a drastic kind) was a failure and repatriation proved to be a non-starter, since no one knew quite where they had come from. In any case they had been in Egypt for hundreds of years and their youngsters spoke no other language, supported Memphis Wanderers, and were entirely part of the local scene!

In fact animosity was so great that, when Pharaoh's ruling Nile Front party passed a law enslaving all Israelites, the man in the street began to feel that at last the government was waking up to its responsibilities.[14]

So the point can be overdone. But this extract from an article by Paul Richards does show how relevant the Bible can be to contemporary issues. Have a look at the first chapter of Exodus and see how many points of comparison you can spot with situations in the world of today.

It is probable that Joseph and his family had come to Egypt during the period when Egypt was ruled by a dynasty known as the Hyksos – an Asian military aristocracy who had invaded Egypt. Their Asian origins may have made them particularly receptive to the immigrants from Canaan – and this may explain why it was possible for Joseph to reach such high office.

Joseph's famous management of the famine years was achieved by the Egyptians having to mortgage their lands to the crown in order to buy food. Expropriation of property by the crown on such a scale can scarcely have been popular with the land-owning classes – though Joseph's policies would undoubtedly have been of benefit to the poorer underclasses. The Hyksos were eventually overthrown and expelled; and the pharaoh of the Exodus period had quite a different attitude to the descendants of Joseph and his brothers (Exod 1:8).

the Bible does not claim that all of the Israelites were literally descended from Jacob

The best evidence for the truth of the Exodus story is that no nation would ever *invent* a story of origins in shameful slavery! Yet this origin as Hebrew slaves was foundational to the faith and religion of Israel.

According to Exodus 12:37, there were 600,000 men plus women and children who went out from Egypt which implies a total population of around two million. Yet the Bible elsewhere implies a much smaller group. For example, two midwives catered for the whole Israelite population in Egypt! The logistics of two million people crossing the Red Sea in one night and the practicalities of their encampment in the wilderness would have been immense.

Various solutions have been put forward for these difficulties. One possible explanation is that the word 'thousand' in English is a mistranslation. The Hebrew word may in fact be a military term, meaning a company or troop. So the verse would instead read: 'six hundred companies of fighting men plus women and children'. This would imply a total population figure of around 40,000 – which seems a much more likely figure than two million.

The Bible does not claim that all of the Israelites were literally descended from Jacob and his sons. It was always possible for people to be absorbed into Israel (as indeed to this day it is possible for someone to become a Jew). The original Hebrew band included

lescendants of the servants and retainers of the earlier patriarchs.
When the Israelites left Egypt a large group of other *Apiru* people
went with them (12:38). In the wilderness years and during the eventual occupation of the land of Canaan other disaffected peoples may
well have been added to their number and absorbed within the
twelve-tribe system.

Chapters 1–6: Yahweh remembers his covenant

As often in the biblical narratives, the description of great affairs of
state is punctuated by episodes from the lives of ordinary people.

After the opening description of the cruelty inflicted on the
Israelites, we read the moving story of the baby Moses, found in the
bulrushes by the Egyptian princess and brought up in the
palace. Moses' first clumsy attempt to do something to
help his own people results in his having to flee from Egypt
- but under God's providence he finds a wife and a home
with Jethro, the priest of the Midianites.

Notice how God prepared Moses for the leadership task
that lay ahead of him. Educated in the royal palace he
would have learned to read and write and gained an understanding of government and law. With the Midianites in
the desert, he would have learned about the functioning of
tribal communities, about animal husbandry, and about desert
survival – all essential skills for the wilderness years ahead. From his
father-in-law, Jethro the priest, he was presumably also able to learn
more about God's character and nature.

the burning bush must be one of the most powerful moments in the Old Testament

The encounter between Moses and Yahweh at the burning bush
on Mount Sinai (chapters 3,4) must be one of the most powerful
moments in the whole of the Old Testament. God had heard the cry
of his oppressed people. He had remembered his covenant with
Abraham, Isaac, and Jacob.

Understandably, Moses is reluctant to accept this seemingly
impossible task which God gives him. The first objection he puts up
is that the rulers of Egypt will demand to know the *name* of the God
who had sent him to Pharaoh. (It seems that in Egyptian religion, to
know the names of the gods was of particular importance.) God then
reveals the full significance of his special name to Moses. He is
Yahweh. He is the I AM – the God who truly exists and who brings all
things to pass.

In answer to his further objections, Moses is given miraculous powers and he is told that his brother, Aaron, will be his 'mouth' or spokesman. Later Yahweh puts it like this: 'See, I have made you like God to Pharaoh, and your brother Aaron shall be your prophet' (Exod 7:1). This verse gives us an interesting insight into the role of a prophet. A prophet is someone who speaks on behalf of God (Abraham had the task of praying to God on behalf of the people).

Chapters 7–10: the first nine signs (or plagues)

The ninth plague used to puzzle me – darkness. Even though it was darkness 'thick enough to be felt', it seemed an anticlimax after the earlier frogs, boils, hail, and other nasties. I thought the Egyptians must have been relieved that it was only darkness this time! What I didn't realise was that the plagues (or signs as they are better called) were demonstrations of Yahweh's power over the gods of the Egyptians! The sun-god was the chief god of Egypt at that time. Darkness which blotted out the sun represented the greatest victory by Yahweh.

Several of the other signs also had a specific religious significance. The Egyptians regarded the Nile as a god – and so changing Nile water into blood was a blow. Frogs were sacred to the Egyptians – but after the plague of frogs the Egyptians must never have wanted to see one again! Yahweh had a sense of humour!

Pharaoh's initial response to Moses was dismissive, 'Who is this Yahweh that I should heed him' (Exod 5:2), but he soon begins to change his mind. He even asks Moses to pray for him to Yahweh – a name he no longer dismisses with disdain. But after each of the signs, Pharaoh's heart is hardened and he again refuses to let the people go. Up until the fifth sign, Pharaoh hardens his own heart. But from the sixth sign onwards, it is God who hardens Pharaoh's heart. He has received enough last chances – and now the hardening of his heart by Yahweh becomes part of his punishment.

Chapters 11–18: the first Passover

It's hard to imagine the grief that the tenth sign must have caused in Egypt – the death of the eldest son in every home, from Pharaoh's son down to the son of the prisoner in the dungeon. Every Israelite home by contrast was spared. This event was called the Passover – because the angel of death 'passed over' the Israelite homes, where the blood of the Passover lamb had been sprinkled on the doorposts in accordance with Yahweh's instructions.

Exodus goes into great detail about the preparations for the Passover meal; and instructions are also given for the future annual celebration of the feast. To this day, the Passover is observed in every Jewish home as the major celebration in the religious calendar. Every year, in fulfilment of Yahweh's command, the youngest child asks, 'Why do we do this?' Every year the story is retold and the explanation given – so that the people will never forget.

Instructions are also given in these chapters for the Festival of Unleavened Bread, which immediately followed the Passover in the religious calendar. The ongoing ritual of 'buying back' (or redeeming) the first-born son in every family was another means of ensuring that the origins of Israel's faith would never be forgotten.

On the night of the first Passover, the people were to eat the specially prepared Passover lamb accompanied by bitter herbs and bread made without yeast. They were to eat the meal dressed ready for a hurried departure. In the end the Egyptians begged the Israelites to go. Ordinary citizens showered them with gifts of jewellery and clothing – which the Hebrews accepted in lieu of payment for the slave labour they had been forced to undertake. There must have been a great sense of adventure as they set out into the unknown, with God's pillar of cloud by day and pillar of fire by night moving before them! But a major hurdle had yet to be crossed – the Red Sea. The Hebrew actually means 'Sea of Reeds'. It most likely refers to a series of lakes and streams between the head of the Gulf of Suez and the Mediterranean.

The story is told of a school in communist Russia, where the atheist teacher was ridiculing the miracle of the crossing of the Red Sea. 'It wasn't a sea at all', he told the class, 'it was just a marshy swamp. Some miracle,' he went on disparagingly, 'to cross water which was only inches deep!' One Christian girl in the class put up her hand. 'If that is true,' she said, 'then it was an even greater miracle for God to drown the whole Egyptian army in two inches of water!'

Whatever the precise location, it is quite clear that the Red Sea of the Bible was no mere marshy swamp! It was a formidable expanse of water. Such was the scale and the power of this miracle that it remained firmly embedded in the communal memory of the

Israelites. If future generations were ever tempted to doubt Yahweh' power – the recollection of this miracle would reconfirm their faith.

In the song of Moses (chapter 15), the events of the Red Se; crossing are portrayed vividly in poetic form. This poem is though to be one of the oldest pieces of literature in the Bible. Try readin; the poem aloud. Even in translation, you can hear the beat of th; horses' hooves in the rhythm of the poem; you can sense the powe of the sea surging forward and back, and you can share the Israelites awe and wonder at the majesty and power of Yahweh.

But the euphoria didn't last long. As soon as the initial supplies o food had run out, the people began to complain. They even wishec they had stayed in Egypt! This is so true to human nature. Wher people have suffered so much for so long, and their hopes have beer dashed again and again, they often find it hard to cope with libera tion when it finally comes.

God miraculously provided food and water for the people. H; boosted their confidence by giving them victory over their first attackers, the Amalekites. On the advice of Jethro, his father-in-law Moses set up a proper judicial system, so that disputes could be settled and justice for all ensured.

Once in the wilderness, the daily ration of manna began. No satis factory natural explanation of this special food has been offered. I; was part of God's miraculous provision. These events were nc ordinary events. They were an integral part of the salvation history by which God was preparing the world for the coming of Jesus Christ.

The story of the exodus has brought hope to many people in times of oppression. But a note of caution is needed. The Bible does not claim that God will *always* intervene miraculously on behalf of the oppressed. We certainly believe that Yahweh, the God of the Hebrews, is the still the God who hears the cry of the oppressed and the poor. But God has other ways of sustaining and meeting the needs of the oppressed – and he expects you and me to play our part. We should not stand by and do nothing in the face of human suffering! The prophets were later to make it abundantly clear that God's anger is directed against those who see their fellow human beings in distress and do nothing about it: 'How does God's love abide in anyone who has the world's goods and sees a brother or sister in need and yet refuses help?' (1 John 3:17).

Christians have always understood the exodus story as an illustra- tion of New Testament redemption. The God who heard the cry of his covenant people in distress, who sent Moses to save them, and who led them through the wilderness to the promised land, is the same God who has heard the cry of his people who are slaves to sin and death, and who has sent Jesus to redeem us and bring us through the wilderness of this world to eternal life.

READ EXODUS 19–39: THE GIVING OF THE LAW

The build-up to the encounter at Mount Sinai must have been awesome. The storm and the lightning, the thick cloud of darkness, the tension and apprehension, and then finally the very voice of Yahweh himself: 'God spoke and these were his words. "I am the LORD your God who brought you out of Egypt out of the house of slaves."' [15]

No wonder the people were terrified! Not only were the Ten Commandments given at Mount Sinai – but a whole range of other laws as well. Almost all of the rest of Exodus is taken up with details of these laws. They were given in the context of a renewed covenant between Yahweh and the people. The basic covenant which had been made with Abraham was expanded and reaffirmed at Sinai.

The original covenant had contained both conditional and unconditional elements. The covenant at Mount Sinai (often known as the Mosaic covenant) focused on the conditional aspect. Ongoing possession of the Promised Land was conditional on the people remaining loyal to God, having nothing to do with other gods, and remaining obedient to God's Law.

Amazingly, the solemn giving of the Ten Commandments was followed almost immediately by the making of the golden calf (chapter 32) – a tragic episode which demonstrates not just the shallowness of the people's faith, but how much they still had to learn of Yahweh's will and nature. Even Moses does not emerge well from the story! The whole covenant relationship of the people with Yahweh had been put in jeopardy. However, though this episode shows God's judgement, it also shows his mercy and his willingness to forgive and allow a fresh start.

Exodus ends with the people of God, forgiven, under God's blessing and protection, equipped and ready for their onslaught into Canaan. But sadly more setback and tragedy was to come before possession of the Promised Land could finally come about.

1.4 LEVITICUS, NUMBERS AND DEUTERONOMY: FROM SINAI TO THE BANKS OF THE JORDAN

Only a brief survey can be given of the remaining three books of th
pentateuch. I hope, however, that you will still find time to rea
through them. Brief comments are given on each of these books; an
this is followed by a separate chapter on all the legal material sprea
through the pentateuch.

READ LEVITICUS: TRUE HOLINESS

Leviticus means 'the priestly book' and it belongs to a very differer
genre from what has gone before. Many people who have set out t
read the whole Bible through from cover to cover have given up whe
they got to Leviticus!

The first part consists of a manual for the priests in their conduc
of the rituals and festivals that made up the religious life of Israe
Much of this may seem irrelevant to us – especially in the light o
Jesus' once-and-for-all sacrifice for sin. However, the Levitical mate
rial teaches us much about God's nature and holiness and abou
worship. The very ugliness of the sacrificial ritual serves as a visua
aid of the ugliness of sin and of the drastic nature of the remed
needed. The regular round of offerings of thanksgiving and praise, a
well as those for sin and guilt, represent all the essential ingredient
in worship. The fellowship offering (or peace offering) was a hol
meal to celebrate the communion of the family of believers with
Yahweh.

A major event in the religious calendar was the annual Day o
Atonement (described in chapter 16). The priest symbolically trans
ferred the sins of the whole community to the 'scapegoat', which wa
then driven out of the camp. This concept of *atonement* is extremel
important in the New Testament. Atonement has been defined as *a
one-ment* – the process by which the believer becomes 'at one' with God

Sometimes it is said that in Old Testament times forgiveness
could only be obtained by the offering of a sacrifice. However, there

are numerous Old Testament examples of people who were forgiven by God without any specific mention of sacrifice. It was *repentance* that led to forgiveness – and the sacrificial ritual was the outward sign of that repentance. Sacrifice without genuine repentance was to no avail. Christians understand the whole Old Testament sacrificial ritual as a pointer towards the sacrifice of Jesus on the cross. Ultimately, it is the shedding of Jesus' blood that has made forgiveness possible for humankind past, present, and future.

The hygiene and food laws in Leviticus are still a major feature of Jewish life to this day. Some of the forbidden practices (such as the prohibition on boiling a kid in its mother's milk[16]) were practices associated with pagan religion. The Israelites who approached Yahweh in worship were to be pure – both physically and spiritually. Physical cleanness was an outward sign of spiritual cleanness.

The strict laws on sexual practice (chapter 18) were designed to make the Israelites stand out as different from other nations. Sexual relationships were to be regarded as holy. The process of creating new life was not to be debased or abused by casual use or by unnatural sex acts. The use of sexual activity in religious ritual (commonplace in the pagan religions of the Ancient Near East) was particularly abhorred.

The second part of Leviticus (from chapter 18 onwards) is often known as the Holiness Code. It includes the regulations for the major religious festivals; but these are interspersed with laws on a range of social and moral issues. The overall message is clear. Holiness is not achieved by ritual and sacrifice alone – but by living in accordance with Yahweh's Law. The whole Holiness Code could be summed up in the words which Jesus later highlighted: 'You shall love your neighbour as yourself: I am the LORD' (Lev 19:18). 'Neighbour' includes the poor and the foreigner. The Israelites were to have particular concern for the alien because of their memory of how they were ill-treated in Egypt.

READ NUMBERS: THE TRAGEDY OF THE WILDERNESS

The book of Numbers is the most tragic book in the pentateuch. Its central feature is the faithlessness of the people after the return of the twelve spies from a reconnaissance trip to the land of Canaan. The result is God's decree that the community must spend forty years in the wilderness before entering the Promised Land (chapters 13–15). Apart from Joshua and Caleb (the only two of the spies with the faith to encourage the people to proceed), no man then over the age of twenty will set foot in Canaan. The tragic nature of events is compounded when even Moses displays a lapse of faith, as a result of which he is told that he will not live to lead the people into Canaan (20:1–13).

Numbers begins with a census; and towards the end of the book (chapter 26) we are told of a second census at the end of the forty wilderness years. This double census is the feature which gives the book its name.

The first half of the book contains a mixture of information from the early wilderness period, including the duties of religious leaders, further legal material, various individual episodes to illustrate life in the wilderness, and a catalogue of complaints by the people leading to their final refusal to accept the word of the two spies who brought back a positive report about Canaan.

The second half (from chapter 15) gives us various cameos from the long years in the wilderness. The very disjointedness of the book represents the disjointedness of those forty sad years. New instructions from Yahweh are interspersed with the ups and downs of wilderness life and the record of skirmishes with various enemy tribes. These include the intriguing story of the unsuccessful attempt of the Moabite King Balak to persuade his prophet, Balaam, to prophecy against Israel (chapter 22). Even Balaam's donkey speaks against Balaam!

READ DEUTERONOMY: THE SECOND BOOK OF THE LAW

The final book of the pentateuch is the book of Deuteronomy – a name which means 'second book of the law'. This book is set at the very end of the forty years in the wilderness, on the eve of the offensive against Canaan. The *genre* of this book is again different from what has preceded. Much of this book is made up of 'sermons' preached by Moses to the people, as they prepared to enter the Promised Land.

The first of these sermons (chapters 1–4) recalls key events from the wilderness years; and contains an impassioned appeal to the people to remember God's past faithfulness as a basis for their future obedience.

The second sermon (chapters 5–26) is the core of the book. Moses repeats the Ten Commandments. He elaborates on the meaning of the first commandment – calling the people to single-minded devotion to Yahweh alone. He develops the practical outworking of the commandments by a survey of many other God-given laws that will apply in the new circumstances of the Promised Land.

The remaining chapters include a description of the blessings that will follow from obedience to God and a chilling description of the 'curses' that will follow from disobedience (chapters 27,28). This is followed by a solemn renewal of the covenant (chapter 29) highlighting the stark choices that faced the people, between good and evil and between life and death.

After Joshua's appointment as Moses' successor, Moses recites a moving song which sums up in poetic form the whole message of Deuteronomy (chapter 32). The book finishes with Moses' final instructions to the people, his final words of blessing for the tribes, and the moving account of his death, which marks the end of the wilderness era. His epitaph is striking: 'Never since has there arisen a prophet in Israel like Moses, whom the LORD knew face to face' (Deut 34:10).

The key theme of Deuteronomy is that God has shown his love for the people by saving them from Egypt and by promising them his ongoing blessing for the future. The memory of this should motivate the people to love Yahweh – not just in words but in practice, by their obedience to his Law. If they do this they will prosper in the land and receive God's continued blessing. The message of Deuteronomy is summed up in those famous words (which Jesus later called the greatest commandment):

> Hear, O Israel: The LORD is our God, the LORD alone. You shall love the LORD your God with all your heart, and with all your soul, and with all your might.[17]

1.5 THE OLD TESTAMENT LAW

Law is positive

Today we are inclined to think of law as a negative thing – a necessary evil. The medieval Jewish rabbis took a different view. For them God's Law was a privilege. Knowledge of his Law allowed them to see into the mind of God. Through the Law they became familiar with God's 'likes and dislikes'. For the rabbis this was an intensely personal thing. Building a friendship with someone is largely a process of getting to know the other person's likes and dislikes. So the Law gave to the Jews the privilege of friendship with God.

A radical new social system

The Israelite Law is often called *covenant* Law since it was an integral part of the covenant between Yahweh and Israel. It covered every aspect of national life – social, economic, constitutional, military, moral and religious. The Law was to be the basis for a new society that was to contrast radically with what the Israelites had experienced in Egypt and also with the oppressive feudalism of the Canaanite city-states.

Yahweh, the God of the Hebrews, was the God of the poor and the oppressed. He especially protected the widow, the orphan, and the foreigner – who had no easy means of self-support[18]. Israelite Law thus had what has been called a 'bias to the poor' in contrast with Canaanite legal systems, which were more concerned with maintaining the privileged position of the rich and the powerful.

Israelite Law was based on the equality of every citizen. Every individual family had their own God-given stake-hold in the Promised Land. The Law was designed to prevent families being forced to sell their land permanently (for example because of debt). Every forty-nine years came the jubilee year when all land was to return to the original owner. This was designed to prevent the rise of large landowners lording it over landless peasants (Lev 25).

Israelite Law provided for an enterprise culture in which all were expected to work for their living. But it was also recognised that

overty or hardship could arise. The Law was designed to make sure
that people could not become so enthralled to debt that they could
ever break out of it. Every seventh year most debts were to be
cancelled so that everyone could start again with a 'clean sheet'.

There was a legal obligation to help your neighbour if he fell on
hard times and there was a complete ban on taking advantage of
someone else's hardship by charging interest on loans. When an
essential item such as a cloak was taken as security for a debt then it
had to be returned to the borrower whenever he needed it to keep
warm! No doubt this system was open to abuse. But the benefit of
the doubt was to be given to the (poor) borrower not to the (rich)
lender.

The Law emphasised protection of the foreigner. The Israelites
were to remember how they had been treated in Egypt and were never
to exploit others in the same way. There was to be one law for the
citizen and the *same* law for the alien. There was an obligation to
provide for a foreigner in need.

The leaving of the gleanings in the field was one of several provisions for the relief of poverty. The harvester was not to reap right to
the edge of the field, nor was he to go back over the field to gather up
grain that had been dropped or missed. This was not charity: the
poor and the foreigner had a right to the gleanings.

The labourer had to be paid fair wages for his work; and his wages
were not to be withheld from him, not even for one day. Proper
respect was to be shown to the elderly and the disabled – for they too
were under Yahweh's special protection.

For soldiers in the citizen army there were terms and conditions
that would be regarded as progressive even today. A soldier had the
right to go home if he was newly married, or if he had essential business to attend to, or even if he had lost his nerve and was afraid! In
war, an enemy was always to be given a proper opportunity to
surrender; and rules made provision for the proper treatment of prisoners of war. This was in effect an early 'Geneva Convention'.

The Law also provided for the protection of the environment.
Fields were to be allowed to lie fallow every seven years. There was
provision for the protection of wildlife – such as birds' nests. Fruit
trees were not to be cut down – even if they belonged to an enemy.

In addition to these social and economic provisions, the Law also
contained basic principles of civil law. There was what today we would
call a 'general duty of care'. For example, if a man did not put a railing
round his flat roof he would be held responsible if someone fell off.

The Law, of course, also covered essential criminal matters – especially crimes of violence. There were extensive rules about sexual morality.

Enough has been said I hope to demonstrate the radical and egalitarian nature of this new legal system. Many of its provisions would still be regarded as far-reaching and progressive today. The principles of going the second mile, of being willing to give, to share and to lend, and of doing the right thing even by an enemy, were more fully articulated in the teaching of Jesus, but these principles were already firmly embedded in the Old Testament.

The Old Testament Law made allowance for what Jesus called human 'hardness of heart'. Redress of wrongs was allowed – but was limited by the principle of 'an eye for an eye and a tooth for a tooth'. Jesus, of course, upgraded this to the principle of 'turn the other cheek'.

It perhaps comes as a surprise that slavery was permitted within the covenant Law. However, slavery as practised in Israel was fundamentally different from slavery in ancient Greece or Rome and from the brutality of slavery in the Americas – where the slave was treated as property rather than as a human being.

A phrase such as *bond-service* might be a better description of Israelite practice. Captives from war could become bond-servants and Israelites could temporarily become bond-servants as a result of debt. The system was preferable to a system where people were theoretically free but in practice did not have any means of livelihood or support. The Law in Israel went much further than was normal in the Ancient Near East in forbidding any ill treatment of bond-servants. And there was the quite radical provision for all bond-servants to become free in the jubilee year.

Another feature that may strike us as very severe in Old Testament Law is the number of offences for which the death penalty was prescribed. However, though death was the nominal sentence for a variety of offences, it appears that it was only carried out in the most serious of cases. Normally the culprit could pay a heavy fine or ransom in lieu of the death penalty.

The different collections of Laws

The various laws are found in the pentateuch in three main collections.

In Exodus, chapters 21 to 24 form a collection which is known as the Book of the Covenant. This selection of laws illustrates what was involved in putting God's covenant into practice in the daily life of the community.

The Holiness Code (Lev 18–25) is a selection of laws designed to illustrate the practice of holiness, both for the individual and for the community. It is summed up by the words: 'You shall love your neighbour as yourself: I am the LORD' (Lev 19:18).

In the second of his great sermons in Deuteronomy, Moses recounts a whole variety of laws on religious, social, economic, constitutional and military issues – most of which are geared specifically towards settled life in the Promised Land (chapters 1–26).

In addition, there is also a great deal of ceremonial law in the pentateuch. Much of the book of Exodus is given over to the instructions for making the tent for worship, the ark of the covenant, the furnishings of the tent, and the vestments of the priests (chapters 25–31 and 35–40). Leviticus (as we have seen) is largely concerned with ceremonial matters.

When was all of this Law given? Was it all given during the initial encounter with Yahweh at Mount Sinai? Was some of the Law given through Moses on various other occasions over the forty years spent in the wilderness? Or did some of the legal material originate later?

Many of the laws are what today we would call case law. They begin, 'if a man does such and such...'. Some of these laws are quite specific and may have arisen from actual decisions that were made in individual cases – perhaps by Moses himself during the wilderness period.

Much of this case law, however, seems to presuppose that the people are already settled in the land of Canaan. Some scholars have suggested that important legal decisions which arose after Moses' time were later inserted into the Book of the Law. They were still regarded as part of the Law of Moses because they represented the ongoing interpretation and application of the Mosaic Law by

divinely appointed leaders. We are in fact told of at least two occ
sions when an Israelite leader wrote new material into the Book
the Law. Joshua does so after the great covenant-making ceremor
(Josh 24:25,26); and Samuel writes down the rights and duties of the
king (1 Sam 10:25).

The greatest commandment

When Jesus was asked what was the most important commandmen
in the Old Testament, he replied:

> 'You shall love the Lord your God with all your heart, and with all
> your soul, and with all your mind.' This is the greatest and first
> commandment. And a second is like it: 'You shall love your neigh-
> bour as yourself.' On these two commandments hang all the law
> and the prophets.[19]

Jesus did not simply say that these were the two most importar
commandments. He taught that all the other laws hang on these tw
basic principles. All Old Testament Law, properly understood,
about putting into practice what it means to love God and to lo
your neighbour.

The parable of the good Samaritan illustrates this well. The prie
and the Levite passed by the wounded man on the other side of the
road – on the pretext that the Law did not permit a temple official t
have contact with a dead body. Do you see how this turned the whol
purpose of the Law on its head? The priest and the Levite actuall
made the Law a reason for *not* loving their neighbour!

The problem with the scribes and Pharisees was that their motiva
tion for keeping the Law was not love for God or love for neighbou
They were motivated by love for themselves! They did the right in th
hope of a reward; and they avoided the wrong for fear of punish
ment. With that attitude they were even able to find a legal reaso
for not looking after elderly parents! Old Testament Law must no
be divorced from its foundation: love for God and love for others.

The Ten Commandments

The Ten Commandments are found in Exodus 20 and are repeate
by Moses in his sermon in Deuteronomy 5. They are often describe
as a summary of the Law. The Ten Commandments forbid stealing
for example. But the detailed Law went further, requiring giving an

...aring. Jesus took this process of interpretation even further. He ...ught that hatred was in the same league as murder and lust in the ...me league as adultery. So the Ten Commandments are not the sum ...tal of what God requires of us. They are ten initial steps towards ...ve for God and love for neighbour.

If our love for God is in any way genuine, we will have no dealings ...ith other gods, or with false religion, we will not take his name in ...in, and we will respect his Sabbath day (the first four command-...ents).

If we cannot honour our own parents then we are not going to get ...ry far with love for our neighbour! And avoiding murder, theft, ...dultery, false witness, and envy of other people's property, is a bare ...inimum requirement of 'love for neighbour'!

The second commandment, against the making of images, made ...raelite religion quite unique in the ancient world. The Israelites ...ere not to make up their own religion. They were not to limit God ...y representing him in earthly forms.

The third commandment, against misusing God's name, was not ...st about swear-words or oaths. To claim falsely that something was ...one in God's name was to break this commandment. King Jehu ...who was commissioned by the prophet Elisha to restore Israel to ...ue religion) went far beyond his brief and carried out an appalling ...urge. For doing this in Yahweh's name, when it was not what ...ahweh had commanded, he was later condemned by the prophet ...osea[20]. There are many such situations in the world today in which ...lers or political leaders seek the support of ordinary God-fearing ...tizens by claiming that God is on their side. To make this kind of ...aim falsely is to take God's name in vain.

You may have noticed that the two versions of the Ten ...ommandments (Exod 20; Deut 5) are not identical. A slightly ...ifferent emphasis is given the second time. For example, in Exodus ...e principle of a Sabbath rest is built into the very fabric of creation. ...n Deuteronomy it is a social reason for the commandment which is ...ighlighted – a right to a day of rest for foreigners and bond-...ervants. Even domestic animals were not to work seven days a week! ...he Israelites were not to exploit as they had been exploited in Egypt.

How does Old Testament Law apply today?

...he theological tradition in which I was brought up taught that the ...ld Testament Law was to be divided up into three categories.

First was the moral law (in particular the Ten Commandments) which was said to be still binding on Christians. Second was the civil law (for example, the gleanings in the fields) – which was regarded only for ancient Israel and therefore no longer binding today. Third was the *ritual* law (sacrifices, food laws) which are rendered obsolete by Christ's once-and-for-all sacrifice for sin.

There may be some value in this three-fold distinction; but it has meant that two thirds of the Law (the civil and the ritual) has been treated as irrelevant by Christians – despite the fact that Jesus said 'Until heaven and earth pass away, not one letter, not one stroke of a letter, will pass from the law until all is accomplished' (Matt 5:18).

I now believe that this division of the Law into three categories is flawed. There is a sense in which the *whole* Law is set aside – because as Christians we are said no longer to be under law but under grace. But there is another sense in which *none* of the Law is set aside.

Sacrificial ritual is no longer necessary because of Christ's once-and-for-all sacrifice. But we can still learn much about God's holiness and about worship from the religious system that God gave to Israel. Even though the details of the civil law were designed for ancient Israel, the principles lying behind these laws are nonetheless a revelation of the mind of God on a whole range of social issues. The civil law still stands in its entirety as a model of how society might be ordered on God-given lines. God still expects us to apply the spirit of this Law in our contemporary society. For example, it is not now practical to leave gleanings in the fields. But the Law shows us that God expects proper provision to be made for the poor by whatever means are appropriate in our circumstances. Many churches became involved in the Jubilee 2000 campaign, which sought to persuade western governments to cancel third world debt. This was an attempt to put into practice the spirit of the Old Testament jubilee laws, which are based on the principle that no one should be allowed to become a permanent prisoner of debt.

The church has a prophetic calling to bring God-given social principles to the attention of those in power and government. In the Law, we have a vast resource of God-given direction on a whole range of issues that intimately affect communities today; a resource which as Christians we have often neglected in the past.

Endnotes

Indeed, the first twelve books of the Bible, from Genesis to 2 Kings, form an integrated collection, which conveys a continuous story right from the creation of the world to the destruction of Jerusalem in 586 BC.

A very helpful book written by a scientist and theologian is JD Weaver's *In the Beginning God,* Regent's Park College, Oxford, 1994.

PR House, *Old Testament Theology*, p 64

See 1 Corinthians 15:20–50

In chapter 17 God changes Abram's name to Abraham (and also Sarai to Sarah). 'Abram' means 'exalted father' and 'Abraham' means 'father of a multitude'.

You may want to explore this topic in the New Testament. See Romans 4; Galatians 3: 6–9; and also James 2:14–24, which emphasises that faith is not true faith unless it results in actions.

Jeremiah 31: 31–34

Malachi 3:1

0 See Hebrews 7

1 The importance of Melchizedek's priestly role will become clearer when we consider David as king of Jerusalem, and also when we come to Psalm 110 – the only other place in the Old Testament where Melchizedek is mentioned.

2 Genesis 20:17

3 Genesis 45:5,8

4 Abridged with minor changes from *False Gods and Wrong Economics*, by Paul Richards, published by Christian Aid.

5 Exodus 20:1 (my own translation)

6 Exodus 23:19 and Deuteronomy 14:21

7 Deuteronomy 6:4–6

8 Exodus 22:21–23; Deuteronomy 15:11

9 Matthew 22: 37-40

0 The story of Jehu's revolution is recorded in 2 Kings 9,10. Hosea's condemnation of it is found in Hosea 1:3–5.

Part Two

The epic history of Israel:
Joshua to 2 Kings

2.1 SPIES, LIES, WARS AND POLITICS

The Old Testament historical books would provide excellent material for an epic TV series. They contain all the essential ingredient war and peace, love and betrayal, spies and political intrigue. Th lives of ordinary people are intertwined with the affairs of state an empire. There is high drama and suspense and there are moments c humour. And, of course, the books deal with God's involvement i history – as part of his saving purpose for the whole world.

The seven books from Joshua through to 2 Kings make up what call the *epic history*[1]. As with the pentateuch, each of the books complete in itself and they are different in character and style fror one another. But they combine to form one continuous and inte grated work, a sequel to the books of the pentateuch.

The epic history of Israel covers a long time span, from th conquest of the land of Canaan under Joshua (around 1200 BC) t the destruction of Jerusalem and the Temple (in 586 BC). In th history of that 600-year period, we are introduced to a variety c fascinating characters; and a range of theological themes are inter woven with the story.

The comparison with a musical concerto or symphony may agai be helpful. Sometimes what is a background theme in the first move ment of a concerto becomes the main melody of the secon movement; and then that same theme may be recapitulated in different way in later movements. Similarly in the epic history, theme which is introduced in the background in one of the book may emerge as a focal theme in the next book; and then is furthe developed in the books which follow.

One of the main themes is that of *kingship* in Israel. This theme i in the background in Joshua, Judges and Ruth. It comes to the for in 1 Samuel and is developed throughout the rest of the books.

When was it written and by whom?

The epic history is anonymous. Until recently scholars thought i terms of a succession of different *editors* who stitched together range of materials to produce the books as we now have then However, scholars now recognise that the books have been pu together with considerable skill and craftsmanship and increasingly they speak in terms of an overall *author* for the final collection.

The author no doubt researched all the available sources – as any good historian would. There are frequent references to royal records. There are several quotations from an ancient book of poems known as the *Book of Jashar*. Earlier eye-witness accounts are incorporated into his work. But this has been done so skilfully that the final work is a literary masterpiece in its own right and not just a patchwork collection of previous writings.

It is widely thought that the collection was first published around the time of King Josiah's reformation in Jerusalem towards the end of the seventh-century BC. However, the story carries on for twenty-five years after Josiah's death, down to the destruction of Jerusalem in 586 BC. So what we now have may be a *second edition* of the original work – re-published after the destruction of Jerusalem, with some updating and revision. The book would have been re-published to help people understand why God had allowed the tragedy to happen.

Modern scholars usually refer to the epic history as the *Deuteronomic history*. This is because the books were clearly intended to be a sequel to Deuteronomy; to illustrate the outworking of the theology of Deuteronomy in the ongoing history of Israel and Judah[2].

In the ancient world, books were written to read aloud to an audience. It is still thrilling to listen to the Bible books read aloud by a skilled narrator. As you read through these books, pause now and again and read a chapter or two aloud, especially where there is dialogue. You will be amazed at how the text can come to life!

2.2 JOSHUA
A GREAT LEADER OF
GOD'S PEOPLE

The book of Joshua belongs to the *genre* of historical biography. It recounts the career of a great man of God; a man of courage and determination, a distinguished general, a wise judge, a gifted ruler, a leader focused on God's Law. It is the story of the conquest of Canaan from the standpoint of this great leader.

The book begins with the words, 'After the death of Moses', signalling that the story has moved into a new era. Just as the miraculous crossing of the Red Sea had begun the wilderness era, so the miraculous crossing of the Jordan marks the transition from wilderness to settlement.

Who were the Canaanites and the Philistines?

There were several different Canaanite tribes. Each Canaanite city-state had its own king who also controlled the surrounding agricultural territory. The typical religion of the Canaanites was a *fertility* cult – often known as Baal religion. The Canaanite economy was based largely on trade. Indeed the word *Canaanite* originally meant merchant. However, the Canaanite city economies were dependent on extorting the agricultural surplus from the peasants of the surrounding countryside.

The Philistines were relative newcomers to the region. Like the Normans (who invaded England in 1066), the Philistines were a military aristocracy who arrived by sea and imposed their rule on the region that is nowadays known as the Gaza Strip. They were noted for their weapons of iron – in contrast with Israelites and Canaanites who still belonged to the Bronze Age. The Philistines were periodically subdued by the Israelites – but they were never completely conquered. Indeed they eventually gave their name to the land. For 'Palestine' originally meant 'Philistine-land'[3].

In addition to these settled groups, there were also large numbers of *Apiru* tribes – who were closely related to the Israelites. During the period of the conquest of Canaan, the whole of the region was still under Egyptian overlordship. Archaeologists have discovered

ealth of diplomatic correspondence belonging to this era –
including letters between Pharaoh's court and the Egyptian commis-
ioners in Canaan, which make regular reference to *Apiru*.

READ JOSHUA 1–12

Chapter 1: Joshua's commission

The inauguration of a new 'head of state' is a great ceremonial occasion for any nation. The first paragraph of the book of Joshua
consists of God's commission to Joshua as new leader of the people.
Joshua's leadership was to be based on Yahweh's Law (v 7). He was
commanded to study the book of the Law 'day and night'.

'Be strong and courageous' is the refrain that runs through God's
instructions to Joshua. These qualities were, of course, required for
Joshua's military campaigns. But Joshua would require even greater
strength and courage to uphold Yahweh's Law. Moral courage is
often much more difficult to sustain than physical courage! Joshua
is never referred to as king – for Yahweh alone was King of Israel. But
he represents a standard of leadership by which the future kings
would be evaluated.

Chapters 2–12: conquest and victory

First spies are sent to Jericho, where they are rescued by Rahab, the
prostitute (chapter 2). This shows how there was room in Israel for
Canaanites who acknowledged the God of Israel. Indeed Rahab was
to become the mother of Boaz and an ancestor of King David! Next
comes the miraculous crossing of the Jordan (chapters 3,4), followed
by a ceremonial act of circumcision at Gilgal, another symbol of the
new beginning for God's people in the Promised Land (chapter 5).
After this we read of the famous fall of Jericho – a miracle to demonstrate that victory for the Israelites would come from God, not from
military prowess.

Chapters 7 and 8 record the tragic story of the greed of Achan and
his family. The people are given a sharp reminder that they can only
have Yahweh's blessing if they abide by his commands and instructions.

With the eventual capture of the city of Ai, the Israelites had firm foothold on the West Bank of the Jordan. For the first time the could truly claim to be in occupation of the Promised Land Chapter 8 finishes with a national act of worship, at which the Law of God is read aloud to men, women, and children – including foreigners who were to be absorbed into Israel.

The next few chapters cover the second phase of the conquest also marked by miracles. The defeat of the Amorites is accompanied by hailstones (a rare occurrence in that part of the world) and then by an even more amazing event:

> And the sun stood still, and the moon stopped, until the nation took vengeance on their enemies. Is this not written in the Book of Jashar? The sun stopped in mid-heaven, and did not hurry to set for about a whole day.[4]

It is not altogether clear what happened here, for it is hard to imagine that the earth's rotation on its axis was suspended Some have suggested an eclipse or a burning meteor a bright as the sun in the earth's atmosphere. What is clear i that it was a miracle from God which made victor possible. Israelites and Canaanites alike were left under no illusion that Israel's victories were not because of superio military skill or tactics. The victory was the LORD's!

Israel's victories were not because of superior military skill or tactics

The next section (chapters 13–22) is a digression from the story of Joshua to describe in detail the allocation o the land among the twelve tribes of Israel. It is difficult fo us today to absorb this geographical detail. In a modern book we might put these lists into an appendix. However, if something is given a lot of space in an Old Testament book, it is usually important! So hopefully, you will at least skim through this section before reading the comments below.

READ JOSHUA 13–22: THE DIVISION OF THE LAND

Every tribe had its own specific allocation of territory, assigned by God after a detailed mapping exercise (18:1–10). Within the tribes individual families each had their own God-given land-holding. This principle was so fundamental to the constitution of Israel that it was important to record the detail.

However, the beginning of chapter 13 makes clear that even by the end of Joshua's life much of this land was still not in Israelite hands

shua had led the initial push across the Jordan and he had consoli-
ated Israel's hold on the central region. It was then up to the
dividual tribes to finish off the job in their own allotted territories.
en in Joshua's lifetime he had reason to be impatient with the
ibes (18:3). Judges reflects even more explicitly the failure of the
ibes to complete the conquest.

Later, the whole system of tribal land holding was steadily eroded
roughout the period of the monarchy. To the people who were the
iginal readers of this book, at the end of the monarchy era, these
aapters were vital in re-establishing their ancestral heritage.

READ JOSHUA 23,24: JOSHUA'S FAREWELL SPEECHES

Joshua's farewell address (chapter 23), Joshua reminds the people
aat they have been victorious only because of God. He stresses again
e need for obedience to God's Law – an emphasis that had marked
e beginning, the middle, and now the end of Joshua's career.

In chapter 24, there is an assembly of all the tribes at Shechem, in
hich the tribes solemnly bind themselves as a community in
venant with Yahweh under Yahweh's Law. This was the formal
auguration of the new state (or confederacy) of Israel – with
ahweh alone as king. Joshua faces the tribes with a stark choice –
ey must choose between Yahweh and other gods. They cannot seek
have the best of both worlds by worshipping other gods side by
de with Yahweh.

Joshua then declares further laws and statutes for this newly inau-
urated Israelite confederacy. He 'wrote these words in the book of
e law of God' (v 26). Probably the laws which Joshua gave on this
ccasion are in fact embedded in the pentateuch as we now have it.
he book finishes with the death of Joshua and also of Eleazar, the
on of Aaron the high priest, marking the end of the transitional
eriod between wilderness wanderings and settlement of Canaan.
he era of the new Israelite confederacy had begun.

Concluding comments on Joshua

What do modern historians make of the conquest story?

Scholars have mostly been sceptical of the Joshua accoun
Commonly it has been argued that there was not a once-and-for-a
invasion, but a long period of gradual infiltration by nomadi
peoples into Canaan. On this approach, Joshua may have been th
leader of one *Apiru* band who were fired up by the memory of
miraculous deliverance from Egypt and who inspired and galvanise
other immigrant groups to join in forming the new Israel.

Other scholars have sought to apply insights from sociology. The
have suggested that the arrival of Joshua and his Hebrew band wa
the spark which ignited a major revolution in which a variety o
oppressed peoples rose up against their Canaanite rulers. Th
struggle between Israelites and Canaanites was thus not betwee
ethnic groups but was a 'class war' in which the oppressed under
classes threw off their overlords.

Joshua's speech in chapter 24 is then understood as laying dow
the terms under which clans and tribes might join the new egali
tarian Israel. Allegiance to Yahweh alone, and to the social ideals o
Yahweh's Law, was the requirement. This theory would explain wh
large areas of Canaan did not need to be conquered. It also fits we
with archaeological evidence.

The conquest and social revolution

However, those of us who have a high view of the inspiration of th
Bible will of course want to stick by the biblical account. But ther
are a number of things that we might usefully take note of from th
various scholarly theories.

The book of Joshua at first gives the impression of a swift and
complete invasion. But closer examination of the text makes clea
that the victorious battles were all in a quite small area. The book o
Judges makes clear that many areas were not conquered and that th
whole process was quite fragmentary. Remember also that it wa
always possible for people to be absorbed into Israel. When th
Hebrew slaves left Egypt a 'mixed rabble' also went with them. In
Joshua 8: 34,35, we read of foreigners who joined the Israelite cause

)ther kindred peoples who were already settled in the land may have
een absorbed into the twelve-tribe structure of Israel. So the
sraelite group may have expanded as the conquest developed. There
re definite hints in the Bible text that suggest that this might have
een so.

There are also insights which we can gain from the sociological
pproach. The new state of Israel which Joshua inaugurated was
ideed to be a classless society very different from anything else in
he Ancient Near East. The constitution of this new state was to be
he God-given Law of Moses – and we should not underestimate the
ocial (as well as the religious) significance of this.

Those who responded to Joshua's challenge in chapter 24 were
ot just signing up to a new religion. They were committing them-
elves to a revolutionary new legal, social and economic system that
ras unique. In rejecting false gods they were also rejecting the
ppressive social and economic systems associated with those false
eligions.

Holy war or ethnic cleansing?

his brings us to a major issue – the slaughter of the Canaanites!
Vhat are we to make of this? What answers are we to give to those
rho protest against it? Was it not a form of ethnic cleansing or geno-
ide? Some Christians simply say that the God of love whom we
now from the New Testament could not possibly have approved of
far less commanded) a slaughter of this kind. And so they argue that
he book of Joshua records what the people *thought* to be God's will –
ot what God actually commanded. The people acted by the stan-
ards of their own age.

It has to be said, however, that the wickedness of the Canaanites
ras considerable. Their Baal worship was not just another religion. It
ras akin to what today we would call the occult. Leviticus 18:24–26
peaks of the enormity of the wickedness of the Canaanites, which
ad defiled the very land itself. God had kept the Hebrews for *four
undred years* in slavery in Egypt in order to give the Canaanites an
pportunity to repent – an opportunity which they did not take. The
onquest of Canaan was specifically excluded from the humane
rovisions for conduct of war set out in Deuteronomy 20.

The Bible consistently presents God as a God of love and as a God
f justice. All peoples and nations are sinful and deserve God's judge-
nent – and indeed the Israelites themselves were to fall under his

judgement in due course. If God were not a God of justice and judgement then evil would ultimately triumph in the universe. One contemporary Christian writer has summarised the conquest like this:

> What occurs ... is divine judgement for sin similar to that which God has reluctantly meted out since the Garden of Eden. Deuteronomy 27,28 has made it abundantly clear that if Israel sins in a similar manner, they will also feel the effects of the wrath of the Lord. Israel has no moral free pass in these accounts. They were simply the instruments of divine intervention in human affairs ...[5]

I do believe that the book of Joshua is the Word of God. However I must confess that I find this the hardest thing in all of Scripture to accept and understand. I cannot see things as God sees them and must accept in faith that somehow the conquest of the Canaanites was in God's providence the best way in which his purposes could be achieved.

Recently, evidence has been produced that the word *Canaanite* may originally have referred not to the population at large but only to the merchant and ruling classes. There is also evidence that the Bible phrase that is translated as '*inhabitants* of Canaan' may in fact have meant '*rulers* of Canaan'. If this were so, then the slaughter would have involved only the oppressive *ruling classes* of Canaan, and not the bulk of ordinary people. Those ordinary (mostly peasant) people would in fact have been set free to join in the new egalitarian Israel. We read in Joshua 8:35 of foreigners who were absorbed into Israel.

There may well be some considerable mileage in this suggestion – and it could prove to be at least a partial solution to our dilemma. However, there are no slick and easy answers to this issue – and we do need to be aware of unconvincingly glib solutions. Whatever else we may say about the fate of the Canaanites in Joshua, it serves as a reminder that though God is a God of love and mercy, we dare not forget his justice and judgement!

2.3 THE BOOK OF JUDGES ISRAEL'S WILD WEST DAYS

Most of us have seen the Wild West movies where John Wayne presides over the wild frontier! The days of the judges were Israel's Wild West days. The disjointed nature of the book reflects and expresses the disjointed nature of the times.

Judges is a very different book from Joshua. Joshua is a biography, charting the career of one great man of God. Judges is a collection of short stories which catalogue the exploits of a range of local leaders (or judges) whose quality of leadership goes from bad to worse. Joshua focuses on success and victory. Judges makes very clear that the conquest of the land was far from complete. According to Joshua, Israel was to be the people of God's Law. In Judges the Law is never mentioned. The people slide further and further away from God-given standards.

The era of the judges lasted for approximately 200 years, from the death of Joshua (around 1200 BC) to the first king of Israel (around 1030 BC). During this period there was no central ruler. There were occasional assemblies of elders from all of the tribes. The ark of the covenant was kept at Shiloh, which served as a focal point for all the tribes. In times of military emergency, God raised up a *judge* – who was a military leader rather than a legal official. Mostly the emergencies which the judges dealt with were of a local nature, affecting only two or three neighbouring tribes.

The book of Judges does not give a continuous history but a selection of cameos from across a 200-year period. These episodes soon make us realise that things were very different from Joshua's vision for the new Israelite confederation. Two bizarre episodes towards the end of the book (from chapter 17 onwards) demonstrate the depths to which Israel was to sink during this period.

Judges illustrates a repeating cycle. The people sin; they fall victim to their enemies; they repent; God raises up a judge who leads them to victory; again the people sin – and the cycle begins all over again.

READ JUDGES 1–16: THE ADVENTURES OF THE JUDGES

Chapters 1,2: the death of Joshua

A new episode in a TV series often begins with a recap of how the previous episode ended. The first two chapters give us a recap of this kind.

Even before Joshua's death the people had begun to compromise with the false religion of the Canaanites. The high ideals of an egalitarian and just society were quickly disintegrating into an everyone-for-themselves philosophy.

The first incident in Judges is the story of the unfortunate Canaanite King Adoni-bezek, who ends up with his thumbs and toes cut off. This incident shows something of the absurdity of the petty kingship of the Canaanites. The behaviour of the Israelite judges may sometimes have been bad – but it was nothing compared with the behaviour of Canaanite rulers! When the Israelites eventually come to Samuel and demand a king 'like other nations' (1 Sam 8:5) we should think back to this episode!

The second half of chapter 2 is a sermon by the narrator. In the epic history, such sermons are regularly used to mark key transitions in the history of Israel. This sermon marks the end of the Joshua era and the beginning of the era of the judges.

Chapter 3: the first judges

Othniel was successful in battle and brought peace and stability for a generation. Next came **Ehud** – the left-handed man with the two-edged sword. We may smile at his trickery and guile, and at the Canaanite King Egan's comical demise. But it is clear that Ehud does not represent anything like the quality of leadership of Joshua! The same can be said of **Shamgar's** frenzied antics with an ox-goad!

Chapters 4,5: Deborah and Barak

The period of **Deborah** and **Barak** was the one brief time in the whole of the judges' era when there was order and stability in Israel. Deborah served as a prophet, and also as a judge to whom people could come for the settlement of disputes. It is significant that she was a woman! Don't let anyone tell you that a woman could never be in a position of authority among God's people!

Chapters 6–9: Gideon and his sons

Chapter 6 brings us to **Gideon**. Several of the stories from Gideon's career are well known – especially his *putting out a fleece* to test God's guidance. Certainly it was good that Gideon wanted to be sure of God's will, but he was not a man of the stature of Joshua, who was in sufficiently direct communication with God to act decisively without putting God to the test! The manner in which Gideon reduced his army from 32,000 to 300 showed again that victory in battle depended on Yahweh and not on military tactics.

Gideon rose to hero status, but like so many of the judges, serious flaws marred his career. He had many wives – and at least one Canaanite mistress. He had seventy legitimate sons and illegitimate children as well! Gideon began his career with a courageous stand against Baal religion; but he ended up making a gold idol for his home town of Ophrah!

At the high point of his military success, Gideon was invited by the people to become king, but he refused on the grounds that Yahweh alone was King of Israel (8:22,23). In the sequel to this in chapter 9, Gideon's illegitimate son, Abimelech, declares himself king of Shechem and murders all seventy of Gideon's legitimate sons except for Jotham. Jotham rebukes Abimelech with a parable about kingship – which (as we shall see below) is an important centrepiece of the whole book.

Chapters 10–16: further decline

The quality of the judges now deteriorates rapidly. Notice in particular the rashness of **Jephthah's** vow leading to the tragic death of his daughter. This episode contrasts with the story of God's command to Abraham to sacrifice his son Isaac. In Jephthah's case, it was his foolish vow that caused the crisis. It was an absurd inversion of moral values to murder a daughter rather than break a rashly-made vow! The Canaanite gods might well have expected Jephthah to fulfil such a vow, but not Yahweh.

Finally in the saga of the judges comes **Samson**. Despite a promising start, Samson represents the lowest point in the era of judges. God is not even mentioned in the course of his career and his womanising lifestyle is his downfall. While we may smile at the way in which he finally avenges himself against his Philistine captors, his life ends in tragedy.

READ JUDGES 17–21: THE WILD FRONTIER!

If the events of the Samson era are amazing; the events of the closing five chapters of the book are mind-boggling! They illustrate the depths to which even God's people could sink. The first is the story of the freelance Levite from Bethlehem, who becomes private priest to a somewhat disreputable businessman called Micah. Later he betrays Micah and becomes priest to the tribe of Dan.

The second even more outrageous story also concerns a Levite. His concubine (or 'mistress') is gang-raped and murdered in the Benjaminite town of Gibeah by men who had previously intended a homosexual orgy. There then follows a terrible revenge on the tribe of Benjamin, so much so that the tribe is in danger of extinction. Since the other Israelite tribes had sworn not to *give* their daughters in marriage to a Benjaminite, the only way for the surviving Benjaminite men to obtain wives was to seize them by force!

Concluding comments

The way in which Judges is structured indicates that the pivotal stories are the Deborah-Barak victory over the Canaanites and the career of Gideon. We will look at these stories in a little more detail.

Deborah's Song

Great victories in battle are often remembered in song. The Israelite victory over Sisera is one of the few stories in the Bible to be told twice – once in prose in chapter 4 and then again in the song of Deborah in chapter 5.

We have already noted that the epic historian marks key points in the narrative with an editorial sermon. In other places a key speech from a major character is used in this way. A poem is another method used by the author to signal to the audience that events have taken an important turn.

Why was this particular episode so important? Deborah's rule was the one period in the judges' era when there was any degree of stability and justice, and it came about when both women and men were given complementary roles in leadership! Another reason is that Barak's victory was the final battle against the Canaanites. The battle took place at Megiddo, which was also to be the site of the *last* major battle in the epic history (Josiah's defeat by the Egyptians in

609 BC). Most of us know Megiddo better by its New Testament name, Armageddon, which according to the book of Revelation is to be the site of one more *last battle*!

Re-read the song of Deborah in chapter 5. Allow yourself through the poetry to become emotionally involved in the events. In the opening verse, be stirred by the willingness of the people to fight for their freedom. As you read on, you will be awed by a sense of the power of Yahweh, before whom even the mountains quake. You will share the vibrant excitement of the people as liberation dawns.

Yahweh is described as the God of Sinai (v 5). The call to battle in Yahweh's name was a call to rally for the Law of Sinai. How dreadful it was that some tribes chose to stay away! We can feel the disdain as we read verses 16–18! But perhaps the most striking thing about the poem is that we see the events through the eyes of three very different women, all of them mother-figures.

First of all, there is Deborah herself described as mother of Israel (v 7). Then secondly comes Jael. Notice the *maternal* symbolism of the milk which she offered to Sisera who had only asked for water. But how are we to regard the way in which she killed Sisera, against all the rules of refuge and hospitality in the ancient world? From one point of view, she was the hero of the hour – but is there not a disturbing question coming through in the song as well? Was this the way for a mother to behave, this betrayal of trust? The poetry brings out in us the mixed emotions of admiration and horror!

this poem is a reminder that even a just war has horrible consequences

Finally there is the pathetic picture of Sisera's mother. Only a hard-hearted reader would feel no sympathy for Sisera's mother – even despite the reign of terror that Sisera had imposed on the Israelites. This was one of Israel's most significant victories and yet the author's final word is the tragic picture of a mother who had lost her son.

What this poem says to me could be summed up something like this: war can be a necessary evil, but the pathetic picture of Sisera's mother is a reminder that even a just war has horrible consequences. No doubt there were many mothers on both sides who wept that day. This is a song which arouses in us the mixed emotions of excitement of victory but also of horror at the inevitable suffering.

Gideon and the Kingship of Yahweh

In chapter 8, after victory in battle, the people come to Gideon and offer him a hereditary kingship. The egalitarian ideals of the confederation of tribes were not working out in practice and there was an increasing desire among the people for a strong ruler – especially for military purposes. Gideon refuses the offer, reminding the people that Yahweh alone is their king. This anti-monarchy view is further reinforced by the episode which follows – the disastrous attempt of Gideon's illegitimate son Abimelech to have himself made king at Shechem.

Then comes the powerful *parable of the trees*, told to Abimelech by Jotham, Gideon's only other surviving son. The olive tree, the fig tree, and the vine are in turn invited to become king of the trees. But they all have much too important a job to do. The only tree that will consider the role is the thorn bush! Abimelech was an example of a thorn-bush king! This parable is the central feature of the book and the reader is at this point persuaded that an earthly kingship would be an affront to the sovereignty of Yahweh.

But then in the remaining chapters of the book, the writer vividly describes the social, moral and religious depths to which Israel sank in those closing years of the judges' era. The book ends with the refrain: 'in those days there was no king in Israel; all the people did what was right in their own eyes[6]'. Now the reader is inclined to think that some form of king is a must – whatever the theological niceties!

The writer has thus very skilfully prepared us for both sides of the pro- and anti-monarchy debate that is to be developed in the book of 1 Samuel. This debate is one of the major themes of the epic history and it does not find a resolution until the New Testament, when Jesus proclaims a totally new understanding of the *kingdom of God*.

2.4 THE BOOK OF RUTH AN IDYLLIC ROMANCE AND MORE!

If ever there was a major change in style and atmosphere between one book and the next, it is the transition between the books of Judges and Ruth. From the cut and thrust of the turbulent times of Judges, we move to the idyllic romance of Ruth and to the well-ordered and law-abiding society of Bethlehem in Ruth's day. We should not, however, be misled by the book's simplicity, for it also deals with serious issues which are as relevant today as they ever were.

> READ THE BOOK OF RUTH

Chapter 1: what's in a name?

It is always interesting to discover what a name means. My first name, James, goes back to the Bible name Jacob, which means 'supplanter' (not very flattering!). Names in the Bible often have a significant meaning.

The first character to be named in the book of Ruth is Elimelech, which means 'My God is King'. This name reminds us of Gideon's rejection of kingship on the grounds that Yahweh alone is King of Israel. It indicates that the book of Ruth has something significant to contribute to the developing debate over kingship.

Elimelech and his family left Bethlehem because of famine and settled in the neighbouring country of Moab. (Famine in Bethlehem is itself an irony over a name – for Bethlehem means 'house of bread'). The journey from Bethlehem to Moab was not long; but it was significant because of the enmity between Israelites and Moabites. However, there is no hint that Elimelech and his family were unwelcome in Moab.

Tragically Elimelech and his sons all die leaving three widows – Naomi and her daughters-in-law, Ruth and Orpah. Naomi prepares to return to her home town of Bethlehem. Orpah eventually decides to stay behind; but Ruth clings to her mother-in-law with the famous words:

Where you go, I will go; where you lodge, I will lodge; your people shall be my people, and your God my God. Where you die, I will die and there will I be buried[7].

Chapters 2,3: love is in the air

Romance between Boaz and Ruth unfolds quickly! Ruth has to find some way of supporting Naomi and herself and she does so by gleaning in the fields. Under Israel's God-given Law, the poor had a right to glean in the fields in this way. We sense God's providence in the background: for Ruth 'happens' to choose the field of Boaz, the man she is going to marry!

Chapter 4: events take a surprising turn

The legal complexities of chapter 4 may require a little explaining. First of all, there is the notion of the *kinsman-redeemer*. One of the basic principles of Israelite Law was that every Israelite family had its own landholding. If a family was forced to sell the land, it was the duty of the next of kin to *redeem* or buy back the land so that it would remain in the family.

The second legal custom is quite alien to us. It is called *levirate* marriage[8]. If a man died leaving a childless widow, then his brother was expected to marry the widow. The first child of that marriage would then be regarded as the heir to the dead brother so that his family line would not die out. This levirate custom did not apply directly to Boaz, since he was a second cousin rather than a brother. But it is characteristic of this book that the characters are willing to 'go the second mile' in doing the right thing by members of their wider family.

At the end of each day's work in ancient Israel, the men would gather at the gates of the town. This gathering functioned as a town council, as a time when wisdom was passed from the old to the young, and as a time when stories of God's past dealings with Israel were passed down. It was also the place where the elders would settle disputes and witness legal transactions as here in the Ruth story.

Boaz was not the immediate next-of-kin. There was a nearer kinsman who had a prior duty to look after Ruth and Naomi and also a prior right to purchase Elimelech's property from Naomi. This ear kinsman is unnamed, and he had not so far come forward to do he right thing by Ruth and Naomi. Why were Ruth and Naomi ving in poverty if they had land at their disposal? Presumably the nnamed kinsman had occupied Elimelech's land for himself. But ow Elimelech's widow has returned 'out of the blue'; and the insman reluctantly agrees that he should pay Naomi the proper rice for the land.

Then Boaz springs his surprise by publicly announcing his inten- ion to marry Ruth. Under Israel's inheritance laws, the land would ventually revert to the heir of the original family line. So if Ruth ere to have a son then Naomi's land would eventually revert to that on. For this reason, the nearer kinsman waives his claim to the land for he does not want to buy land that will not in the end pass to his wn son. The handing over of a shoe in the presence of the elders was he formal symbol of a legal agreement (in the days before written ocuments).

Boaz's marriage to Ruth fulfilled the spirit of the *levirate* custom. That is why the child when born is welcomed by the townspeople as a on and heir for Naomi (rather than for Boaz).

When the townspeople congratulate Ruth and Boaz on their ngagement, they liken the couple to an ancestral figure of their tribe alled Perez (v 12). Perez was the son of Judah by an inces- uous union with his daughter-in-law, Tamar! To nderstand the significance of this, turn back and read Genesis 38. Tamar was also a foreigner who married into srael, but unlike Ruth, she was not treated well and she ad to go to extreme lengths to get justice.

And if this reference to Boaz's ancestor comes as a urprise – even more of a surprise comes in the closing erses in which we discover that Ruth and Boaz are ances- ors of King David, and also therefore, of Jesus Christ!

the Old Testament story is the story of how God chose *unlikely* people for his purposes

The opening verses of Matthew's Gospel trace the ncestry of Jesus, from Abraham, through Ruth and Boaz own to David, and then right down to Joseph and Mary. As was ormal in ancient genealogies the focus is on the male line. But Matthew mentions four of the women who were ancestors of Jesus: Tamar (mother of Perez), Rahab (the prostitute of Jericho and mother of Boaz), Ruth, and Bathsheba (with whom David had his dulterous affair). Much of the Old Testament story is the story of how God chose *unlikely* people for his purposes, despite their sinful- ess and shortcomings! These women are all foreigners who had married into Israel. The genealogy serves to remind us that Jesus was Saviour for all the nations, not just for the Jews.

Ruth and the kingship question

The book of Ruth swings the pendulum back to the *God-alone-is-king* viewpoint! The bizarre events of Judges 17–21 had certainly suggested that a strong ruler was needed. Yet the book of Ruth is set in that same period when there was no king in Israel; and Ruth's Bethlehem is the nearest thing in the epic history to the full implementation of Yahweh's Law.

The rules requiring provision for the poor were properly observed. The elders administered justice fairly. Women obtained their rights. Family members did the right thing by one another. The widow, the orphan, and the foreigner are properly looked after – even a Moabitess (from a long-standing enemy nation) was made more than welcome. God's Law is kept on every count and there was no need for an earthly king to make this happen!

This teaches a lesson which is surely of relevance in many contemporary situations. I am writing at a time when the peace process in Northern Ireland is floundering. Political process is, of course, most important in any country. But ultimately, if the hearts of the people are not right then there will not be true peace, whatever the system of government. And that does not just apply to Northern Ireland!

Hesed: love and loyalty

A very important Hebrew word used in Ruth is the word *hesed* – which means *love and loyalty*. It implies commitment, faithfulness, and a generosity of spirit. It is a word commonly used in the Old Testament – especially of God's own *steadfast love* for his people.

In Ruth all the main characters do *hesed*, that is, they go the second mile in their relationships with one another. It is this very quality of *hesed* which was the true mark of the kingdom of Yahweh. The kingdom of God exists on earth whenever people do *hesed* with one another in the fulfilment of God's law. This understanding clearly points forward to the concept of the kingdom of God as taught by Jesus.

The book of Ruth demonstrates *hesed* in relations between men and women. The book promotes marriage. It also reminds us of our responsibility to make provision for the poor and disadvantaged.

Ruth and Boaz never knew that they were destined to be ancestors of King David, let alone of Jesus Christ! But God used their faithfulness in their own small corner as part of the outworking of his saving purpose for the whole of the world!

2.5 THE BOOK OF 1 SAMUEL THE TRAGEDY OF KING SAUL

Few things are more tragic than when someone of great potential ends his life in calamity and despair. It is even more tragic if the disaster arises from the person's own sin or folly. We are familiar with Shakespeare's tragic figures such as Macbeth and Hamlet. In the dramas of classical Greece, the hero was a man of super-human qualities with a tragic flaw or weakness which was his downfall.

The book of 1 Samuel is the tragedy of King Saul, who began his reign with hope and promise, but who in the end took his own life in hopelessness and despair. Once again there is a change of *genre*. We have had biography in Joshua; a collection of Wild West stories in Judges; and an idyllic romance in Ruth. Now we have tragedy.

I have suggested earlier that I would love to see the whole of the epic history produced as a great TV series. If I were allowed to make a film of just one of these books, I would choose the tragedy of King Saul. It is a superbly written book with all the ingredients for a box-office success. There are scenes of intense emotion, yet also moments of humour. Heights of courage and great acts of kindness are juxta-posed with depths of brutality and cruelty. Great affairs of state alternate with the lives and struggles of ordinary people. Trust and friendship contrast with acts of betrayal. There are both victories and defeats in battle. The famous duel between David and Goliath is followed by the unnerving frenzy of Saul's increasing madness. The book culminates in the macabre visit of Saul to the Witch of Endor. And most important, the hand of God is behind it all; the God who is able to bring good out of evil and to achieve his purposes through the most unlikely of people and circumstances.

> ### READ 1 SAMUEL 1–7: SAMUEL – A GREAT MAN OF GOD

Chapters 1–3: Samuel's birth

The opening episode is the moving story of the birth and boyhood of Samuel. We can feel for Hannah in her childlessness and we can share her joy at the eventual birth of Samuel. We can smile when Eli

ne priest mistakes her distress for drunkenness! We can be moved
nd stirred by the song of thanksgiving and praise which Hannah
ings. The touching simplicity of young Samuel's late-night call from
ahweh is one of the best-known Bible stories. The tragic figure of
li, whose family line will be replaced as God's priests, is a forerunner
o the coming tragedy of King Saul.

Chapters 4–7: Samuel as judge

These chapters pick up where Judges left off. Religion has so degen-
rated that the ark of the covenant is regarded as little more than a
alisman which might bring good luck if taken on to the battlefield!
The Israelites are defeated and the ark of the covenant is captured –
ut the Philistines find it 'too hot to handle' and soon return it to
sraelite soil. The Israelites do not quite know what to do with it and
o it is shunted to a backwater in Kiriath Jearim.

Eventually, however, under Samuel's guidance, the people repent,
heir enemies are defeated, and a period of peace and stability
eturns, in which Samuel rules as Yahweh's representative. For a brief
eriod the tribal confederation seems to be working well – but it was
ot to be for long.

READ 1 SAMUEL 8–12: THE RISE OF SAUL

Chapter 8: the demand for a king

Samuel is getting old. His sons (like Eli's) were greedy and corrupt.
There was no effective military leadership and law and order was
breaking down. The people came to Samuel and made their
demands: 'You are old and your sons do not follow in your ways;
ppoint for us, then, a king to govern us, like other nations[9].'

Samuel's initial reaction is very human, arising from a sense of
ersonal hurt and rejection. (It is reassuring for us to know that even
he great men of God can feel like this sometimes!) Yahweh rebukes
Samuel. It is Yahweh they are rejecting not Samuel! Give them a
king, says Yahweh, if that is what they want; but warn them what
hey are letting themselves in for.

Samuel's warning to the people could be summed up in two
words: *taxation* and *conscription*[10]. The picture which Samuel paints of

how kings behave was no doubt based on the local Canaanite kings. The Israelites were asking for the very form of government which their forefathers had fought to be free of! Despite Samuel's warning the people persist. They want a king. They want to be like other nations. God tells Samuel to give them what they want.

Chapters 9–11: the reluctant king comes to the throne

There are three separate episodes in the process by which Saul eventually becomes king.

First comes the light-hearted story of the country boy who set out to find his father's lost donkeys and ended up finding a throne! Notice the way in which Saul's servants speak of the prophet (9:6–8). They look on him as some kind of fortune-teller who will find their lost donkeys if they give him the smallest coin they can find!

Three important things are stressed about Saul at this point. First of all, he was young, handsome, and a head taller than anyone else. Secondly, we are shown his natural humility. Thirdly, we are told that after he was anointed king God gave him 'a new heart'. He had everything going for him!

The second main episode takes place at a formal assembly of the Israelite tribes. Saul is chosen by the casting of lots. But where was Saul when his name was announced? Hiding behind the baggage! This is certainly a humorous touch. Is it evidence of Saul's humility or is it an early hint that Saul, the reluctant king, will crack under pressure?

'Long live the king!', the people shout. It is clear from the text, however, that there were still all shades of political opinion in Israel on this issue of kingship. In the middle ground were those who accepted the need for a permanent ruler but avoided the use of the word *king* itself [11]. The process by which Saul became king established two ongoing principles for the appointing of kings of Israel. A king had to be anointed by Yahweh's prophet and had also to be accepted by the people.

Though Saul was now called king, he was not 'head of state' for Samuel clearly regarded himself as still in charge. He expected Saul's ongoing obedience to his instructions. In chapter 11, when a major military crisis arose, the newly-appointed King Saul was found working in the fields. He may have been declared king – but he still had no palace and no permanent army! Saul was in many ways still ke the judges of old. He carried on with his normal working life ntil an emergency arose in which his leadership was needed. It was nly when Saul led the people to victory over their enemies that oubts about his appointment are finally banished.

Chapter 11 records the third episode in the process of Saul's elec- on, what we might call a coronation celebration. The writer pecifically draws our attention to Saul's generosity and mercy to his olitical opponents. Saul had begun his reign well.

Chapter 12: Samuel's farewell speech

his section of the book ends with a major speech from Samuel. This peech formally marks the end of the days of the judges and the eginning of monarchy. Samuel summarises the history of the sraelites to date and the events leading up to the monarchy. The eople acknowledge that they have been sinful in asking for a king, ut Samuel assures them that God can bring good out of the situa- on if both king and people remain faithful.

READ 1 SAMUEL 13–27: SAUL AND DAVID

Chapters 13–15: Saul is rejected

he enthronement ceremony is over. The day-to-day business of king- hip now begins. Chapters 13–15 describe military campaigns in vhich Saul is successful – despite the foolish oath which almost led o Jonathan's death. At least Saul was more flexible than Jephthah ad been in the matter of his oath! However, it is quickly apparent hat Samuel has not bowed out of the picture. On two occasions he lashes with Saul (chapters 13,15) and this leads to Saul's total rejec- ion by Samuel as king. God will now choose a successor to King Saul.

Chapters 16–18: David's rise to fame

God tells Samuel to go to Bethlehem to the family of Jesse (a descen- lant of Ruth and Boaz). He is to anoint one of the sons of Jesse as he next king. To everyone's surprise, David, the youngest son is hosen. For: 'The LORD does not see as mortals see; they look on the outward appearance, but the LORD looks on the heart' (1 Sam 16:7).

Many of the episodes of David's early career are well known: David as the court musician soothing King Saul's rages; his famous victory over Goliath; Saul's increasing jealousy of David's military success and popularity; David's enduring friendship with Saul's son Jonathan; and finally Saul's outright persecution of David.

Chapters 19–27: Saul persecutes David

We are told that Yahweh's spirit had left Saul and that an evil spirit sent by Yahweh tormented him[12]. This evil spirit sent by Yahweh is hard to explain. Was it simply the tormenting voice of conscience? Was it a spirit of temptation – such as Jesus himself was later to experience (and conquer)? Was the evil spirit a punishment from Yahweh to bring about Saul's final downfall? We cannot be sure.

However, we might have some sympathy for Saul. His successor has been anointed by God's prophet and is rapidly gaining in popularity. Yet somehow Saul has to struggle on and discharge his responsibilities as king. No wonder he cracks under the pressure. His persecution of David and his murder of the priests of Nob (chapter 22) are instances of outrageous behaviour, however Saul is presented as a possessed madman rather than as a calculating evildoer.

David is now the rising star. His military prowess had become proverbial. Forced to flee from Saul, he became a Robin-Hood-style outlaw figure. He spared Saul's life on two occasions when he could have killed him – professing his ongoing loyalty to Saul (chapters 24,26). He played a kind of double game of pretending allegiance to Israel's Philistine enemies, while doing his best to help his own people when he could.

However, the picture of David is not all rosy. Saul agreed to David's marriage with his daughter Michal – but only on the absurd condition that David must bring to Saul the foreskins of one hundred dead Philistines! So David murdered not just one hundred but two hundred Philistines and mutilated their bodies. And what are we to make of David's campaigns in chapter 27, where men, women, and children are slaughtered so that no one will remain alive to report on what David had done? These two episodes show a ruthless side to David's character – for which David did not have the excuse of a tormenting evil spirit!

READ 1 SAMUEL 28–31: SAUL'S FINAL DOWNFALL

...ul is finally driven to the depths of despair. Samuel, the only
...rson whom he could have turned to, was already dead (25:1). There
...en follows the macabre scene of Saul's visit to the Witch of Endor.
...e raises up an apparition of the spirit of Samuel. A final judge-
...ent on Saul is pronounced and the apparition of Samuel foretells
...e death of Saul and his sons in the forthcoming battle.

Some years ago, I had the sad task of counselling a young widow
...hose husband had been tragically killed in a bomb explosion. She
...ceived letters from a spiritualist group in England who claimed to
... able to put her in touch with her late husband. She had a strong
...hristian faith and she was not tempted to become involved in
...iritualism. But she was greatly distressed that the spiritualist
...oup might in some way be disturbing her late husband's rest. She
...oted the words spoken by the apparition of Samuel, 'Why have
...ou disturbed me?' I was able to reassure her that biblical teaching
... the subject was clear, and that her loved one remained safe in the
...ms of Jesus until the day of the resurrection. The Witch of Endor
...ory is a unique and puzzling Bible story – and not one from which
... can derive a doctrine about departed spirits.

But what are we to make of Samuel's re-appearance from the
...ead? Some suggest that the episode was all in Saul's tormented
...bconscious. Others suggest that what Saul saw was not the real
...amuel at all, but a false apparition conjured up by the witch.
...hatever the explanation, Saul's initial reaction was one of total
...espair. But eventually he pulled himself together, ate a meal with
...is men, and finally went out to do what a king should be doing –
...reparing for battle against his country's enemies.

Saul died a tragic but heroic death on the battlefield. True, he
...ok his own life, but only to avoid the worse fate of capture,
...ockery, torture, and mutilation at the hands of his enemies. The
...hilistines could not be allowed to say that they had killed Yahweh's
...nointed.

...ingship and Messiah in 1 Samuel

...nd so the first experiment with kingship in Israel ends in tragic
...ilure. We may have some sympathy for Saul and his final heroic
...eath. But we must also acknowledge that the fatal flaws which led
... his downfall were ultimately of his own making. It may, therefore,

come as somewhat a surprise to discover that Saul is the first persc
in the Old Testament to be described as Yahweh's *messiah*!

In chapters 24 and 26, David is given an opportunity to kill Sau
He refuses, saying that he will not lift up his hand against 'Yahweh
anointed'. Samuel also refers to Saul on a number of occasions a
'Yahweh's anointed'. The Hebrew word for 'anointed' is *messiah*. Th
king was Yahweh's messiah. We will trace the development of this th
messiah title as it develops into the messianic hope which finds i
ultimate fulfilment in Jesus.

2.6 THE BOOK OF 2 SAMUEL
THE ENIGMA OF KING DAVID

you are familiar with Shakespeare's play *Julius Caesar*, you will
member the great speech made by Mark Anthony after the murder
Caesar. Mark Anthony refers to the involvement in the murder by
esar's close friend Brutus. He says several times: 'For Brutus was
honourable man'. By the end of the speech he has placed a strong
ubt in the audience's mind that Brutus was maybe not as
nourable as he seemed[13]!

David was described early in 1 Samuel as a 'man after God's own
art'. But by the end of the story, we are maybe wondering how on
rth a 'man after God's own heart' could have behaved the way
avid did!

We have already noticed the different genre of each of the books
the epic history. This book adopts the format of the *court history*; a
nre which was common in the royal courts of the Ancient Near
st. But 2 Samuel is a court history with a difference. For this book
es not hesitate to bring out David's faults and shortcomings as
ll as his success and greatness.

READ 2 SAMUEL 1–5: DAVID BECOMES KING

ese opening chapters of 2 Samuel are transitional; they could
ually have been the closing chapters of 1 Samuel. David puts to
ath the messenger who had claimed to have killed Saul. There is
en a moving poem by David lamenting the deaths of Saul and
nathan. The first days of David's kingship (like Saul's) are marked
a magnanimous attitude to his rivals and opponents.

David at first became king only of Judah, his own tribe, for Saul's
n, Ishbaal, had declared himself King of Israel. In practice,
wever, it seems that Ishbaal only had a 'government in exile' in a
sert stronghold. Abner, who had been Saul's right-hand man, even-
ally transferred his allegiance to David – only to be murdered by
avid's henchman, Joab. Soon Ishbaal was murdered as well. This
ft the way clear for David to become king of the whole of Israel at
e request of an assembly of all the tribes (5:1–5). David had now
lfilled the twin requirements for kingship: anointing by Yahweh's
ophet and acclamation by the people.

The writer emphasises how David distanced himself both from the murder of Abner and that of Ishbaal. He makes a great show of lamenting Abner's death, but he does nothing to punish the culprit Joab. Was David (like Brutus) really as honourable as he seemed?

The next significant event is David's capture of the fortress of Jerusalem. It had been a Jebusite city, an almost impregnable fortress, and David captured it by a surprise attack through the water tunnel. David did not wipe out the Jebusite people – indeed many of them became his advisers and officials. Jerusalem served as a neutral capital, since it was not part of the territory of any one of the Israelite tribes[14]. A modern parallel would be the way in which Washington DC is a separate territory and not part of any one of the United States.

This gave David the opportunity to do what Saul had never been able to do, to accumulate the trappings of kingship: a fortress capital, a professional army, a government team of ministers and advisors – and even a harem (an indispensable attribute of kingship in the ancient world, it seems!).

David had now become king of three separate jurisdictions (Judah, Israel, and Jerusalem), each by a different process. He more and more became a 'king like other nations', doing all the things that Samuel had warned against (taxation and conscription), and defying the instructions which Moses had laid down in Deuteronomy 17. David's reign moved Israel a further stage away from the egalitarian ideals of Joshua's vision.

READ 2 SAMUEL 6,7: THE COVENANT WITH DAVID

David became a 'king like other nations', doing all Samuel had warned against

In the world of the Ancient Near East, kings usually claimed to be descended from the gods. Indeed in Egypt the Pharaoh claimed actually to be a god. In Israel, of course, the people knew that David was not descended from any god. He was the shepherd-boy son of Jesse. In chapter 7, however, we have a totally new development.

Through the prophet Nathan, Yahweh establishes a covenant with David, in which David is promised an everlasting dynasty. David's son (Solomon) will build a Temple for God in Jerusalem and will be adopted as God's *son*. Similar language is used about the king in Psalm 2. A new dimension is thus added to the concept of the king as Yahweh's anointed (or messiah). The king was in a sense, 'son of God'.

David had earlier brought the ark of the covenant to Jerusalem
(chapter 6). The ark had been the main focus of faith in Yahweh in
the pre-monarchy days. David offered sacrifices on that occasion. We
are told that several of David's sons later acted as priests. Yet,
according to the Law, only descendants of Aaron were to act as
priests. Samuel had earlier rebuked Saul for offering a sacrifice[15].

The explanation is that when David brought the ark of the
covenant to Jerusalem, he was in fact combining two religious tradi-
tions: the tradition of Israel (stretching back to Moses), and the
Jebusite worship of 'God Most High' (stretching back to
Melchizedek). You will remember the mysterious figure of
Melchizedek, who is described in Genesis 14 both as king of
Jerusalem and also as priest of God Most High[16].

It seems that the Davidic kings of Jerusalem took on this ancient
priestly role of Melchizedek. This did not give them the right to usurp
the role of the Israelite priesthood (as King Uzziah was later to learn to
his cost[17]). But it seemed to give the Jerusalem kings an overarching
priesthood and the right to offer sacrifices on special state occasions.

It may seem odd that David had a different religious function in
the city of Jerusalem from his function as king of Judah and Israel.
Interestingly, however, we have a parallel in the United Kingdom.
The Queen, when she is in England, is Supreme Governor of the
Church of England. When the Queen crosses the border into
Scotland, she becomes a Presbyterian, for the national Church of
Scotland is Presbyterian. When it comes to Wales and Northern
Ireland, the Queen has no official religious role at all, for in those
jurisdictions there is no longer any state church.

In practice, the end result of David's religious policy was that the
ark (and the tablets of the Law which it contained) ceased to be the
focus of the faith and religion of Israel. Indeed once the ark was
moved to Solomon's Temple we never hear of it again – hence the
scope for explorers and film-makers to indulge in searches for the
lost ark! The religious focus of the people is now the king himself.

READ 2 SAMUEL 8–24: THE COURT HISTORY OF DAVID

These chapters have an eyewitness flavour which suggests that they
were originally written by someone with a first-hand knowledge of
David's court. Unlike the court histories which were commonplace
among the kingdoms of the Ancient Near East, these chapters do not
gloss over David's sin and failure.

David was in many ways better suited to the 'outlaw' lifestyle of his earlier years. He did not cope easily with the government of what had become a large empire. The same was true of many of those who were closest to David. Joab had made an excellent leader of the warrior band, but he was not cut out to be minister of defence in a settled empire!

Chapters 8–12: success and failure

Like Saul, David's reign had started well (chapters 8–10) with military victories and generosity to opponents. But as so often in the history of Israel, high-sounding ideals did not always work out in practice.

In chapters 11 and 12 we read the notorious story of David's adultery with Bathsheba, and the staged murder of her husband Uriah the Hittite. The stinging rebuke of the prophet Nathan to David, and David's eventual repentance, are well known. But Nathan has to tread carefully. He approaches in a deferential manner, and has to bring his rebuke indirectly by means of a parable. The king, not the prophet, is now very much the boss! By Solomon's time, prophets seem to have been eliminated from Jerusalem altogether.

Chapters 13–21: court intrigue and a palace coup

David's lack of control over his own family – a situation only possible because of his many wives and their rival sons – led in the end to the disastrous rebellion by his son Absolom. Absolom was able to play on popular discontent that the king was remote from the people and made little effort to enforce justice or to settle disputes (chapter 15). David had become like the oriental despot – aloof and uninterested in the needs of his people. Samuel's warnings were coming to pass!

Chapters 22,23: David's farewell songs

After Absalom's rebellion things did seem to settle down; but under the surface the country was deeply divided with all kinds of tension and undercurrents. When we come to chapter 22 and read David'

ong of thanksgiving and victory and then his final song in chapter
3, we might well wonder if these songs were written by the same
avid we have just been reading about!

Chapter 24: the census

his story of the ill-fated census is the last word on David in
Samuel. It is not altogether clear why Yahweh was so angry at this
ensus. Any census, of course, was inevitably to do with taxation and
onscription – the very things that Samuel had warned against. But
he real point (which even Joab seems to have realised) is that in
arrying out this census David was usurping a role reserved for God
one. David's repentance over the census led to the purchase of the
hreshing floor of Araunah as a site for an altar. This points forward
o 1 Kings – for this was the site on which Solomon was to build the
emple.

Samuel and the monarchy

he book of 2 Samuel begins with that popular hero picture. David
ad been described as 'a man after God's own heart'. But as the story
rogresses we soon realise that the hero-image is not the whole story.
he reader must seriously ask the question, was David really the man
hat he is sometimes made out to be?

Early in David's reign he was faithful to God and obedient. There
as much about his kingship that was positive: indeed the later
ooks regularly praise those kings who followed the example of
avid. He was given a special covenant relationship with Yahweh
omething which Saul had never enjoyed). So much potential, yet by
he end of David's reign, Israel had moved further than ever from the
ocial and religious ideals of Moses and Joshua.

Certainly he made Jerusalem the capital of a considerable empire,
mposing burdens of taxation and forced labour on conquered
eoples. But was that the kind of success God wanted? Look at
euteronomy 17:14–20 and measure King David by the standards
hich Moses had set out for future kings. David did not fall so far
hort as Solomon. But in some ways even Saul departed less from the
osaic ideal than David!

It is for these reasons that I believe that David's reign was a
ragedy. The outward appearance of success was the kind of success

looked for by pagan monarchies – and even this worldly success is badly dented in David's closing years. The people had got what they asked for and were warned against, 'a king like other nations'.

David's shortcomings, however, could not undermine God's over-riding purpose. The covenant which Yahweh made with David and his descendants was sure and steadfast, despite the demerits of David and his descendants. That covenant ultimately found its fulfilment in 'great David's greater Son' – Jesus Christ.

2.7 THE BOOKS OF 1 AND 2 KINGS
A TALE OF TWO CITIES

hink of a country partitioned into north and south, with one reli-
ous group in the majority in the north and another religious group
the majority in the south, and not much love lost between them.
m I thinking of Ireland, or another part of the modern world? In
ct I am thinking of ancient Israel!

After the death of Solomon, Israel was partitioned into two sepa-
te states. The southern kingdom of Judah was based on Jerusalem
nd was ruled by a descendant of David. The separate northern
ingdom was eventually based at Samaria. The books of Kings could
e called 'A Tale Of Two Cities.'

The books of Samuel had covered a relatively short time span –
nly sixty years or so. The books of Kings cover a much longer period
over 400 years from David's death (around 970 BC) right down to
he destruction of Jerusalem (in 586 BC).

READ 1 KINGS 1,2: DAVID'S LAST DAYS

aul had died on the battlefield fighting for his country.
ontrast this with David's death-bed scene in 1 Kings 1,2.
e is now an old man, confined to bed, unable to keep
arm, unable to have sex, and manipulated by women. A
ar cry from the powerful ruler once renowned for both his
ilitary and his sexual prowess!

nowhere are we actually told that God had chosen Solomon to be king

Two of David's sons are hovering in the wings as rival
laimants to the throne. The eldest surviving son is called
donijah. Notice that the author makes a point of empha-
ising that he was a good man (vs 5,6). His name means
'ahweh is Lord' – a name which is a reminder of the old Israelite
deology that Yahweh was the real King of Israel. The other rival
laimant is Solomon, son of Bathsheba. His name is derived from the
ame Hebrew root as the name of Jerusalem. Their names suggest
hat the struggle between Adonijah and Solomon was also a struggle
etween Israelite and Jerusalemite concepts of kingship.

Both of the rival claimants had the support of powerful figures in

David's court. On Adonijah's side was David's long-standing
henchman, Joab, commander of the army. Adonijah also had the
support of Abiathar, the high priest whose family had for genera
tions been guardians of the ark of the covenant. On Solomon's side
was the other high priest, Zadok whose name connects him closely
with the ancient Jerusalem traditions of Melchizedek. Solomon also
was supported by Nathan (the prophet), by Benaiah (chief of palace
security), and, of course, by his mother, Bathsheba.

The drama begins when Adonijah holds a feast at which his
supporters proclaim him to be the new king. Bathsheba hurriedly
approaches David, claiming that David had promised that her son
Solomon would one day be king (although we have no record of such
a promise). David summons Zadok, Nathan, and Benaiah. He orders
Zadok and Nathan to anoint Solomon as king. The interesting thing
about all this is that nowhere are we actually told that God had
chosen Solomon to be king. It was David who gave the order!

The people cheer 'Long live King Solomon!' though the narrative
strongly hints that Adonijah would have been the people's preferred
choice. Benaiah's crack troops were no doubt on the streets making
sure that the people would cheer! Adonijah had to plead for mercy to
Solomon – and for a time he was spared.

In chapter 2 we read David's last words, his final instructions to
Solomon. The opening words of his speech are pious words of good
advice. But then David instructs Solomon to get rid of Joab – despite
the fact that Joab was the man on whose support David had
depended totally from his outlaw days right through to the end.
Solomon is also told to deal with Shimei. David had promised to
spare Shimei; but he had not promised that Solomon would spare
him! These final death-bed words of David's are hardly endearing.

It is not long before Solomon finds an excuse to send Benaiah, his
hatchet man, to murder Adonijah. The only supporter of Adonijah
who escaped death was Abiathar, the priest. He was banished to the
country town of Anathoth, while his rival Zadok remained as
Solomon's sole high priest.

It seems that when Solomon banished Abiathar to Anathoth, the
ancient Mosaic traditions of Israel were effectively banished from
Jerusalem with him. There was not even a celebration of the Passover
in Jerusalem from the time of King Solomon, right down to the time
of King Hezekiah, over 200 years later.

The focus of religion in Jerusalem was now the covenant which
God had made with David and the associated promise that

rusalem would always be God's chosen city. This covenant with
avid had not been intended to replace the Mosaic covenant tradi-
ons; but in practice that is what happened in Jerusalem. The
[osaic traditions, however, were remembered at rural shrines such
; Anathoth.

READ 1 KINGS 3–11: THE REIGN OF SOLOMON

Chapters 3,4: the early years

[istory often repeats itself, and like David and Saul, Solomon's reign
:arted off well. When God asked Solomon what he would want as a
pecial gift, he chose wisdom, not wealth, or military success. The
:ory of the dispute between the two prostitutes (3:16–28) was but
ne example of the practical wisdom for which Solomon was to
ecome famous.

Chapter 4 gives a list of Solomon's officials. We are tempted to
kim over lists like this. But notice two things. Firstly, Solomon had
eplaced the God-given twelve-tribe structure of Israel with officials
ppointed from Jerusalem (v 7), whose primary job was to collect
axes to pay for the cost of the ever-expanding royal court. Secondly,
.otice that there was an official in charge of forced labour (v 6)! The
sraelites, whose forefathers had fought against Canaanite oppres-
ion, now found that their own king was subjecting them to the
askmaster's whip.

Solomon certainly brought wealth to the country through trade,
opper mines, manufacture of chariots, and customs duties on
:oods passing through his territory (on the main highway from
:gypt to Mesopotamia). But the wealth which Solomon created was
oncentrated in the hands of a few and did little to benefit the popu-
ation as a whole.

Chapter 4 ends with a summary of Solomon's famous wisdom –
ncluding the writing of 3000 proverbs, many of which are no doubt
ontained in the book of Proverbs. It has been remarked, however,
hat Solomon did not apply his unique God-given wisdom to the
ust and equitable government of his people!

Chapters 5–8: the building of the Temple

Solomon's crowning achievement was the building of the Temple in Jerusalem. The writer emphasises the meticulous preparation and planning, the high quality of the craftsmanship and materials, and the rich and ornate finishing. It took seven years to build; and the whole project involved the forced labour of 30,000 Israelite men and 150,000 non-Israelites! The Temple was highly ornate though in fact quite small: 27 metres long, 19 metres wide, and 13.5 metres high – about the size of a standard swimming pool today.

The author also gives us the dimensions of Solomon's palace. The palace took thirteen years to build – six years longer than the Temple. The banqueting hall alone was 44 metres by 22 metres – four times the size of the Temple! These dimensions are symbolic of the fact that religion had become an annex to the state, rather than the foundational principle on which the state was built.

Over the years, the people of Jerusalem increasingly put their faith in the Temple rather than in the God of the Temple. Sacrifice and ritual became a substitute for keeping God's Law – as the prophets were so often to proclaim. A spurious belief that God would never allow his Temple to be destroyed gave the people of Jerusalem a false sense of security.

In the epic history, important events are often marked by a major speech. The opening ceremony for the Temple is marked by Solomon's great prayer of dedication (chapter 8). The prayer acknowledged Yahweh as the true King of Israel and there are numerous references to Yahweh's Law. Sadly, however, as so often, the high ideals of king and people were not to be matched by reality once the celebrations were over!

Chapters 9–11: overview of Solomon

Yahweh responds positively to Solomon's prayer of dedication for the Temple, though there are stern words of warning that not even the Temple will protect the people from Yahweh's judgement if they disobey his Law. The second part of chapter 10 (vs 14–29) is a catalogue of the apparent successes of Solomon's kingship, but is also a catalogue of how Solomon did all the things that the Law of Moses had forbidden the kings of Israel to do!

In chapter 11 the author writes explicitly of the downside of Solomon's reign. By the end of his career, the empire which he had inherited from David was fast unravelling. The extent of God's anger

comes clear when Ahijah the prophet graphically proclaims to
roboam that Yahweh will take ten of the twelve tribes away from
olomon's son and successor (11:29–36). There will always be a
escendant of David on the throne in Jerusalem, but the northern
ibes will in future be a separate kingdom with a separate monarchy.
olomon was hated so much by his people that the majority of them
fused to have his son as their king. Yet another tragic end to a
romising reign.

READ 1 KINGS 12–16: THE DIVIDED KINGDOM

Chapters 12–14: Rehoboam and Jeroboam

1 Jerusalem and Judah, Solomon's son Rehoboam succeeded to the
hrone without much ado. But the people of Israel demanded that
Rehoboam should come to Shechem and submit himself for election
y the assembly of the tribes. If Rehoboam had been more concilia-
ory he might have won the people over to his side. But it was not to
e so. In fulfilment of the prophecy of Ahijah, Rehoboam is chased
ack to Jerusalem and Jeroboam becomes king of a separate
orthern kingdom. God's will in the matter is confirmed to
Rehoboam by the prophet Shemaiah, from Judah.

From this point the terminology is confusing. The name *Israel* is
ow used as the name of the separate northern kingdom,
hich included only ten of the twelve tribes. However, the **there were**
ame *Israel* continued to be used in its older sense, **many in**
enoting the twelve-tribe religious community of Israel, **Israel who**
ound together by allegiance to Yahweh. **resented the**

Similarly, the name *Judah* continued in use as the name of **Jerusalem**
ne of those twelve tribes. But Judah was now also the name **Temple**
f a nation state which included the territory of the tribe of
Benjamin and a large number of other non-Israelite inhabi-
ants as well.

The kingdom of Judah preserved the Davidic model of kingship.
The northern kingdom reverted to the Saul model, in which kings
ould be hired and fired by the tribal assembly and in which
Yahweh's prophets (such as Elijah) did not hesitate to rebuke or even
verthrow kings in Yahweh's name. The harsh reality was that over
half of the kings of the northern kingdom come to the throne by
ssassinating their predecessor (what we would call a *coup d'état*). By

contrast, the southern kingdom of Judah had a stable succession with only one brief break in the rule of David's descendants.

Jeroboam, the first king of the separate northern kingdom, imme diately took steps to discourage his people from travelling to Jerusalem to worship. He rebuilt the ancient shrines at Bethel (on his southern border) and Dan (in the far north). Bethel was associated with Jacob, the forefather of all of Israel. Priests who were descended from Moses served at Dan.

Jeroboam, however, set up a bull calf at each of these shrines. These bull-images were highly reminiscent of the golden calf which Aaron had made in the wilderness. They were probably not intended to be worshipped as idols, however, but rather to represent Yahweh's throne – as the ark of the covenant did in Jerusalem. The bull was an obvious fertility symbol, much used in Canaanite Baal religion. Jeroboam was trying to weld together the Israelites and Canaanites in his kingdom by a mixture of Yahwism and Baalism. The words which Jeroboam used when he set up these shrines are significant: 'Here are your gods, O Israel, who brought you up out of the land of Egypt' (12:28).

the Yahwism of ancient Israel was similarly divided into at least three distinctive streams

What Jeroboam was cynically trying to do was to win the loyalty and allegiance of those who resented all the changes in religion that David and Solomon had introduced – those who wanted to get back to the faith of their fathers, to the worship of the God who had brought them out of Egypt. There were many in Israel who resented the Jerusalem Temple set-up and who yearned for a return to what they saw as their traditional faith and worship. The shrines in Bethel and Dan did not, of course, represent true tradi tional religion, but Jeroboam manipulated the feelings of ordinary religious people. Yahweh, of course, was not impressed, and he sent a prophet to pronounce a terrible judgement on Bethel (chapter 13)!

Chapters 15,16: Jeroboam and Omri

These chapters summarise the reigns of the first few kings of the divided Israel and Judah. Some kings were better than others; but the author makes clear that none lived up to God's standards.

The next king of importance is Omri (16:21-28) who became king of the northern kingdom after a military coup around 885 BC twenty-five years or so after Jeroboam). He built a splendid new capital city at Samaria (to rival Jerusalem), and established lucrative trading relations with Israel's neighbours. Omri's son, Ahab, was married to Jezebel, a princess from Phoenicia. His grandaughter, Athaliah, was married to the king of Judah, bringing about cooperation between the northern and southern states for the first time since Solomon's day. The Bible historian, however, cursorily summarises Omri's reign in a few lines, for he was unimpressed by political success. He had led the people of Israel into sin just as his predecessors had done.

Elijah ... and Elisha tower like giants of faith over this period

If Omri's reign was dismissed by the author in a few verses, the same was not to be the case for his son, Ahab, whose reign takes up most of the rest of 1 Kings. This is because of the crisis which took place in Ahab's reign, in which the true worship of Yahweh came under threat of total extinction. This was the era of the wicked Queen Jezebel and her implacable foe, Elijah, one of the greatest prophets of Israel.

READ 1 KINGS 17–22: ELIJAH THE PROPHET

We are well used today to the different streams of tradition (or denominations) in Christendom. The Yahwism of ancient Israel was similarly divided into at least three distinctive streams.

First of all, there was the Temple in Jerusalem. It focused on Yahweh's promises to David's descendants and on his eternal choice of Zion (Jerusalem). The more ancient Israelite traditions and the Law of Moses, however, were largely forgotten.

Secondly, there were the national shrines of the northern kingdom at Bethel and Dan, and other similar centres. These were supposedly shrines for the worship of Yahweh, but they were paganised by the influence of Baal religion.

As well as these official state-sponsored religious centres, there was also an ongoing allegiance among ordinary people to traditional *Mosaic* Yahwism – the kind of simple faith and allegiance that we saw operating in Ruth's Bethlehem. This third stream of tradition within Yahwism was not an institution or an organised religious system. It was a movement among the ordinary people of both Israel and Judah. The greatest exponents of this prophetic movement were Elijah and his successor Elisha, who tower like giants of faith over this period in the history of Israel.

In addition to these different streams of tradition in the worship of Yahweh, there also persisted in both Judah and Israel widespread worship of false (Baal) gods, particularly among those sections of the population of Canaanite descent.

It was to this already diverse melting pot of religion that Ahab's Phoenician Queen Jezebel added a new and explosive ingredient – the worship of the Baal god of her home city of Tyre in Phoenicia. There is no evidence that Ahab himself consciously forsook his nominal allegiance to Yahweh. His sons had traditional royal names which implied allegiance to Yahweh. He was probably swayed by arguments similar to those we hear today. In a pluralist society should there not be room for every religion? If people wanted to worship other gods as well as Yahweh, why shouldn't they? And if Phoenicia was the senior partner in a defence and trade pact with Israel, was it not only diplomatic courtesy to have a shrine for the god of Phoenicia in Israel's capital?

Chapters 17–20

Jezebel soon found that faithful Yahwists would not tolerate any compromise with Baal worship; and in the end she embarked on a crusade to eliminate them. Against this backcloth the prophet Elijah steps onto the stage of history (chapter 17). Elijah's first act was to throw down the gauntlet to the Baal god. For Tyrian Baal was especially known as the god of thunder and rain. Elijah declared that there would be no more rain until Yahweh said so! He then went into hiding and was sent by God to the widow of Zarephath in Phoenicia – Tyrian Baal's own patch! The miracles of the food which never ran out and of the healing of the widow's son were clear confirmation of Yahweh's power – even in Phoenicia.

the Israelite king was supposedly subject to God's Law

Three years pass before Elijah's public contest with the prophets of Baal at Mount Carmel, on the border between Israel and Phoenicia. Again it was an 'away match' – for it took place on the Phoenician side of the mountain. Before the contest Elijah utters his famous words: 'How long will you go limping with two different opinions? If the Lord is God, follow him; but if Baal, then follow him' (18:21). 'Maybe he is daydreaming, or relieving himself,' he mocks (18:27, GNB) when their god is unable to respond. The Baal prophets cut themselves and pray in a frenzied manner, but to no avail. Yahweh alone is the God who sends fire. The people cry,

'Yahweh alone is God!' (18:39).

After victory on such a scale, you might think that Elijah would be on the crest of the wave! But such is Jezebel's anger that Elijah has to flee from Israel altogether, travelling to the southern wilderness, to Mount Sinai, the very mountain where God had given the Law to Moses. Elijah's journey to Sinai was symbolic of what his ministry was all about. In calling for a return to the God of Sinai, Elijah was not just calling for religious reform. The Law of Sinai was the Law which demanded social justice. Baal religion, by contrast, was the means by which rulers justified oppression and inequality.

Elijah at Mount Sinai is at first totally despairing. However, Yahweh demonstrates vividly by earthquake and fire that he and not Baal is the God who controls the elements of nature. Yahweh has the power to deal with the situation. But it is with the still small voice of calm that he finally reassures Elijah (19:12).

Elijah is told to do three things. He is to anoint a new king for Syria (demonstrating that Yahweh is the God who controls the destiny of all nations, not just Israel). Secondly, Jehu is to be anointed as the next king of Israel. Thirdly, Elisha is to be appointed as Elijah's successor.

Chapters 21,22

Finally in Elijah's career we come to the incident of Naboth's vineyard (chapter 21). Ahab had set his heart upon a piece of land adjacent to his summer palace in the staunchly Israelite (rather than Canaanite) town of Jezreel. Naboth refuses to sell, which annoys Ahab greatly. Jezebel arranges for Naboth to be put to death on trumped-up charges. Ahab takes possession of the property only to be confronted by Elijah's stinging rebuke. It was, of course, an outrageous abuse of power by Jezebel. As such it became proverbial in Israel as the low point of Ahab's rule. But the story raises a whole range of other issues as well.

Elisha's ministry is the most similar to that of Jesus himself

Naboth was right to refuse to sell his land. Under Yahweh's Law, no one was allowed to sell his land permanently. This traditional law, however, was largely flaunted; and increasingly small farmers were forced to sellout to large landowners, creating a poverty-stricken underclass of landless workers. This was one of the main causes of the poverty which later prophets such as Amos preached against.

The incident also involved a clash of kingship ideology. The Israelite king was not an absolute ruler. He was supposedly subject to God's Law and expected to be obedient to God's prophets. This was for Jezebel a contradiction in terms. In any other nation the king's word was the law. The vineyard incident at Jezreel became symbolic for the clash of social and political as well as religious systems.

Elijah's words of judgement to Ahab are chilling. None of the kings had devoted himself so completely to wrongdoing in Yahweh's sight as Ahab (21:25). But notice that in the end Ahab repents and God accepts his repentance. But for Jezebel the sentence is uncompromising. Dogs will one day eat her body in the very town of Jezreel where the murder of Naboth had taken place!

The last episode of Ahab's reign comes in chapter 22. Jehoshaphat, the king of Judah, had joined with Ahab in battle against Syria. Ahab calls on 400 so-called prophets of Yahweh, who all tell him what he wants to hear! Pressed by Jehoshaphat, Ahab finally consults Micaiah, the one prophet who would tell the truth – but Ahab ignores the prophet's warning. Like Saul, Ahab dies in battle – though scarcely a heroic death, having disguised himself as a common soldier and put Jehoshaphat in the firing line.

READ 2 KINGS 1–8: CAREER OF ELISHA

Elijah is one of only two men in the Old Testament who did not die (the other was Enoch[18]). Amid a whirlwind, God took him up to heaven in a chariot of fire. For this reason he is regarded by the Jews as the most outstanding of the prophets.

His successor was Elisha. It has been said that Elisha is the Old Testament figure whose ministry is most similar to that of Jesus himself. His early ministry took place during the reign of Ahab's second son, Joram. Times had changed since Elijah's day. Faithful Yahwists were once again able to come out into the open. Elisha is able to move about among ordinary people, teaching and working miracles, much as Jesus was later to do. Elisha had a band of disciples; and he even ran a training school for aspiring young prophets!

There are many miracles told about Elisha. In chapter 2 he parts the waters of the Jordan – a miracle which recalls Joshua's crossing of the Jordan. He purifies the water supply for the adjacent city of Jericho. Chapter 3 brings the deception of the Moabites with a mirage of blood-red water. In chapter 4, Elisha brings help to a poor woman who is in debt, and then raises from the dead the son of the rich woman of Shunem. At the end of the chapter, he provides food in a time of famine for the prophetic school at Gilgal. This is followed in chapter 5 by the healing of Namaan, the Syrian enemy general who so reluctantly agreed to bathe in the River Jordan as a cure for his leprosy. The recovery of the borrowed axehead (chapter 6) shows how Elisha could identify with the dilemmas of everyday life. These miracles demonstrate Yahweh's concern for ordinary people, rich and poor, Israelite and foreigner.

Later in chapter 6, during the crippling siege of Samaria, we find Elisha at home, calmly declaring to the unbelieving king and his officers that Yahweh is in complete control. The king had blamed Yahweh for the city's misfortune and even threatened to have Elisha beheaded! How true to human nature to blame God instead of realising that the fault was in himself. This siege served as a warning and a forerunner of the later siege of Samaria in 721 BC, which resulted in the total destruction of the city and the end of the northern kingdom.

There is one notorious incident in Elisha's career which presents problems for us today. In chapter 2, forty-two 'boys' from Bethel are mauled by two bears because they had made fun of the prophet by shouting 'bald-head' at him!

The explanation of this harsh treatment seems to lie in the fact that the boys were from Bethel. The religious centre at Bethel had compromised with Jezebel's Baal religion and would have been utterly condemned for this by prophets such as Elisha. In Northern Ireland, paramilitary groups are often referred to colloquially as 'the boys' or 'the lads'. It may be that we have a similar usage in Hebrew, and that the boys from Bethel were not innocent children but some form of paramilitary hit-squad! And it may be that the Hebrew word which they shouted was something more abusive than the English bald-*head*!

READ 2 KINGS 9–11: JEHU'S REVOLUTION

European history has seen a number of bloody revolutions – of which the French and the Russian revolutions are the best known. Often in such revolutions high-sounding ideals (such as liberty, equality, fraternity) were so swamped by violence and bloodshed that the end result was worse than what had gone before.

These chapters record a revolution in Israel of this kind. Discontent had been mounting against the rule and policies of the Omri and his descendants. Joram, son of Ahab, was now on the

throne and Jezebel was still a force to be reckoned with. Support fo:
the Omrides lay mostly with the city dwellers, the wealthier classes
many of them of Canaanite descent. The Israelite section of the
population, mostly small landowners, had suffered from the
economic oppression of the Omride era. They had seen their culture
eroded, their traditional God-given Law undermined, and their reli
gion threatened with extinction. The episode of Naboth's vineyard
had become proverbial for all that was hated in Omride rule. The
religious communities under Elisha's leadership fostered much of
the resistance to the Omrides. The army also were resentful
of Omride policies. The stage was set for a military *coup* –
with considerable popular support.

Jehu manipulated the loyalty of ordinary religious people for his own personal ambition

It was Elisha who 'lit the touch paper' in 841 BC that led
to the bloodiest explosion in the history of the northern
kingdom. The sequence of events in chapter 9 should be
noted carefully. First of all, Elisha instructs one of his
trainee prophets to go to the army camp, to find General
Jehu, to take him aside privately, to anoint him as king in
Yahweh's name, and then to run off as fast as he can!
However, the zealous young prophet goes far beyond what
Elisha had instructed. He instructs Jehu to kill King Joram
and every member of his family circle. Jehu then advances to King
Joram's summer residence in Jezreel. Not only is Joram killed, and his
body dumped in Naboth's field, but Jehu also kills Ahaziah, the king
of Judah, who was unfortunate enough to be visiting Joram at the
time.

The chapter finishes with one of the most melodramatic passages
in the whole of the epic history. We can visualise the proud Jezebel
arranging her hair and putting on her make-up as she prepares to
face her assassins! She is thrown out of the palace window to the
ground, where Jehu drives his horses and chariots over her body
before calmly entering the palace for his dinner! As Elijah had foretold, the dogs eat the body of Jezebel at Jezreel, the scene of her most
notorious crime. Jehu's purge did not stop there. Chapter 10 records
the deaths of seventy descendants of Ahab and other visiting rela-
tives of the king of Judah. By means of trickery the leading
worshippers of Tyrian Baal were gathered together in their own
temple and slaughtered. The remains of the temple of Baal were
turned into a latrine!

Jehu's revolution was supposedly in Yahweh's name. It was
intended to restore true religion and social justice to Israel. But,

eferring to Jehu's revolution, Yahweh later declares through the prophet Hosea: 'I will punish the house of Jehu for the blood of ezreel, and I will put an end to the kingdom of the house of Israel' Hos 1:4,5).

How did it all go so badly wrong? Jehu had used and manipulated he loyalty of ordinary religious people in order to advance his own personal ambition. This is ultimately what is forbidden in the third commandment – claiming that things are done in God's name when in fact the real motive is personal advancement[19]. We see this in Northern Ireland, where some politicians seek to gain political support by manipulating religious loyalties. It is to be found in American fundamentalism. It is a feature of sections of the Muslim world. No country is immune!

Jezebel's foreign Baal religion had now been extinguished in Israel; but native paganism still remained. The preaching of Amos and Hosea makes clear that, far from reversing the oppressive social policies of the Omrides, Jehu and his successors allowed things to go from bad to worse. By the time of Jeroboam II, a descendant of Jehu, there was more wealth in the country than there had ever been – but there was also more poverty than ever before. For the wealth was concentrated in the hands of the elite few.

READ 2 KINGS 12–17: THE END OF THE NORTHERN KINGDOM

Jeroboam's son was overthrown, and then king after king, coup after coup, marked the final slide of the northern kingdom to oblivion. Eventually, the Assyrians besieged and destroyed Samaria, devastated the land, deported the leading citizens as prisoners of war, and resettled the land with peoples from other parts of the Assyrian empire. The northern kingdom of Israel had now been wiped off the map forever. Only the southern kingdom of Judah remained.

As at other key points in the narrative, the epic historian marks the fall of Samaria with a powerful editorial sermon, in which he explains the theological reasons for the destruction of the northern kingdom (17:7–23). The sermon also warns that the same fate awaits the southern kingdom.

READ 2 KINGS 18–21: HEZEKIAH AND ISAIAH

So far, monarchy has proved a costly mistake for the Israelites. While some kings were better than others, none had succeeded in implementing the kingly rule of Yahweh. Much of the rest of the book is taken up with the story of two kings in whom there was a last hope of making the monarchy work in Jerusalem – Hezekiah and Josiah.

When Hezekiah came to the throne in 716 BC, Judah was firmly a part of the Assyrian Empire. This involved paying crippling taxes to the Assyrians, as well as practising Assyrian religion in the Jerusalem Temple. Early in his reign, Hezekiah had witnessed the horror of the destruction of Samaria by the Assyrians. Throughout his reign Hezekiah had the support and advice of the prophet Isaiah. Isaiah's message was constant. The king and people should depend on God alone. Neither armies nor weaponry nor political alliances would save them.

Against Isaiah's advice, Hezekiah eventually joined a coalition of neighbouring states in a rebellion against the Assyrians. It was an ill-judged move, and it led to the invasion and devastation of Judah by the Assyrian emperor, Sennacherib, and to a prolonged siege of Jerusalem. The story is often quoted of how Hezekiah took Sennacherib's letter of ultimatum to the Temple to lay it before Yahweh in prayer (19:14). Eventually Jerusalem was miraculously delivered (19:35–37) – an event foretold by Isaiah.

From the point of view of the epic historian, however, the most important thing about the reign of Hezekiah had been his extensive reform of religion and his attempt to implement the Law of Moses (chapter 18). The reform movement was no doubt spurred on by the destruction of Samaria, and fear that the same fate might befall Jerusalem. Sadly, however, Hezekiah's reforms died with him; and his son Manasseh is regarded by the historian as the most wicked of all the kings of Judah.

READ 2 KINGS 22,23: JOSIAH, THE GREAT REFORMER

A palace *coup* was a common event in the northern kingdom but it was rare in Judah. However, in 640 BC, palace officials assassinated King Amon of Judah (21:19–25). The assassins apparently belonged to a party who were impatient with Amon's continued policy of submission to the Assyrian Empire. The assassins, however, were quickly overthrown by another group called *the people of the land* (21:24). This expression refers to the landed gentry, the people of rural Judah. For them, Sennacherib's invasion and his devastation of Judah were still a bitter memory; and they were not going to invite another Assyrian invasion by rebellion at the wrong moment. They were also steeped in the ancient Mosaic traditions that had been forgotten in Jerusalem. They put the boy-king Josiah on the throne at the ripe old age of eight!

For the epic historian, the most significant event in Josiah's reign was the finding of a copy of the book of the Law discovered by the workmen undertaking repairs to the Temple. It is generally assumed that this book was what we know as Deuteronomy. The book of the Law was read aloud to King Josiah, and he was greatly dismayed by the warnings in the book of the consequences of disobedience. Josiah had already instigated a religious reform similar to that of his great-grand-father, Hezekiah, but was it too little too late? Josiah sends for advice from a prophetess called Huldah. Her answer was that a disastrous fate for Jerusalem was inevitable – but Josiah himself would be allowed to see out his days in peace because of his own faithfulness.

For the first time since the days of Joshua, the Law was read aloud to the whole people. Josiah renewed the covenant which Joshua had made for the people with Yahweh all those years before. Later the Passover was celebrated – the first time this had been done properly in Jerusalem since before the monarchy.

In Jerusalem a belief had developed that Yahweh could never allow Jerusalem or the temple to be destroyed. However, prophets such as Jeremiah were warning the people that Samaria had fallen, and that the same fate would befall Jerusalem if she did not mend her ways.

The reformation of Josiah was not just about the abolition of pagan and foreign religion. It was also a bringing together of the two main streams of tradition within Yahwism. The Jerusalem establishment once again came to terms with the Mosaic Law which they had long neglected.

For the epic historian, Josiah's reformation was the climax of the history of Israel. Law and covenant had been the focus of Joshua 24 – the inauguration of the new Israel by Joshua. This emphasis on Law and covenant was restored in Josiah's reformation. If ever there was a chance for the monarchy to work, this was it! Josiah (who had none of the demerits of King David) was seeking to implement the Law in a way that had never happened before. Would the kingship of Yahweh and the rule of Yahweh's Law at last be implemented in the earthly community? Alas, it was not to be! As Huldah had foretold, the hearts of the people were not right. No king could bring about the change that was needed.

Josiah was defeated and killed at Megiddo (or Armageddon) in 609 BC. A battle at Megiddo had long before marked the end of the

conquest of the land from the Canaanites. This marked the beginning of the end of the Israelite monarchy.

Josiah's reforms lapsed on his death, and to that degree his reign
ended in failure. His immediate successors fostered a return to religious syncretism. However, in the longer term, after the exile, the
twin pillars of Josiah's reformation re-emerged as the basis of later
Judaism: adherence to the Law and centralisation of worship in the
Temple in Jerusalem.

READ 2 KINGS 24,25: THE FINAL DESTRUCTION OF JERUSALEM

After Josiah's death, events went from bad to worse until the
inevitable destruction of Jerusalem by the Babylonians. Do not
underestimate the scale of the calamity of 586 BC. The city was left
uninhabitable. The Temple was reduced to a pile of rubble. The
leading citizens who were marched off to exile in Babylon were the
fortunate ones! The majority of the population died in the fighting
or from the famine and disease which followed. Many fled to Egypt
and beyond. From a population of a quarter of a million in Josiah's
time, it is estimated that no more than 25,000 were left alive amid
the devastation. The book of Lamentations is a moving poetic
response to the tragedy.

Kingship and the Messiah

Ultimately, Yahweh himself is King of Israel. But how is the kingly
rule of Yahweh to be realised on earth? How is the nation to be
governed, how are God's laws and commands to be implemented?
Can this be done without an earthly king?

Yahweh was angry at the people's demand for a king. Yet various
references in the pentateuch had made clear that a kingship had
always been part of Yahweh's purpose. But the people wanted a king
for all the wrong reasons – and the king they wanted was to be 'like
all the nations' rather than a ruler who would uphold Yahweh's
unique Law. Eventually God conceded the people's request for an
earthly king. Saul and David represent two different models of
earthly monarchy; two different attempts to work out how the
concept of Yahweh as heavenly king might be reconciled with an
earthly ruler.

On the death of Solomon, the kingdom of Israel was divided. The
northern kingdom of Israel continued (disastrously) with a 'Saul'

model of monarchy; while in Judah and Jerusalem the descendants of David continued to rule. However, Israel and Judah had both moved very far from the Mosaic ideal. The prophets vividly portray the increasing lack of social justice. Attempts at reform by Hezekiah and Josiah raised high hopes – but they proved to be too little too late. Eventually, the faithlessness of the kings of both jurisdictions led to the final destruction first of Israel by the Assyrians in 722 BC and then of Judah and Jerusalem by the Babylonians in 586 BC.

As readers we are left with an unanswered question. Was the monarchy a failure? Would people have been better off without an earthly monarchy – as the prophet Samuel had tried to tell them?

Of course there is another important aspect of this theme of kingship. For Yahweh had entered into a special and unique relationship (or covenant) with David and his descendants. Christians believe that God's promises to David found their true fulfilment in David's descendant, Jesus Christ, who is both Son of David and Son of God and it is Jesus who is the ultimate answer to the questions of kingship when he announces the advent the kingdom of God.

Endnotes

1   The epic history is not the only collection of historical books in the Old Testament. The books of Chronicles, Ezra and Nehemiah form another collection which we will look at later.

2   Indeed the epic history is a sequel not just to Deuteronomy, but to the whole pentateuch.

3   It is striking when reading an Israeli newspaper to realise that the modern Hebrew word for Palestinians is almost the same as the Bible word for Philistines. There is a sense in which the wars of the Old Testament are still being played out 3,000 years or so later!

4   Joshua 10:13

5   PR House, *Old Testament Theology*, IVP (US), 1998

6   Judges 17:6 and 21:25. Also 18:1 and 19:1

7   Ruth 1:16,17

8   The word levirate comes from a Latin word meaning brother-in-law. See Deuteronomy 25:5,6

9   1 Samuel 8:5

10 1 Samuel 8:10–18

11 Indeed, when anointing Saul, Samuel himself avoids the word king and uses a more general Hebrew word meaning ruler.

12 1 Samuel 16:14

13   Act 3, Scene 2

14   Jerusalem never became fully integrated with Israel or Judah. Even in the New
     Testament we always read of 'Jerusalem and Judea'.

15   Samuel also offered sacrifices – and he was not a descendant of Aaron either!

16   We will discuss Melchizedek more fully when we consider Psalm 110, the only
     other place in the Old Testament where he is mentioned.

17   2 Chronicles 26:16–23

18   Genesis 5:24

19   Exodus 20:7 in the NRSV: 'You shall not make wrongful use of the name of the
     LORD your God, for the LORD will not acquit anyone who misuses his name.'

Part Three

The people look back:
the later
historical books

3.1 THE BOOKS OF
1 AND 2 CHRONICLES

Two authors might write about the same historical events, but produce two books very different in the way the events are described and in their interpretation of the past. The books of Chronicles re-tell the history of the Jerusalem monarchy from the perspective of a much later generation. These books cover a similar period to the epic history – but they are significantly different in ethos and interpretation. The two histories offer us two distinct commentaries, from different perspectives, on the events of Israel's past.

'The day of small things'

The epic history had probably been completed shortly after the fall of Jerusalem in 586 BC. The likeliest date for the composition of the Chronicles is around 350 BC – 200 years or so after the Jews had been allowed to return to Jerusalem and to rebuild the Temple.

This small community of Jews were struggling to keep the faith alive in a partially rebuilt Jerusalem, with a Temple which was small and plain compared with the great Temple of old. As a tiny community in a remote corner of the Persian Empire, the people must have found difficulty in conceiving Yahweh as a major player among world religions! The era in which the chronicler lived and wrote has sometimes been called the 'day of small things'[1].

The books of Chronicles were written to remind this beleaguered community of the richness of their past, to explain the historical basis for their religion, and to assure them that they still had a central place in God's plan for the nations. The chronicler refers to writings by prophets such as Samuel, Nathan and Gad; to works by the prophet Isaiah; and to a variety of other documents and archives.

More than half of the text of Chronicles is identical to that of Samuel-Kings – and almost certainly the epic history was the chronicler's major source. However, he omitted a great deal of material which was not relevant to his purpose, and he also added to the earlier text where appropriate.

Summary of contents

- 1 Chronicles 1–9: genealogies from Adam right down to the time of the return from the exile

- 1 Chronicles 10–29: David's reign

- 2 Chronicles 1–9: Solomon's reign

- 2 Chronicles 10–36: from Solomon's death to the fall of Jerusalem, finishing with a reference to Cyrus' decree of restoration which allowed the Jews to return to Jerusalem.

READ 1 CHRONICLES 1–29

Chapters 1–11: from Adam to David

The first nine chapters almost entirely consist of genealogies. We are inclined to pass over such passages, but it is worth at least skimming these chapters to get a feel for the writer's purpose. They trace the ancestry of the Davidic monarchy right back to Adam. Chapter 1 serves to place Israel within the family of nations. The genealogies then detail the unbroken line of descent right down almost to the naming of those individuals who had returned and resettled Jerusalem. The people of the chronicler's own day are thus firmly linked in to God's overall purposes in history.

Significantly, Moses, Joshua, and the days of the judges are passed over. The chronicler's emphasis is on David as God's chosen king, on Jerusalem as God's chosen city, and on the importance of the Temple.

Chapters 10–29: the reign of David

Saul's death is described in chapter 10, but we are told nothing else of his life story. For the chronicler the story begins properly in chapter 11 when David becomes king not just of Judah and Israel but also of Jerusalem. The demerits of David's reign are passed over (no mention of the Bathsheba incident, for example). This is not to whitewash David or to present a distorted impression of his reign. It is simply that the chronicler's specific interest is in David's role with regard to the Temple. The chronicler credits David with much of the detailed planning for the Temple – even though it was Solomon who actually oversaw the building. For the chronicler it is David's Temple as much as Solomon's!

READ 2 CHRONICLES

Chapters 1–9: Solomon

As with David, Solomon's shortcomings are omitted. Great detail of the construction and dedication of the Temple makes clear that this is the focus of the chronicler's work.

Chapters 10–36: Jerusalem and the Temple

After the reign of Solomon, the chronicler relates only the history of Judah, not that of the northern kingdom of Israel. He omits the narratives of the northern prophets such as Elijah and Elisha. There is a particular focus on three of the kings of Judah – Jehoshaphat, Hezekiah and Josiah. The writer elaborates on matters to do with the Temple, with religion, and with worship. For example, he gives a much fuller account than in the epic history of the reformations of Hezekiah and Josiah and of the Passover celebrations held by these two kings.

Particular questions faced by the chronicler

Neither the epic historian nor the chronicler wrote history for its own sake. Their purpose was to offer a theological interpretation of history, selecting material relevant to their purpose, and seeking to address the questions and issues of their own day.

First, there was the ongoing question of whether there would ever be a monarchy again in Israel. For the chronicler, the Temple was the legacy of the monarchy of old, and God's future plans for his people did not depend on a restoration of the monarchy.

Secondly, there was tension between the Jews of Jerusalem and the inhabitants of the old northern kingdom (the ancestors of the Samaritans of New Testament times). In particular the chronicler wished to attract northerners away from the Samaritan worship centre at Mount Gerizim near Shechem[2]. Part of the author's immediate purpose was to persuade descendants of the old northern tribes at they too had a place in the Jerusalem community and that the mple worship was as much for them as for the people of Judah.

Thirdly, the chronicler is particularly concerned to show that the mple worship in Jerusalem was the *only* legitimate worship of hweh, that its roots go deep into history, and that the Temple was .e assurance of God's continued blessing and the basis for the :ople's future hope.

ighlights from the chronicler's message

he people of God

he chronicler was keen to stress that northerners and southerners l belonged to the *theological* Israel – a totally different concept from rael as the name of the old northern kingdom. He makes frequent se of the phrase 'all Israel'.

ingship

s with the epic historian, kingship is a major theme for the chroni- er. The epic historian had focused on the failures of the kings hich led to the destruction of the two kingdoms. The chronicler resses those achievements of the Davidic dynasty which hold out ope for the future. Like the epic historian, the chronicler empha- ses that Yahweh is the real King of Israel. The books could be ummed up as 'the kingdom of Yahweh in the hand of the sons of avid' (2 Chron 13:8).

he Temple and worship

he chronicler's interest in the kings was primarily in the system of emple worship which they had set up. His references to Moses and he Law, to the ancient tabernacle, to the ark of the covenant, to avid, Solomon and the later kings, are all designed to show that hese different streams of tradition eventually flow into the temple orship. The chronicler greatly expands on the detail of religious ccasions, especially the bringing of the ark to Jerusalem, the dedica- on of the temple, and the Passovers of Hezekiah and Josiah.

He had a particular interest in the role of the Levites, whose role in he temple was to assist the priests in a variety of temple duties, ranging from preaching and choir music to security and maintenance. It has been suggested that the chronicler himself was a Levite.

Links to the New Testament

The books of Chronicles bridge the gap between the Old Testament monarchy and the New Testament Messiah. They speak of a community who re-affirmed their heritage in David and in the Jerusalem of old; who stood firm by the temple and the Law which were the visible assurance of the ongoing kingship of Yahweh; and who awaited the coming of a Son of David, who would usher in the Kingdom of God in a totally new way.

3.2 THE BOOKS OF EZRA AND NEHEMIAH RESTORATION FROM EXILE

due course Babylon, once all-powerful, fell before the armies of the sing Persian Empire in 539 BC. The Babylonians had held their npire together by a reign of fear and terror. Cyrus, the Persian nperor, however, sought to win the affection and loyalty of nquered peoples. He allowed exiled peoples to return home if they ished; and he encouraged the revival of local religions and culture. particular, he issued an edict in 538 BC which allowed the Jews to turn and to re-settle Jerusalem. It is to this era of restoration that he books of Ezra and Nehemiah belong.

The compiler of Ezra-Nehemiah brought together a number of different written sources. He has included autobiographical sections that is, accounts in the first person written by the characters themselves. These are often referred to as the *memoirs* of Ezra and of Iehemiah. There are also third-person narratives, summarising the ey historical events. Official government documents and correspondence are often quoted. Several genealogies are included.

ummary of contents

Ezra 1–6: the edict of restoration by Cyrus and the initial return to Jerusalem and the re-building of the Temple (in the time of the prophets Haggai and Zechariah)

Ezra 7–10: Ezra reorganises religion and worship in Jerusalem

Nehemiah 1–7: the re-building of the walls of Jerusalem in the face of opposition from Samaria

Nehemiah 8: Ezra reads the Law to the people

Nehemiah 9–13: the remainder of Nehemiah's governorship, further measures by Nehemiah told in the third person, various lists and records.

The official documents and correspondence

It used to be widely held that the documents and letters quoted in Ezra could not have been authentic. It seemed unlikely that King Cyrus would have referred to Yahweh as the God who had made him ruler (as in the decree quoted in the opening verses of Ezra) or that the Persian emperor would have agreed to pay for the re-building of the JerusalemTemple.

Archaeology has helped us here. We now know that Cyrus frequently wrote letters in which he spoke in reverential terms of the gods of the people to whom he was writing. So there is now a much greater willingness to accept the authenticity of the documents. After all, Ezra was a senior civil servant in the empire, and could well have had access to official archives and records.

READ EZRA 1–6: EVENTS BEFORE THE TIME OF EZRA

The book opens with the decree of restoration by Cyrus. Detailed lists are given of those who returned to Jerusalem. In fact very few did return. The leaders of the first band of returnees were Zerubbabel (a descendant of David) and Joshua (the chief priest). Zerubbabel, however, disappears from the scene without explanation. The Jewish community in Jerusalem, from this point right through to New Testament times, was ruled by the priests. No significant attempt was ever made to restore a descendant of David to the throne.

Eventually the Temple was re-built, though on a much more modest scale than the splendour of old. Haggai tells us of the discouragement of the people and of their slowness to get round to the re-building job. Times were hard and the obstacles the people faced were formidable. There was much opposition to the re-building, especially by the forerunners of the Samaritans of later times.

The sequence of events in chapter 4 is confusing. After explaining about opposition to the building of the Temple (around 530 BC), the author digresses (from verses 6–23) to tell of other later episodes of opposition to rebuilding work in Jerusalem. The events described in this digression span several generations. Then in verse 24 the author picks up where he had left off in verse 5 and resumes the story of the initial re-building of the Temple.

READ EZRA 7–10: THE CAREER OF EZRA

zra was a Jewish scribe – but he was also a Persian government
fficial. He was sent to re-organise the religion of the Jews back on to a
roper footing. He has been described as the empire's 'Secretary of State
r Jewish Affairs'. Ezra is often referred to as the father of Judaism. He
as the one who gave shape to the future religion of the Jews. He may
ell have been the compiler of the book which bears his name.

Ezra is particularly severe on those Jews who had intermarried
ith local inhabitants. His measures were a response to an emergency
tuation in which the very identity of the Jews as a separate people
as under threat and their religious purity was in danger of being
st. It would be unwise to generalise from these events.

READ NEHEMIAH 1–7

hese autobiographical chapters tell the story of Nehemiah and the
-building of the walls of Jerusalem. Nehemiah's organisational
bility, his out-manoeuvring of his opponents, and his inspiring of
e people to hard work are proverbial and they have encouraged the
eople of God whenever they had to build or farm with a tool in one
and and a weapon in the other.

READ NEHEMIAH 8–13

emple, city, and walls are now complete. So it is fitting that Ezra
hould appear on the scene again to read the Law. The Law (and not
tonework defences) would be the real security of the Jerusalem
ommunity.

According to the prophets, the destruction of Jerusalem had been
ecause of failure to keep the Law. So there was a great emphasis on
aw in the period after the exile. The Jews were not going to make the
ame mistake again! However, there was a tendency to focus on the
remonial aspects of the Law, rather than on provision for the poor,
e widow, the orphan, and the foreigner. Circumcision, sabbath
bservance, food laws, and temple ceremonial become dominant. We
e in these closing chapters of Nehemiah the beginning of the
rocess that was to lead to the legalism we are familiar with from the
lew Testament.

It is easy today to make the same kind of mistake. Which form of
aptism we approve of, what style of worship we prefer, whether or

not we exercise charismatic gifts – these issues are not unimportant. But we can focus on these matters to such an extent that we forget the real imperatives of Jesus' teaching – to go the second mile, to love our enemy, to turn the other cheek.

The book of Nehemiah brings to an end the mainstream history of the people of Israel. The stage is now set for the birth of Jesus – and for the New Testament understanding of the kingdom of God.

However, there is one more historical book which we have to consider – the book of Esther, which provides us with one intriguing episode in the history of those Jews who did not return to Jerusalem but remained scattered across the Persian Empire.

3.3 THE BOOK OF ESTHER

he power of a good story lies in its capacity to speak to the whole
erson – imagination, memory, emotions, and reason. A story
ecomes great when it transcends the boundaries of the time and
ace of its first telling and proves not to be limited to a particular
storical context[3].

Esther is one of the most fascinating books in the Old Testament.
is not just a good story but a great story. It also is a puzzling and
erplexing story. Surprisingly, God is never mentioned! On the
urface the story seems thoroughly secular and nationalistic –
ough God is working providentially in the background. It has been
id that God is made conspicuous by his absence!

The hero is a Jewish woman who marries a pagan king as a result
f a beauty contest, in which each of the contestants spends a night
ith the king! The book is the nearest thing in the Old Testament to
comedy. I do not mean that it is flippant or without a serious
essage. But it is full of satire and of larger-than-life characters.
umour, of course, can be used to convey a serious and challenging
essage.

The book of Esther has been a source of hope and inspiration for
ws at so many times of persecution across the centuries of their
istory. It is the most popular book in many Jewish circles after the
ve books of Moses, though there have also been times in history
hen Jews have debated whether it should be in the Bible at all.

Esther has had a mixed reception across the years among
hristians. For example, Martin Luther complained: 'I am so hostile
 this book that I wish it didn't exist, for it Judaises too much and it
as too much pagan perversity'. There is debate as to whether we
ould regard Esther as an actual historical story. In the Jewish Bible
 is not found among the *history* books but among the *wisdom* books,
hich may suggest that it should be understood as a story with a
oral.

In the book of Esther, the king is called Ahasuerus. We have no
ther knowledge of a Persian king of that name. Some scholars think
at Ahasuerus is another name for the Emperor Xerxes; and indeed
ome Bible translations actually call him Xerxes. However, it is diffi-
ult to fit many of the details of the book of Esther with what we
now of the historical King Xerxes from Greek and Persian sources.
he Hebrew name Ahasuerus seems to mean something like King

Quiet and Poor, which is an unlikely name for an emperor! So it cou be a Jewish nickname for one of the Persian emperors – or even stage name for a typical Persian emperor.

As you read the book you will become aware of how carefully tl story has been structured. For example, almost everything in th story comes in pairs: two wives for the king; two feasts and then tw banquets; two royal decrees on the plight of the Jews; two periods fasting; two letters to establish the feast of Purim. There are ten feas in all and they are used by the narrator to mark the rise and fall of th different characters. Much use is made of irony – as when Haman hanged on the very gallows he had built for Mordecai.

READ THE BOOK OF ESTHER

Chapter 1: who rules?

My family love watching 'whodunnits' on television! We play a gan in which there is a prize for the first to guess the culprit. Often w find that there is a vital clue to the mystery in the very first momen of the programme. This is true not just of TV programmes but most books as well. The opening gives vital information for unde: standing the book as a whole.

In the case of Esther, the opening verses describe the extent of th wealth and power of the new King Ahasuerus. He ruled an empir that stretched from India right round to Ethiopia. Yet it quickl becomes clear that he has no control even over his own household; h does not know what is happening in his own court; and those wh surround him manipulate him at every stage! This seemingly al powerful potentate turns out to be a more like a dim-witted buffoo whose life is totally taken up with wine, women, and song!

The opening verses of the chapter emphasise the lavish nature c the king's lifestyle – with feasting lasting six months for all th noblemen, and then a garden party, seven days long, for all the me: of the city of Susa. The men were allowed to drink as much wine a they wanted. It must have been quite a party!

At the end of the seven days, the king, now well under the influ ence of the wine, decides to show off the beauty of Queen Vashti t all the assembled menfolk. He commands that she should appea wearing her royal crown. The text may in fact mean that she was t

ear *only* her royal crown! And if that was so then we can well under-
:and why Vashti refused to come!

The king is furious. So what does he do? He calls for those whom
e is accustomed to consult for 'expert opinion on questions of law
nd order' (v 13 GNB)! This is an excellent example of the tongue-in-
heek way in which the story is told, pointing up the absurdity of the
ing's behaviour – though presumably true enough to the kind of
1ing which actually happened in the court of ancient emperors.

The absurdity of the situation intensifies when these top legal
dvisers give their opinion. If Vashti is allowed to get away with it,
1en it will not be long till every woman in the empire is refusing to
bey her husband! And so they devise a law, not only to strip Vashti
f her status as queen, but also to declare that that 'every man should
e master in his own house' (v 22). Whatever the Bible may have to
1y elsewhere about male and female roles, this is a ridiculous
ttempt to impose male supremacy.

Just as we began with a seemingly all-powerful king who was not
1 fact in charge of anything, so we have this emphasis on male
1premacy at the beginning of a story in which all the men are even-
1ally controlled or manipulated by women! Even Haman, the
illain, does what his wife tells him. It is men that cause the crisis;
nd it is a woman who solves it.

Chapter 2: a beauty contest with a difference

ashti's banishment means that a new queen has to be found and an
laborate beauty contest is duly organised, the arrangements for
'hich would make today's Miss World seem a minor event by
omparison!

Esther is presented to us as a charming personality, who quickly
'ins the favour not just of the king but of all the royal officials,
1ough she does keep a secret of the fact that she is a Jew. But should
respectable girl from a Jewish family be taking part in a contest of
1is kind – chosen on the basis of a night spent in the king's bed?

I remember reading of the dilemma faced by a Jewish woman in
Iazi Germany. She was able to pass for a Gentile. By acting as the
1istress of high ranking Nazi officials she was able to obtain infor-
1ation that led to saving the lives of many of her fellow Jews. Was her
ction in sleeping with Nazi officials right or wrong, moral or
nmoral, in these special circumstances? The book of Esther does

not offer an easy answer. But it does make us aware that such ethical questions are complex.

In chapter 2 we are also introduced to Esther's cousin and guardian, Mordecai, who had uncovered a plot to assassinate the king and who saves the king's life.

Chapter 3: to bow or not to bow?

Now we meet the villain of the piece – Haman. He was a descendant of Agag, the Amalekite king, whom King Saul had defeated in battle long ago (1 Sam 15). This does not mean much to a modern reader. But any Jew would have known of the age-old enmity between Jews and Amalekites, stretching back across the 500 years or so from King Saul's time down to the time of Esther.

Haman had been appointed prime minister and all the palace officials were required to show their respect by bowing down to him. But Mordecai refuses to do so and sets in motion a chain of events that almost leads to the extermination of all the Jewish people in the empire. Why did Mordecai refuse to bow down? We are told that it was because he was a Jew. Did he have a good *religious* reason for refusing to bow down? Certainly the Ten Commandments forbade the Israelites from bowing down to any *god* other than Yahweh or to any idol or image. In Daniel chapter 3, Shadrach, Meshach and Abednego had been thrown into the fiery furnace because they refused to bow down before the statue that the Babylonian King Nebuchadnezzar had built.

why did Mordecai refuse to bow down?

But was it forbidden for a Jew to show the customary respect of bowing down before a king or appropriate royal officials? It was certainly not regarded as a problem for Joseph's brothers to bow down before the governor of Egypt; and there are numerous other examples throughout the Old Testament. It is not certain that there was any genuine religious reason for Mordecai's behaviour.

There is no suggestion in the book that Mordecai refused to bow down to anyone else, such as the king himself. But there was no way that he was going to bow down to an Amalekite! Mordecai might have argued that the Amalekites were God's enemies in order to give a semi-religious justification for his actions. But I suspect that today we would describe his behaviour as motivated by racism or sectarianism.

When I was first ordained to the ministry, an older minister gave me some good advice. 'Do not turn all your opinions into principles,' he said. 'Have opinions, have strong opinions, but do not turn them all into principles, for when they become principles you have to die for them⁴!' Mordecai could have done with hearing those words. He made a principle out of a 500-year-old antagonism, and he nearly had to die for it, and all the Jews of the Persian Empire with him!

However, Haman's reaction is totally over the top. He hatches a diabolical plot to have all the Jews in the empire killed. Notice how the king was persuaded to go along with the plan – by a promise of considerable income for the royal treasury. How little things change in the affairs of nations! This kind of language has been used countless times as a means of justifying persecution – not just against the Jews but against minority populations of all kinds. *They keep themselves separate, they have strange customs, they don't keep our laws and they have too much money!*

The king authorised the plot without even asking who was to be killed! He handed over his signet ring to Haman and told him to get on with it. Haman issued an edict that on a certain date, ten months ahead, all Jews, men, women, and children, were to be slaughtered and their property confiscated. The closing words of the chapter are very chilling: 'The king and Haman sat down to drink; but the city of Susa was thrown into confusion' (v 15). There is in fact no suggestion in the book of any real antagonism among the Persians against the Jews. The hatred stemmed entirely from Haman, the Amalekite.

all Jews, men, women, and children, were to be slaughtered

Chapter 4: 'at such a time as this'

In chapter 4, Mordecai manages to get word to Esther of the crisis. At first she is reluctant to become involved, for even the queen was not allowed to approach the king uninvited – on pain of death. Mordecai then sends Esther his famous warning:

> Do not think that in the king's palace you will escape any more than all the other Jews. For if you keep silence at such a time as this, relief and deliverance will rise for the Jews from another quarter, but you and your father's family will perish. Who knows? Perhaps you have come to royal dignity for just such a time as this (Esther 4:13,14).

The words 'if you keep silence at such a time as this' have rung out across the centuries as a challenge to many people who have been tempted to keep silent for the sake of their own safety but who knew it was their duty to speak up. From this point on it is no longer Esther who obeys Mordecai. Esther now gives the orders and Mordecai obeys.

Chapters 5–7: Esther to the rescue

The action now moves swiftly towards the conclusion. The king holds out his sceptre and spares Esther when she approaches unin-vited. Esther slowly and carefully prepares the ground for the right moment to bring her plea before the king.

The extent of Haman's bitterness is vividly portrayed. He cannot enjoy any of his wealth and power because of his resentment towards Mordecai. How true this is to human nature. If bitterness, hatred, jealousy, sectarianism, or any such negative emotions, are allowed a foothold in our lives, then they destroy us from within and prevent us from enjoying the good things of life. The supreme irony of the book is when Haman finds himself organising a triumphal proces-sion for Mordecai when he thought the triumphal procession was going to be for himself!

In chapter 7 Esther finally brings the matter before the king. Haman's attempt to plead for mercy rebounds on him and he ends up hanged on the very gallows he had built for Mordecai!

Chapters 8,9: self-defence or cruel revenge?

Esther acquires Haman's wealth and Mordecai becomes prime minister. But the problem still remains of the edict for the destruc-tion of the Jews. Not even the king himself could change the law of the Medes and Persians. The king simply abdicates all responsibility for the matter. It is left to Esther to find a way of undoing this bizarre situation.

The solution Esther comes up with is to issue a new decree autho-rising the Jews to defend themselves when the day of slaughter comes. However, as chapter 9 continues, it becomes clear that the Jews did far more than just defend themselves. They took the oppor-tunity to rid themselves of those they regarded as their enemies: 'So the Jews struck down all their enemies with the sword, slaughtering and destroying them, and did as they pleased to those who hated them' (v 5).

The Jews killed over 75,000 people throughout the empire (v 16). In the city of Susa itself, 500 were killed on the first day; and then Esther requested the king's permission for a second day of slaughter. Not one Jew was killed, which suggests that there were few who actually tried to attack them. What are we to make of slaughter on this scale? Surely this cannot be justified? This issue will be discussed more fully below.

The chapter ends with the institution of the feast of Purim – a new feast in the Jewish calendar - as a memorial of these events. Now it is the turn of the Jews to indulge in feasting and celebration. Notice that a letter from Mordecai to the Jews throughout the empire is not enough to establish this new feast. The matter has to be confirmed by Esther. The book which began with a declaration of male supremacy ends on a note in which a woman is the final authority, even in religious matters.

Chapter 10: happy ever after?

The final chapter of the book seems to be a happy-ever-after ending in which the king, aided by Mordecai, emerges from his lifestyle of revelling and feasting to take on proper government of his vast empire. The king is now living up to his responsibilities. Mordecai is respected and loved by his own people. However, forced labour was imposed on many of the peoples of the empire.

Concluding comments

How are we to interpret this book overall? Like any great work of literature it is a complex tapestry of many meanings. Like many a Bible book it says different things to different people at different times. It will speak to Jews who have survived the modern holocaust in a way that it cannot speak to those of us who have never had such experiences. For those of us who live in Northern Ireland it has much to say about the dangers of sectarianism cloaked in religious garb. For those who live in England the warning may be to do with institutionalised racism. For some it will be the feminist issues that come to the fore. The book certainly offers us assurance about the providence of God, who looks after his own people even when they seem to pay little attention to him.

But in many ways this book raises more questions than it answers. The most disturbing thing is the revenge that the Jews exact on their enemies in the closing chapters. There are many things which happen in the Old Testament which are recorded because God abhors them not because God approves of them. In the book of Esther, the writer records the events without making any comment as to the rights and wrongs of the matter. There is no hint in this story that the slaughter was in any way authorised (still less commanded) by God or that God approved of it. We are left to make a judgement in the light of the rest of Scripture.

Through God's providence the Jews were saved from disaster. Yet whatever comedy or satire there may have been earlier in the book, the story ends in tragedy. The tragedy is that God's people were no better than any other nation. Indeed their behaviour was arguably worse than that of the very Persians whom they despised as pagan and godless. So often in history this same pattern has been found. Oppressed people who have been liberated often behave worse than their original oppressors. An example of this would be the current situation in the former Yugoslavia. However, Jesus said:

> Love your enemies, do good to those who hate you, bless those who curse you, pray for those who abuse you. ... If you love those who love you, what credit is that to you? For even sinners love those who love them (Luke 6:27-36).

Jesus makes clear in this passage that it is not enough for his followers simply to do what anyone else would do. Even sinners love those who love them – what credit is there in that?

Endnotes

1   This expression comes from the prophet Zechariah 4:10
2   See the conversation between Jesus and the Samaritan woman in John 4.
3   KJA Larkin in *Ruth and Esther,* Sheffield Old Testament Guides, Sheffield, 1996.
4   I am indebted to Rev Martin Smith for this advice – which I still try to remember!

Part Four

*Praise, thanksgiving, lament
and love:
the poetic books*

4.1 OLD TESTAMENT POETRY

Much of the Old Testament is written in poetry rather than in prose. In poetry much more can be said in fewer words than in prose. Poetry rouses the emotions as well as communicating information. Poetry makes great use of picture language, of metaphors, and of other figures of speech. Poetry involves structure and discipline in the use of language. The composer has to abide by certain rules of harmony and rhythm, otherwise what he produces is just noise rather than music! Similarly the poet works within a discipline.

In English we associate poetry with the disciplines of rhyme and rhythm. But the structures of poetry vary greatly from language to language. Hebrew poetry uses a complex system of *parallelism*, in which the same thought is expressed twice in two successive lines but in a slightly different way. Like poetry in any language, Hebrew poetry is rich in picture language.

Poetry is very difficult to translate from one language to another. No two languages have the same structures and rhythms. Hebrew poetry works with a rhythm of *ideas*, so it is easier to translate into other languages. Even in English, much of the poetic quality of the original Hebrew remains.

In this chapter we will look at three of the poetic books of the Old Testament – Psalms, Song of Songs, and Lamentations.

4.2 THE PSALMS

The psalter

The *psalter* (the collection of psalms) is perhaps the best loved of all of the Old Testament books. The psalms are used in worship in almost all Christian traditions. Individual psalms have been cherished by believers across the centuries, because they are able to bring people close to God at crisis points in their lives.

The psalter is a collection of hymns and prayers. The collection was made after the Jews came back to Jerusalem from exile, so it is sometimes referred to as the hymn-book (or prayer-book) of the Second Temple. However, many of the individual psalms in the collection date back to the time of King David or even earlier.

Who wrote the psalms?

There is a very strong connection between the psalms and King David. Many of the psalms have a title which includes the words 'A Psalm of David'. This phrase has traditionally been taken to mean that David wrote these psalms himself. However the Hebrew phrase that is translated '*of* David' could also mean '*to* David' or '*for* David'. So it may be that some of the psalms of David were written in his honour, or in his memory, or dedicated to him.

David did have a reputation as a musician and song-writer and it is possible that he composed some of the psalms. However, the majority make no specific mention of David in their title. A few psalm titles refer to other authors such as Asaph. Many have no indication at all of authorship. However, the psalter as a whole came to be known as 'Psalms of David' because he was the main historical inspiration.

The three main types are the *hymn*, the *lament*, and the *thanksgiving*. An example of each of these types is included in the selection which follows.

> ## READ PSALM 29: A HYMN OF PRAISE

I once was asked to take an open-air service for a regiment of soldiers. I began by reassuring them that I was not going to preach a 'hell fire and thunder sermon!' However, no sooner were these words out of my mouth than a forked sheet of lightning flashed across the sky followed by a tremendous roll of thunder! There was some amuse ment that I could apparently call up celestial audio-visual aids! Bu such is the awe-inspiring effect of thunder that the soldiers listenec to the message that day with more than usual attention!

In Psalm 29, the imagery of thunder is used to give a sense of th awesome presence of the Almighty. Such is the quality of Hebrew poetry that even when we read the psalm in English we can feel th build up of the thunderstorm as it sweeps down from the turbulen waters of the north (v 3), across the Lebanon forests, and down through Israel and Judah to the desert of the south (v 9). With tremendous skill and economy of words, the psalmist conveys th crescendo beat of the storm by vivid verbal pictures – such as th dance of the mighty forest oaks (v 9).

Most psalms begin with a call to worship. However, in this psaln the call is addressed not just to the temple congregation but to th heavenly court as well. In the climax of the storm in verse 9, heavenl and earthly worshippers together utter that great cry, 'Glory!'

Try and visualise in your mind's eye the thronging crowd of worshippers in the temple courtyards. Imagine the choir of Levite: leading the singing of the psalm, building up the tension so tha everyone can feel the power of God in the storm, until the massed crowds join in that climactic shout.

There might then be a dramatic silence, full of the sense of God': presence. The worshipper can visualise the King of Kings taking hi: seat on the throne of the universe (v 10). Then comes the punchline 'May the LORD give strength to his people! May the LORD bless hi: people with peace!' (v 1). It is this very God who has chosen Israel for his own. He is awe-inspiring, yes, but from that very awe comes our security and our assurance, if we are his people.

What then can we learn about praise from this and the other hymns in the psalter? First of all, note the difference between praise and prayer. The hymn is not addressed *to* God as a prayer would be In a hymn, the worshippers sing *about* God, reaffirming their faith and declaring God's power and his deeds to the world at large.

Secondly, the subject matter of our praise should not just be pious platitudes. It should actually engage with the issues which the worshippers face. In Canaanite religion, Baal was especially known as the god of thunder. Psalm 29 challenges that pagan world-view proclaiming the kingship of Yahweh over and against the false ideology of the Canaanites. The false gods of our society may be materialism, nationalism, or whatever. Our praise should engage with them, proclaiming the sovereignty of the one true God.

We believe that God allows and uses our prayers to change things. We should also expect to change things by our praise! Both in our praise and in our prayers we participate in ushering in the kingly rule of God on earth. We should never emerge from worship the same as we went in. True praise should always change us.

There are many hymns of praise in the psalter; hymns which celebrate Yahweh's greatness, goodness, wisdom, power, and love. Other examples are Psalms 8, 19, 33, 93, 96, 98, and 145–150.

READ PSALM 6: A PERSONAL LAMENT

People visiting Israel sometimes buy plaques with modern Hebrew inscriptions which they then ask me to translate. A Christian businessman recently brought back from Israel a prayer for a business, which he thought he would hang in his office. It said things like, 'may my customers' cheques never bounce, and may my creditors be long-suffering.' It was very direct and to the point! This Jewish tradition of being direct when talking to God goes right back to the psalms, and especially to the psalms of lament!

Laments form the biggest single group of psalms in the psalter. They vary greatly in length but they all follow a similar pattern. The psalmist first describes his distress. Sometimes the worshipper acknowledges that he deserves to suffer because of his sin; but other laments record the anger of those who feel they have suffered undeservedly. Then there follows an appeal to the God of Israel to intervene. Usually the psalm does not give us the end of the story. But the psalm ends on a note of assurance and faith that God will hear and answer.

Psalm 6 follows this pattern. It can be divided up like this:

Verses 1–3: lament and appeal to God

Verses 4–7: appeal to God and lament

Verses 8–10: assurance that God will deal with the situation.

It is virtually impossible to work out exactly what was the cause of the psalmist's distress. Verse 2 suggests sickness and pain; verse 3 suggests spiritual anguish; verse 5 suggests danger or death; in verse 6 it seems more like grief; in verses 7 and 10 enemies are mentioned; and in verse 8 it seems that evil-doers are the cause of the distress. Of

course, these do not necessarily contradict one another. But it is difficult to work out the exact circumstances.

It is this very lack of specifics that has enabled countless people
across the ages to make the lament psalms their own. As you read the
psalms you can find your own particular distress or suffering or grief
in the words. Some of the psalms may have been specifically written
for use in this way. If people were in distress in ancient Jerusalem
they could go to the temple, explain their predicament to the priest
who would then select from a 'library' of psalms the one which would
best fit the particular circumstances.

Most of the laments have a sudden change of mood towards the
end. The first seven verses of Psalm 6 speak of despair. But by verses
8–10, the worshipper has suddenly found a new confidence and hope
in God. It may have been that the worshipper in the temple would
use the first seven verses to bring his or her particular distress before
God. The priest would then pronounce a word of assurance that God
had heard the prayer. The worshipper would then use the closing
verses of the psalm as a declaration of personal belief that God would
answer the prayer[1].

reasons given to God to persuade him to intervene are often very frank and to the point!

It is very interesting to note the reasons that are given to
God to persuade him to intervene or come to the rescue.
They are often very frank and to the point! In Psalm 6, the
worshipper reminds God that if he dies then God will have
one less person to praise him (v 5)! Sometimes the
worshipper in a lament points out that God would not
want to lose his reputation as a righteous and fair judge (for
example Ps 7:9–11)!

On other occasions, the psalmist almost tries to bargain
with God, by promising to do something specific if God
answers the prayer. In Psalm 22, the worshipper promises to make
public all that God has done (v 29) and to offer a sacrifice (v 25). In
Psalm 51, David promises to teach God's commands to others (v 13).
In other cases God is reminded that those who insult God's people
are also insulting God himself (for example Ps 69:6–8).

The Israelites were not afraid to say to God what was on their minds
– especially in times of distress or anger. Expressing our feelings to
God is often the first step in working through the anger and distress.

There are many personal laments in the psalter. Other examples
are Psalms 3, 5, 7, 13, 22, 31, 42, 43, 51, 64, 69, 71, 120, 130, 140, 141,
142 and 143.

READ PSALM 74: A COMMUNITY LAMENT

hose who remember war-time will remember national days of ayer. In recent years those of us who live in Northern Ireland have d days of prayer for peace. The same was so in Israel of old. As well the personal laments, the psalter also contains community ments, spoken on behalf of the nation as a whole in times of war or her national crisis. Psalm 74 belongs to this group.

Note the reasons that are given to God to encourage him to come the rescue. God is reminded that the enemies are not just mocking rael, they are mocking the God of Israel as well (v 10)! If the ople's cause is lost, God's cause is also lost (v 23). Yahweh's reputaon will suffer if he does not act!

The psalm may have arisen after the catastrophic destruction of rusalem and of the Temple is 586 BC. However, several references in e psalm suggest that it may belong to a later period. In verse 8, for ample, enemies are said to have burned all the *meeting places* of the nd, which suggests a much later period when meeting places (or nagogues) had begun to appear in all the towns and villages. So it as been suggested that the psalm may belong to some later period hen the second Temple was desecrated – perhaps even as late as 57 BC, when Antiochus Epiphanies defiled the Temple.

Another possibility is that the psalm did originate with the tragic ents of 586 BC, but that it was then used again and again :ross the generations at different times of crisis and efeat. New lines or phrases could have been added to lapt the psalm to the new situations. There is quite a lot f evidence that psalms were updated in this way, and also at new psalms were written using well-known words and hrases from older ones. The psalms can readily be used in is way to serve as a template or pattern for us to bring to od the laments and thanksgivings which affect our lives and >mmunities.

the Psalms can be used as a template to bring us ... to God

For other examples of community laments, look at Psalms 44, 79, 0, 83, 85 and 126.

READ PSALM 116: A PSALM OF THANKSGIVING

ome years ago I was away from home on Fathers' Day. The children osted an elaborate home-made Fathers' Day card to me – but they rgot to put a stamp on it so I did not get it on time! However, all five of them spoke to me on the phone on the Saturday night. Even the baby was able to say, 'I love you, Daddy'. I left the phone box with tears in my eyes. It is often said that the one of the biggest moment in any man's life is the first time his little one says to him, 'I love you Daddy!'

In Psalm 116, the worshipper begins by expressing exactly that sentiment to our heavenly Father. He says 'I love Yahweh!' Worship i when we join with others in God's family to express our love to him. believe that God delights in our expressions of love just as an earthly father delights in the 'I love you' of a child.

Psalm 116 is one of many thanksgiving psalms in the psalter. The opening verses show the close connection between giving thanks to God and expressing our love to him. The psalmist's love springs from gratitude to God for his care. As John was later to write: 'We love because he first loved us' (1 John 4:19).

In many of the thanksgiving psalms, it is clear that the author ha been in distress or danger, but (as with the laments)it is often diffi cult to determine precisely what the distress was. Here in Psalm 116 the worshipper was clearly at death's door (v 3). But what has caused this state of affairs? There are hints that the cause might have bee illness (v 3), or false imprisonment (v 16), or enemy action (v 8), or some combination of all of these. We are lef unsure.

true thanksgiving is about *doing* something to demonstrate our gratitude

After the psalmist's description of how God has rescued him, there comes a vital question in verse 12: 'What shall return to the LORD for all his bounty to me?' What shall return? The psalmist's answer is that he will lift up the cup of salvation. He will offer a sacrifice of thanksgiving. He wil publicly declare his allegiance to God. He will fulfil his vow in the presence of God's people.

True thanksgiving is not just about singing a psalm. It i about *doing* something to demonstrate the reality of ou gratitude. As we read in the New Testament: 'Little children, let u love, not in word or speech, but in truth and action' (1 John 3:18) True thanksgiving is costly!

When the psalmist penned these words he no doubt had in min the worship of the Jerusalem Temple. When we read of the cup o salvation, we naturally think of the communion service, and of wha that service represents. Through this psalm, we can celebrate not onl God's earthly dealings but also our eternal salvation in Christ.

How can I sum up what this psalm means to me? It is a dee

xpression of heartfelt love and thanksgiving to God in worship. It
eminds me of how often God has answered prayers in times of
istress. It underlines how true love and thanksgiving must be
xpressed in action, not just in words. We should seek to say by our
ctions as well as with our lips: 'I love you, Heavenly Father!'

The psalter contains many thanksgiving psalms. Other examples
re Psalms 3, 92, 124 and 137. There are also thanksgiving psalms to
e found not in the psalter itself but in other parts of the Old
estament, for example, Hannah's song of gratitude for Samuel's
irth (1 Sam 2:1–10) and Jonah's song of thanksgiving from the
side the great fish (Jonah 2:1–9).

READ PSALM 110: A ROYAL CORONATION SONG

Iost of us nowadays are not old enough to remember the corona-
on ceremony for the Queen in 1953. It was the first great royal event
iat people could watch on television. There was pageantry, pomp,
id ceremony as the leaders of church and state carried out the act of
oronation. Music is always an important part of such an occasion.
ew hymns and anthems are composed. You may remember the
oyal weddings of more recent years, which were also occasions for
omp and ceremony.

The psalter contains a number of psalms that were originally
omposed for great royal occasions in Jerusalem. Psalm 110 seems
riginally to have been a coronation psalm either for King David or
or his successors on the throne in Jerusalem. Certain New
estament passages seem to refer to David himself as the author.

When we read the psalm in English, it is important to distinguish
etween the word LORD (spelt with four capital letters) and the word
ord (spelt with just one capital letter). LORD (you will remember) is
sed in our English versions to represent the Hebrew *Yahweh,* God's
pecial name. Whereas *Lord* translates a different Hebrew word which
sually denotes an important human being such as the king. So the
pening line of the psalm, 'The LORD says to my Lord', could be trans-
ted, 'Yahweh says to the king'.

Another interesting feature of this psalm is the reference in verse 4
> Melchizedek. Melchizedek is only referred to on one other occa-
on in the Old Testament, in Genesis 14, where he is described both
s *king* of Jerusalem[2] and also as *priest* of God Most High. Abraham
lowed himself to be blessed by Melchizedek. He gave Melchizedek a
:nth or tithe of the booty from the battle. He acknowledged

Melchizedek as a priest of the one true God. Melchizedek is recognised in the New Testament as having a priesthood higher even than the priests of Israel who were descended from Abraham[3]. When King David captured the city of Jerusalem from the Jebusites and made it his own personal capital city, it seems that he acquired this priest-king role. This royal priesthood gave the king a unique relationship with God. Psalm 110 celebrates the installation of the king into this Melchizedekite role.

As you read Psalm 110, try to imagine the coronation scene in your mind's eye. All the leading citizens are present. The people are crowding in and cheering. The choir of Levites are leading the worship and praise. Then the new king of Jerusalem is led to his throne at God's right hand, probably at the right hand side of the ark of the covenant.

The opening words of the psalm in Hebrew are a special expression only ever used by God's prophet. He enthrones the king in Yahweh's name – first as military leader of God's people (vs 1–3) and then into this special priesthood of Melchizedek (v 4). The remaining verses of the psalm use highly poetic language to give the newly enthroned king an assurance of God's help and victory.

This psalm is particularly meaningful for Christians, since the New Testament writers clearly understood the psalm as a prophecy of the enthronement of the Messiah. The ultimate 'priest forever according to the order of Melchizedek' is Jesus Christ – as is explained in Hebrews chapters 7 and 8.

Psalm 110 is one of quite a number of psalms originally written for royal occasions. Psalm 2 probably also belongs to the coronation ceremony in Jerusalem. Psalm 18 celebrated the king's victory in battle. Psalms 20 and 21 are respectively prayer for and praise after a royal victory. Psalm 45 is an anthem for a royal wedding.

READ PSALM 22: A POINTER TO THE SUFFERING OF JESUS

It would be quite impossible for us to read this psalm without thinking of the cross. The psalm opens with the words which Jesus quoted: 'My God, My God, why have you forsaken me?' The jeering of the crowd (vs 7,8), the thirst (v 15), and the gambling for clothes (v 18) all find unmistakable echoes in the crucifixion story. And yet it also seems clear as we read through the psalm that it was originally written as a personal lament arising out of one individual's private anguish.

The opening cry of despair is uttered by someone who feels totally abandoned by God. If you have had experiences which have led you to doubt God's presence, or to question your faith altogether, it may be reassuring to know that this psalmist felt the same way and felt able to say so to God. It is not easy to pray in such circumstances. Yet telling God how we feel is often the first step to re-establishing contact with him and re-building our relationship.

Notice the alternation between despair and hope in the psalm. Verses 1 and 2 are despair; but in verses 3 and 4 the psalmist recalls how God had heard and responded to the cry of his forefathers in distress. Then verses 6–8 describe more of the writer's personal suffering, while verses 9–11 are an expression of faith and trust. By verse 22, the psalmist is promising God what he will do if God spares him. He will proclaim God publicly as the God who rescues the poor and the suffering.

Then in the closing verses of the psalm, the writer is inspired to lift his eyes beyond his own personal plight and indeed beyond his own people Israel.

> All the ends of the earth shall remember
>   and turn to the LORD;
> and all the families of the nations
>   shall worship before him. ...
> Posterity will serve him;
>   future generations will be told about the Lord,
> and proclaim his deliverance to a people yet unborn,
>   saying that he has done it (Psalm 22:27,30,31).

It is these verses that especially enable us to see the whole psalm as fulfilled in Jesus. He was the one who above all felt forsaken by the Father as he took the world's sin upon himself. It is likely that Jesus did not just quote the first verse of the psalm from the cross, but that he in fact recited it all, moving from the forsakenness of verse 1 to the note of triumph of the closing verses.

READ PSALM 1: YAHWEH'S *TORAH*

We would be unlikely to talk about *enjoying* reading a book of laws! Yet this is exactly what the psalmist says here in Psalm 1: 'Their delight is in the law of the LORD, and on his law they meditate day and night' (v 2). The Hebrew word for 'law' is *torah*. *Torah* means something much broader than the English word, 'law'; it means teaching or instruction. The first five books of the Bible are thus called the *Torah*.

It is possible that *Torah* here refers to the first five books of th
Bible, but more likely, *Torah* here means teaching and instruction in
more general sense; and it may in fact refer to the teaching of th
Psalter itself. Psalm 1 is therefore an introduction to the psalter as
book of instruction and teaching designed for daily meditation. Ju
as a tree planted by the water's edge has a regular supply of wat
which enables it to bear fruit in its season, so men and women wh
regularly study God's *Torah* or teaching will be solidly rooted in the
faith and will 'bear fruit' in righteous deeds.

Another psalm which speaks of the importance of the regul
study of God's *Torah* is Psalm 119 which is, in fact, a collection
twenty-two short psalms encouraging believers, young and old, t
build their lives on Yahweh's teaching.

The psalms touch on of all the main themes of the Bible – God
mighty acts in history, his steadfast love, his covenant with h
people, his care and concern for the poor and needy, his power ar
majesty, his future purposes, and, of course, pointers to the Messia
and to the gospel. This is why the psalter has always been so centr
in Christian worship. It is still a tremendous resource for daily med
tation and teaching on all the great truths and themes of Scripture.

READ PSALM 137: SUFFERING AND REVENGE

Psalm 137 is a community lament from the exile period when th
Jews were transported to Babylon and were trying to piece togeth
again their faith after the horrific destruction of Jerusalem in 586 B

Did the destruction of Jerusalem mean that God had abandone
his people for ever? Did it mean that he had not been powerf
enough to save them? How would the people respond to the demar
to sing songs of Zion for their captors' entertainment? Was
possible to use Yahweh's songs in worship in a foreign country, aw
from God's Promised Land, his chosen city, his holy Temple?

These are the kind of questions in the mind of the writer of th
psalm. In the end, having worked through these doubts, the psal
reaches a climax in verses 5 and 6, in which he declares that he w
remain loyal to the faith of Jerusalem, even amid the bewilderment
captivity.

However, the second half of the psalm is very disturbing for
because of the horrific way in which the psalmist prays for reveng
'Happy shall they be who take your little ones and dash them agair
the rock!' (v 9). No doubt the Israelite exiles had seen enemy soldie

deal in this brutal way with their own people but even so, to call for a revenge of this kind horrifies us. How on earth can we reconcile this prayer of the psalmist with the teaching of Jesus? 'Love your enemies, do good to those who hate you, bless those who curse you, pray for those who abuse you' (Luke 6:2, 28).

It has to be said that this psalm is a cry from the heart of someone whose people have undergone suffering and tragedy on a holocaust scale. How the psalmist must have been traumatised by this experience is far beyond what most of us are able to imagine. We are in no position to judge!

We have already noted how the Israelites of old had no inhibitions about telling God how they felt. They brought their innermost feelings to God in their prayers – whether those feelings were feelings of anger, bitterness, or even revenge. They did not try to hide their feelings from God by pretending that emotions such as revenge were not in their hearts. But as the psalmist spilled out his innermost emotions to God, God was no doubt able to begin the process of healing.

One of the best discussions of these revenge prayers in the psalms is by Walter Brueggemann in a book called *Praying the Psalms*[4]. He points out a great paradox of the psalms. On the one hand they are very human. They contain the honest and frank prayers that people of old brought to God. On the other hand these very human words are also part of God's Word to us.

This paradox means that our interpretation (or hermeneutic) of the psalms is not straightforward. Psalm 137 is certainly not there to encourage us to feel vengeful! A favourite saying of mine is: 'What the Bible *does* to you is as important as what it *says* to you.' What the closing verse of Psalm 137 *does* to me is to churn up my emotions with horror against such thoughts of revenge. I realise as I look into my own heart that I am not immune from vengeful thoughts even in circumstances trivial by comparison with the suffering of the Jewish exiles! I then think of the teaching of Jesus and I realise the need to work through, before God, my own thoughts of revenge.

This is just one example of the way in which reading the Bible can do things to you. Of course, emotions and feelings cannot be a substitute for doctrine and truth. We must remain firmly anchored by the doctrine and truth which the Bible gives us. However, the Holy Spirit also uses the emotional impact of the Bible to bring about changes in our thinking and in our lives. As Brueggemann says, we must find a way of working *through* the revenge prayers of the psalms, not a way of working *round* them!

4.3 THE BOOK OF LAMENTATIONS AN A TO Z OF SUFFERING

As I write, the TV news screens are full of unfolding horror of the ethnic cleansing of Kosovo in 1999. It is hard for us to imagine human suffering of such proportions – although the 20th century saw numerous examples of 'man's inhumanity to man' on a massive scale.

I happen to be writing on the anniversary of the Battle of the Somme, when thousands of men from my own homeland of Northern Ireland were killed, leaving hardly a family in Belfast without a loved one lost. The vast numbers killed in the trenches of the First World War; the horror of the Holocaust; right through to genocide in Rwanda, Sudan, Bosnia, Kosovo; these have all involved suffering and loss of life on a scale that most of us are just unable to take in.

A friend of mine is an army chaplain. His regiment spent six months in Bosnia. They were camped beside a river and one of the soldiers' daily tasks was to bury the dead bodies, many of them children, which had floated down the river during the night. The soldiers (whose average age was about twenty) came home traumatised by this experience. Their lives could never be the same again. At the regimental church service on their return home, the chaplain based his sermon on the book of Lamentations which vividly describes suffering and tragedy on a similarly vast scale. The soldiers were fascinated to discover a Bible book relevant to the kind of trauma they had experienced. Lamentations has been used to express the suffering of God's people, both Jews and Christians, in many other tragic situations across the centuries.

This poignant book is an extended lament for the destruction of Jerusalem by the Babylonians in 586 BC. The five poems in this book express in emotional, poetic terms the events which are described in narrative by the books of 2 Kings and 2 Chronicles.

It is hard for us to imagine the scale of the destruction and suffering. It has been estimated that the population of Judah before the invasion may have been as many as a quarter of a million. Afterwards only 25,000 or so were left alive in the ravished country.

de and amid the ruins of the once great city of Jerusalem. It was
thnic cleansing on a vast scale. Many of the leading citizens were
aken into exile in Babylon and re-settled there. They were the fortu-
ate ones! For the vast majority, the destruction of their homeland
neant death; either in the fighting itself, or from the famine and
isease that followed. Most of the survivors fled as refugees. This is
ne tragic backcloth to the moving poems of Lamentations.

Each of the five chapters of the book is a separate poem. The first,
econd and fourth are *acrostics*, that is, each of the twenty-two verses
egins with a different letter of the Hebrew alphabet. Chapter 3 is a
imilar acrostic, except the verses are in groups of three. It is because
f this *alphabetic* pattern that Lamentations has been called an 'A to Z
f suffering'. The first, second, and fourth poems are specifically
ritten in the style and format of Israelite *funeral songs*; songs of grief
or the funeral of Judah and Jerusalem and for the many whose lives
ad been lost.

There is a tradition that the book was written by the prophet
eremiah – though in fact the book itself does not give us any
uthor's name. There are vivid scenes in the book that seem to reflect
ne emotions of an eyewitness to the aftermath of events of 586 BC –
nd that would certainly fit with Jeremiah. The author was not just
n eyewitness but a profound theologian, a poet of great skill, and a
rue patriot, heartbroken at the tragedy for his own people.

READ LAMENTATIONS

f it is hard for us to conceive of the almost total destruction of a
ation, it is probably even harder for us to understand what the
estruction of Jerusalem must have meant for the faith and religion
f the few who survived, whether for the exiled Jews in Babylon, or for
he few survivors struggling to eke out a living amid the rubble of
erusalem.

Did it all mean that Yahweh, the God of Israel, had simply not
een powerful enough to protect his chosen people? Did the tragedy
nean that the gods of Babylon were in the end more powerful than
he God of Israel? Or was it rather that Yahweh had rejected the Jews
or ever because of their sin? Was it possible for the faith of Israel to
urvive the destruction of the Temple? Was it possible to worship
srael's God in a foreign land? Many must have questioned whether
hey could still believe in a God who would allow such a disaster to
vercome his chosen people.

Through the ministry of prophets such as Jeremiah and Ezekiel
such questions were eventually to be answered in a way that enabled
the faith of Israel to re-emerge from the ashes. There are clear signs
that the book is written from a foundation of faith – though it is a
faith that has been tested to the limit. The poet is able to declare: 'the
steadfast love of the LORD never ceases, his mercies never come to an
end' (3:22). Glimpses of hope shine through, especially in the latter
part of chapter 3. The poet even speaks of turning the other cheek
while waiting for God's intervention (3:30)!

It is all too easy for us to look back across more than 2,500 years
and say that the destruction of Jerusalem was God's punishment for
the peoples' disobedience and unfaithfulness, and that they deserved
it! For those struggling to come to terms with the awful realities,
those who had seen their loved ones suffer and die, the innocent with
the guilty, there were no easy answers – just as there are no easy
answers for the victims of suffering in today's world.

Two and a half thousand years later there is still a theological
problem as to how a God of love can allow large-scale suffering. Part
of the explanation is the free-will that God has given to humankind,
which is an essential aspect of what makes us human. The consequence of free-will is that human beings can cause incredible
suffering to one another. We do believe that one day God will
somehow right these wrongs, if not in this world, then in eternity.

Israel, of course, *was* a special case. God had promised that the
Israelites would have his special protection and blessing in the land
of promise, so long as they remained faithful to him and to his word.
God's mighty acts in history on behalf of his people, especially at the
time of the exodus, were the evidence that he could and would intervene on their behalf. This covenant-relationship between God and
Israel, however, was exceptional – because God was using Israel as a
means of working out his ultimate purpose for all humankind. So
long as the Israelites remained faithful to God they had no fear of the
great empires of the day – for God would protect them. However, in
the event of their continued unfaithfulness and disobedience, God's
special intervention would be withdrawn. Lamentations helps us to
understand 'both the doom and the hope of a people for whom dire
judgement was the necessary prelude to grace'[5].

At the time it must have seemed as if God himself was directly
inflicting the suffering on Israel. The writer of Lamentations even
goes so far as to suggest that God had become Israel's 'enemy' (2:5).
There is, of course, a sense in which nothing good or evil happens

unless God allows it. But Lamentations does not minimise the wickedness and guilt of the enemy nations who caused Israel's suffering. The writer of Lamentations calls for them to be punished as they deserve (1:22).

Lamentations gives a lifeline of faith to those who are overwhelmed by suffering. And this lifeline is not just for those caught up in the large-scale disasters of this world. The personal tragedies that most of us have to face at some stage in our lives can be as overwhelming. Reading Lamentations, and making its words our own, can be a significant step to building a bridge back to God out of a despair which threatens the very foundations of faith.

4.4 SONG OF SONGS
LOVE SONGS FROM ISRAEL

Your lips cover me with kisses;
Your love is better than wine.
There is a fragrance about you;
The sound of your name recalls it.
No woman could help loving you.[6]

People are often astonished to discover that there are love songs in the Bible! Yet these words from the opening of Song of Songs would do well on any Valentine card!

The Song of Songs (also called Song of Solomon) is a collection of love songs in which both female and male speakers express their love for each other. The lyrics are rich in romantic imagery and there are explicit physical descriptions of both the woman and the man.

Song of Songs is closely associated with the wisdom books. As with most of them, the Song is closely linked with Solomon. Certainly Solomon had a reputation as a lover! In fact, however, the Hebrew of the opening verse is more likely to mean 'commissioned by' or 'dedicated to' Solomon than written by Solomon. Though there are parts of the Song which could have come from a royal author, overall the Song seems to be about the love of ordinary people. Solomon (who had seven hundred wives and three hundred concubines) was scarcely an appropriate role model on matters of love and romance!

READ SONG OF SONGS

It is not clear whether we have one continuous love song, tracing the ups and downs of one young couple, or a collection of several separate songs that were popular in ancient Israel at the time. Some have suggested that it is possible to trace a continuous story throughout the book. The storyline would be something like this: girl loves shepherd boy, girl meets king and leaves shepherd boy, boy wins girl back!

It could be that Song of Songs is a collection of lyrics associated with a story that everyone would have known at the time. A modern parallel might be a CD of the soundtrack of a musical. It would not be easy to work out the storyline of the musical if you only had the songs. Similarly the storyline of Song of Songs is not completely clear since we only have the words of the songs and not the whole of the drama!

Another suggestion is that Song of Songs contains pieces that were regularly sung at wedding ceremonies or celebrations, perhaps to accompany a traditional pageant in which the bride and groom would take part. On these matters we can't be sure. What we can be sure of is that the Song celebrates romantic love between a woman and a man, described in poetry that is sometimes very explicit.

Christians have often had a negative attitude to human sexuality. Song of Songs makes clear that physical love between a woman and a man is something which God intended to be enjoyed to the full – within the safeguards of marriage. I well remember a young couple whom I taught in Bible college coming home from their honeymoon and telling us: 'Marriage is so good that only God could have thought of it!' That sentiment is very much in line with the thinking of Song of Songs.

It has been suggested that Song of Songs was written as a poetic commentary on two key verses from the beginning of Genesis, namely: 'So God created humankind in his image, in the image of God he created them; male and female he created them[7],' and 'Therefore a man leaves his father and his mother and clings to his wife, and they become one flesh[8].'

Literal or allegorical?

Across the centuries there has been debate (among both Jews and Christians) about how this book should be interpreted. Some of the early rabbis taught that the book was not really about romantic love. Such matters could have no place in Scripture! Instead they taught that the book was an *allegory* of the love between God and Israel.

Similarly, Christians have often interpreted Song of Songs as an allegory of the love of Christ for his church. If you open an Authorised (King James) Bible, and turn to the Song of Solomon, you will see page headings such as 'the Church glorieth in Christ' and 'the graces of the Church'.

An allegorical book is one that seems on the surface to be about one thing, but which actually means something else altogether. Some of the parables of Jesus are allegories. For example, the parable of the prodigal son is, on the surface a story, about a human father and his sons, but it is really intended to teach the reader about the heavenly Father's love for his children. The best known example of an allegory in English literature is John Bunyan's *Pilgrim's Progress,* which on the surface is about one man's pilgrimage to the heavenly city, but which is in fact an allegory of the Christian believer's pilgrimage through life.

An allegorical approach to all Bible books was common in the early church and it led to wild and fanciful interpretations. The trouble with allegorical interpretation is that you can make a text mean whatever you want it to mean – and you can all too easily disregard the obvious meaning! Allegorical interpretation is only valid where the text itself makes clear that it is intended as allegory (as, for example, in the parables of Jesus).

There is no such indication in the text of the Song of Songs. Anyone reading the book for the first time, who did not know about the allegorical debate, would naturally conclude that the book is a collection of romantic love songs. However, it is not necessarily a case of *either* literal *or* allegorical. The Old Testament elsewhere uses the marriage relationship as a helpful parallel towards understanding the love of God for Israel. In the book of Revelation, similar imagery is used in picturing the church as the bride of Christ.

So although Song of Songs speaks primarily about love between woman and man, that in turn teaches us about the love of Christ for his church. What an obligation it places on us as Christians to have the kind of marriage relationships that will mirror the love of Christ for his church!

Endnotes

1   An informal example of this process is the conversation between Hannah (Samuel's mother) and Eli, the priest, in 1 Samuel 1:12–18.

2   Salem is short form of Jerusalem.

3   Hebrews 7:9,10

4   Walter Brueggemann, *Praying the Psalms* (St Mary's Press, Winona, Minnesota, 1993).

5   Quoted from: La Sor, Hubbard, and Bush, *Old Testament Survey* (1996), page 529.

6   Song of Songs 1:2,3 (GNB)

7   Genesis 1:27.

8   Genesis 2:24.

Part Five

'Learning how the world works':
the wisdom books

5.1 HOW THE WORLD WORKS

When the National Curriculum was launched some years ago, the Department of Education distributed a leaflet entitled, *Learning How The World Works*. The books that we call the *wisdom books* teach us something of *how the world works*. These books are Proverbs, Job, and Ecclesiastes and sometimes Song of Songs.

Unlike most Old Testament books, the wisdom books make little reference to Israel as a special or chosen nation. They concerned humankind as a whole. In this sense they are 'universalist'. The authors of these books drew on the wisdom traditions of other neighbouring cultures. They did not refuse 'light from any quarter'. For example, there is a portion of Proverbs[1] which is very similar to a passage from an early Egyptian work called *The Wisdom of Amen-em-opet*.

The wise women and men of ancient Israel (often called *sages*) sought to deduce *how the world works* by God-guided observation and study. The words of Paul from the New Testament sum it up well: 'Ever since the creation of the world his [God's] eternal power and divine nature, invisible though they are, have been understood and seen through the things he has made'[2].

From earliest times in Israel, short wisdom sayings and proverbial stories were exchanged and handed down among ordinary people. The old and wise would pass on the wisdom of the generations to their children and grandchildren. Jotham's parable (Judg 9:7–15) is an early example of this wisdom. Certain individuals were famed for their wisdom, such as the wise woman of Tekoa (whom Joab sent to influence David)[3].

King Solomon was particularly famed for his God-given wisdom, and as a collector of proverbs and wise sayings. It seems likely Solomon founded in Jerusalem a royal wisdom school (or university), as was the practice in the royal courts of the Ancient Near East. This school would have been a centre for study of *how the world works*, a centre where wise sayings and traditions were collected, not just from all over Israel, but also from the other cultural centres of the Ancient Near East. However, the Israelite sages adapted this material to the faith and religion of Israel. They asserted that without faith in Israel's God it is not possible to have true wisdom. As Proverbs says: 'The fear of the L ORD is the beginning of wisdom, and the knowledge of the Holy One is insight' (Prov 9:10).

The wisdom books do not deal with the Law of Moses, the covenant, or the sacrifices in the Temple. Despite the close connection of these books with King Solomon, there is no interest in Yahweh's covenant with David, or in Jerusalem as God's chosen city. Sometimes the wisdom books are referred to as human-centred – because they start from ordinary everyday situations. The books do not normally record direct intervention by God in the affairs of history.

The wisdom books are less well known among Christians than other books of the Old Testament. This is partly because the theme of wisdom does not easily plug into New Testament themes such as law and gospel, salvation, sacrifice, or the promised Messiah. However, Jesus' own teaching had deep roots in Old Testament wisdom. Parables, for example, are a wisdom means of communication. The Sermon on the Mount contains many echoes of the wisdom books. Paul makes many references to wisdom themes (eg Galatians 6:7,8) and the whole of the book of James very much has a wisdom ethos. So do not neglect the wisdom books!

5.2 THE BOOK OF PROVERBS 'THE FEAR OF YAHWEH IS THE BEGINNING OF WISDOM'

A Highway Code for life

Most of us are familiar with the Highway Code; the book of the rules of the road in the UK. It contains all kinds of good advice for safe motoring. My favourite line is about level crossings with no gates. It says, 'Stop, look both ways: always give way to trains!' Sometimes even commonsense things need to be spelled out!

The Highway Code is not in itself *law*. This is made quite clear in the introduction. It is a collection of good *advice* about safe motoring – although, of course, it includes things which are legal requirements (such as stopping at traffic lights). The Highway Code is *proverb* rather than *law* – an important distinction which was discussed in Part One.

The book of Proverbs might be described as a 'Highway Code for Life'. It is full of good, God-given, instruction for getting the best out of life. Like the Highway Code it is not primarily a book of law, though it emphasises the wisdom of choosing right rather than wrong. Just as the physicist observes that what goes up must come down, and calls it the law of gravity, so the sages sought to observe laws and principles of human relationships. The sages saw a close connection between wisdom and righteousness, just as there is a close connection between folly and wrongdoing. Prosperity and happiness is offered as the reward for the wise. Disaster is the consequence of folly and sin.

A doctrine of rewards?

Sometimes there has been misunderstanding on this last point. For you do not need to look very far in the world around you to realise that good people often suffer, and wicked people often prosper. The sages of old must have realised this just as much as anyone would today. Now, of course, it is true that God did promise to Israel that righteousness would bring prosperity and that disobedience would bring about disaster. But these promises were to the *nation*, not to the individual. When Israel prospered, the wicked in her midst prospered along with the good. When Jerusalem was destroyed, the righteous suffered along with the guilty. Nor does God's promise to Israel imply that every wicked nation will always suffer and that every righteous nation will always prosper. On the contrary, God's relationship with Israel was exceptional and special; through them God would bring blessing to all the nations.

So whether we are talking about nations or individuals, let us be clear that the Bible offers no guarantee that the good will always be rewarded or that the wicked will always be punished, not at least in this life. Indeed one of the very first episodes in the Bible is the story of Abel, a righteous man who was undeservedly murdered – and the rest of the Old Testament is full of similar examples. Far from offering his followers a guarantee of prosperity, Jesus spoke of taking up a cross and of denying self [4].

What then are we to make of the passages in Proverbs which seem to give a promise of prosperity to the wise and an assurance of punishment and disaster to the foolish and wicked? There are quite a number of such passages, for example:

> 'Hold on to wisdom and insight, my son ... They will provide you with life, a pleasant and happy life' [5].

> 'The sins of a wicked man are a trap ... His utter stupidity will send him to the grave' [6].

> 'Those who keep the commandment will live; those who are heedless of their ways will die' [7].

The parallel with the Highway Code is helpful. People are much more likely to be safe on the road if they follow the good advice of the Highway Code. Those who disregard it are much more likely to have an accident. However, even the most careful drivers can still be involved in road accidents. It may be caused by something totally beyond the driver's control. It could be black ice, it could be someone else driving carelessly. Keeping to the Code means you are much more likely to be safe but it cannot be a guarantee. The reverse is also true. We probably all know people who drive as though they have never read the Highway Code – and yet survive unscathed!

Who wrote the book of Proverbs?

The book has always been closely connected with the name of Solomon whose personal wisdom was, of course, proverbial[8]. The heading given to the book in its title verse is: 'The proverbs of Solomon, son of David, king of Israel'. This could mean that Solomon himself was the author – and indeed he was a collector of proverbial sayings. It is equally as likely, however, that the Hebrew phrase means to or for Solomon. This would imply that Solomon commissioned or sponsored the book. Or it may have been compiled at a later date and dedicated to his memory.

Proverbs as we now have it seems to have been arranged and expanded over the years after King Solomon's time. The book itself tells us that new material was added in the reign of King Hezekiah (25:1). The book also includes other material – such as the words of Agur in chapter 30 and the advice in the closing chapter given to King Lemuel by his mother.

Reading Proverbs as a book

Proverbs may not be as easy as other books to read right through because most of the book appears to be a random collection of proverbs. A look at the structure and layout of the book can help us. The book divides into three main sections:

● Chapters 1–9: the importance of God-given wisdom and an introduction to what Old Testament wisdom is all about

● Chapters 10–30: a compendium of individual proverbs covering a wide variety of subjects

● Chapter 31: an epilogue in two parts: advice to King Lemuel by his mother, and a closing poem on the qualities of the capable wife.

So a possible *first* reading of this book might be done like this:

● Read right through the first nine chapters, if possible at one sitting

● Read at least part of the central section, perhaps chapters 10 and 11, in order to gain a flavour of the variety of proverbs

● Jump forward and read the final chapter of the book.

This approach will give you a good feeling for the book as a whole; and then at a later stage you can come back and read the complete central section of the book. I remember once hearing Billy Graham say in a radio interview that he read through five psalms and two chapters of Proverbs every day; so valuable did he find Proverbs in facing everyday situations.

READ PROVERBS 1–9

As always the opening and closing sections of any book contain important clues to what that book is all about. The *Good News Bible* translation of the first three verses is very good:

> Here are proverbs that will help you to recognise wisdom and good advice, and understand sayings with deep meaning. They can teach you how to live intelligently and how to be honest, just, and fair.

In the New Testament, Paul says that the Christian should come to have 'the mind of Christ'[9]. The person who becomes familiar with Proverbs will increasingly be able to discern the mind of God in everyday life.

I remember once asking a senior CID officer how police constables were selected to transfer from the uniformed branch to the CID. 'What I look for in a young copper,' he replied, 'is someone who doesn't bother his superiors with things he could have decided for himself; but also someone who knows when he needs to ask advice.'

I have often thought that there is a lesson for the Christian seeking guidance from God. Of course, we can always come to God for guidance. But God has given us minds and intellects and he expects us to use them. Just as a parent brings up a young person to be able to make decisions for herself or himself, so God wants us to become mature spiritually, so that we can instinctively make right decisions.

Do remember again how important it is to distinguish between law and proverb. In the story of the good Samaritan, the priest and the Levite passed by on the other side – for there is no specific law in the Bible which says you must help a man in distress. If, however, the priest and Levite had taken a proverbial rather than a legalistic approach, they would have realised that, law or no law, it could not possibly be the mind of God for them to walk past a man in such need!

The fear of Yahweh is the beginning of wisdom

Verse 7 of this first chapter is one of the keys to understanding the whole book: 'The fear of the LORD is the beginning of wisdom.' As we have seen, much of the material in the book of Proverbs was known outside Israel. It was the shared wisdom of the Ancient Near Eastern world. However, the claim of Proverbs is that true wisdom and knowledge is only possible for those who reverence the God of Israel. Certainly people of other nations, cultures, and religions could attain to a certain measure of wisdom, and the Israelites could learn from the wisdom and experience of others. However, true wisdom is nonetheless God's gift, and it begins with him alone.

Do you remember puzzle books as a small child? A common type of puzzle is a maze with treasure at the centre. There are several entry points to the maze – but it is only possible to reach the treasure at the centre if you chose the right entry point. Choose the wrong one and you soon reach a dead end. If we begin at the right place, with reverence for the God of Israel, will it be possible to attain the 'treasure' of wisdom?

Proverbs is for everyone

Again the *Good News Bible* translates chapter 1: 4,5 well: Proverbs 'can make an inexperienced person clever and teach young men to be resourceful. These proverbs can even add to the knowledge of wise men and give guidance to the educated ...'. Proverbs are primarily for ordinary people, especially for the young and for the inexperienced. Indeed, paradoxically, it is the worldly-wise who may find difficulty with Bible wisdom. The apostle Paul was later to write, 'God's foolishness is wiser than human wisdom' [10].

Reading on, it soon becomes clear that much of Proverbs is directed towards younger people - to equip them to cope with the decisions and temptations of adult life. These references are specifically addressed to young men – probably because of a long tradition of handing down proverbial wisdom from father to son. However, when we remember that proverbs are particular sayings to illustrate general truths, then clearly the book of Proverbs will be of value whether we are young or old, female or male.

The young man is warned several times about the immoral woman waiting to seduce him [11]. It has sometimes been suggested that the book contains a negative view of women – as if young men would naturally be upright and pure were it not for women! This wrong impression only arises if these passages are taken out of the context. The book warns the young man just as much against the different temptations that will be put before him by other men.

Wisdom *herself* speaks

Wisdom is represented as speaking on several occasions – and, significantly, wisdom is personified as female [12]. Chapters 2 and 3 consist of advice from 'mother wisdom' to the young person setting out on life's journey. This is, of course, the wisdom of God himself. It is often said today that there is a need to think of God in a more gender-inclusive way – not just as a *father* figure but also as a *mother* figure. God is neither male nor female, and we have been wrong in the past in using *only* masculine imagery to portray God's character.

In chapter 8, Wisdom makes her appeal to the whole human race. The chapter is a beautiful and challenging poem – well worth reading carefully. Wisdom says: 'The LORD created me at the beginning of his work, the first of his acts of long ago' (v 22); and: 'When he marked out the foundations of the earth, then I was beside him, like a master worker; and I was daily his delight, rejoicing before him always, rejoicing in his inhabited world and delighting in the human race' (vs 29–31). God's wisdom is woven into the very fabric of creation. Wisdom laments that, though she calls out in the streets and the market places, only a few people pay heed to what she has to offer.

It is very interesting to read these verses side by side with New Testament passages such as John 1:1–5 and Colossians 1:15–20. From these it becomes clear that the wisdom of Proverbs is not just the wisdom of God the Father, but also the wisdom of Jesus Christ, the Word of God, through whom everything in the universe was created, and through whom 'God was pleased to reconcile to himself all things, whether on earth or in heaven, by making peace through the blood of his cross' (Col 1:20).

READ PROVERBS 10–30

I have suggested that at this point you read at least two chapters of this central section. Of course if you are able to read through the whole of this section of the book, so much the better.

Sanctified common sense

One of my activities is training people for life-saving qualifications. Some of the skills that are taught in these courses are basic and common sense. Sometimes the initial reaction of students is that it is almost beneath them to have to learn and practise such simple things! Yet experience has shown that in emergencies common sense often goes to the winds, and otherwise sensible people end up doing very silly things. The same is true in life. When we are under pressure, common sense can evaporate and even the most basic Biblical principles are easily forgotten. The more familiar we are with Scripture, the more likely we are to act properly under pressure or temptation. Remember how the writers of the Highway Code felt it necessary to say, 'Always give way to trains'!

Proverbs and the New Testament

I will not say much more at this stage about individual proverbs. They speak for themselves. But let me emphasise how much the Proverbs prepare the way for the teaching of Jesus. After you have read through these chapters, it would be useful to read Jesus' Sermon on the Mount (Matthew 5–7) and to notice the many ways in which he echoes the wisdom teaching.

Here are just a few examples of specific links between the book of Proverbs and various other parts of the New Testament:

- Read Proverbs 10:12 and compare James 5:20 and 1 Peter 4:8

- Read Proverbs 25:6,7 and compare Luke 14:8–10

- Read Proverbs 25:21,22 and compare Romans 12:20 and Matthew 25:31–45

- Read Proverbs 27:1 and compare James 4:13–16.

READ PROVERBS 31

The closing section of any book is always important – if only because the last thing we read in any book is what sticks in our minds. Significantly, women are central to this epilogue chapter.

The first nine verses are the advice given by the mother of King Lemuel to her son. We do not know who King Lemuel was. It may be another name for King Solomon (though his mother, Bathsheba, was scarcely a paragon of virtue!). Possibly it is a name for a 'typical' king. The focus of the passage is not on the king himself but on the advice his mother gives him. Even powerful and successful men can be much more dependent on women than they care to admit!

Whoever Lemuel is, the closing chapter of Proverbs makes clear that even kings and rulers must pay attention to ordinary wisdom – a salutary message for those with power and influence to this day.

The book ends with a pen-picture of the 'capable wife'. She is able to combine traditional roles of wife and mother with an initiative and industry that are modern in scope. 'She is far more precious than jewels' (v 26). This closing section of the book represents a remarkable stand against the prevailing 'chauvinism' of the ancient world. These last words of the book suggest that good women do not get the credit they deserve. Let's not forget the all-important place of women in a godly society – women whose God-given wisdom may indeed exceed that of their husbands and sons!

5.3 THE BOOK OF JOB: DOES JOB FEAR GOD FOR NOTHING?

The book of Job begins with a wager between God and Satan! It deals with profound questions arising from the suffering of a righteous man. Almost all of us at some point in our lives have felt a keen sense of injustice at undeserved suffering. 'Why did God do this to me?' 'Why did it happen to such a good person?' These are the kind of questions that are faced in the book of Job.

Job as a drama

Probably the best way to interpret the book of Job is as a *drama*. It has many similarities to the tragic dramas which we know from the ancient Greek world. The core of the book is a series of *dialogues*; debates between Job and his friends. A modern equivalent might be a radio play without any need for stage or scenery. The book of Job could be 'performed' very effectively. A church might even consider a performance in their local hall. Why shouldn't friends and neighbours come, as they might to a Shakespeare play? This could be an innovative means of communicating God's Word!

Recently I saw a school production of George Bernard Shaw's play *The Devil's Disciple*. It is set during the American war of independence, mostly in the camp of the British general, who was nicknamed Gentleman Johnny. Now the thrust of the play is that the British forces were so incompetent that it was no wonder they lost the war! Gentleman Johnny himself scarcely knew one end of a rifle from the other! However, that is not what the characters on stage actually say! They speak of how wonderful they are! The message of the play as a whole is the *opposite* of what individual characters are saying.

In the book of Job, the main characters are Job and his three friends, or 'comforters' as they have come to be known. They enter into lengthy debate on the issue of Job's suffering and each of them puts forward his viewpoint. When God himself appears in the final scene, it becomes clear that none of them, not even Job, was right in what he had said. So the overall message of the book is different from what the individual characters are saying. It is therefore particularly dangerous to take a verse out of context from the middle of Job and quote it as an authoritative word from God.

History or parable?

Does the book of Job relate actual historical events or is it an extended parable? The Job story was known in the literatures of other cultures in the Ancient Near East.

So it almost certainly has a strong basis in historical fact. The author may have taken a well-known proverbial story and made it the basis for a dramatic exploration of theological issues. There is no indication of who the author might be.

The dialogue is in verse and the language is highly poetic. There is a widespread convention in drama that the characters should speak in verse. Ancient Greek and Roman drama was in verse. Shakespeare's characters speak in verse. One of the reasons is that more can be communicated in fewer words; poetry can touch the audience's emotions more readily than prose.

The drama divides clearly into four Acts, each with a number of scenes. We will look at these four Acts in turn.

> **READ ACT 1: THE PROLOGUE (CHAPTERS 1,2)**

The prologue is in prose. The scene is set in God's heavenly court and the conversation is between God and Satan. The prologue divides into six brief scenes.

Scene 1 (1:1–5)

The narrator opens with important information about Job himself, stressing both his wealth and his righteousness. He even offered sacrifices in case his children sinned unintentionally! God himself later says about Job: 'There is no one like him on the earth, a blameless and upright man who fears God and turns away from evil' (v 8).

Scene 2 (1:6–12)

The royal court of the heavenly King is sitting for judgement. The courtiers are God-like beings though we are given no other information about them. It is difficult to know to what extent we should understand this episode as a literal description of God's heavenly court. A parallel is Jesus' parable of the rich man and Lazarus (Luke 16:19–31). In that parable, the rich man in hell is able to call across to Lazarus who is in heaven and then receive an answer from Abraham. However, we are not intended to assume that conversations between heaven and hell are normally possible! It is a hypothetical picture.

The same may well be true of the Job prologue. Hypothetical does not mean untrue. The author is describing the indescribable! The reality would be beyond our power to imagine, far less to describe!

The most surprising feature of the scene is the appearance of Satan among God's courtiers. The Hebrew word *satan* is not in fact a proper name. It means the *adversary* or *prosecutor*. His role here in the heavenly court is what we might call 'counsel for the prosecution'. He prosecutes the charges against God's people. Not content with being the *prosecutor* he has taken upon himself the role of putting people up to wrong-doing in the first place – which is why we have come to know the Satan as the tempter. He tempts King David in 1 Chronicles 21:1. By New Testament times the name Satan has become a proper-name equivalent to the Devil.

the most surprising feature is the appearance of Satan among God's courtiers

Satan's words in verses 9–11 are extremely important: 'Does Job fear God for nothing? ... You have blessed the work of his hands, and his possessions have increased in the land. But stretch out your hand now, and touch all that he has, and he will curse you to your face'. The textbooks often describe this as a *wager* between God and Satan! The scene ends with God giving Satan permission to take away all that Job has in order to put him to the test.

Scene 3 (1:13–22)

In the third brief scene, Job loses everything – even his family. The scene ends with Job determined to remain faithful despite what Satan has done to him: 'Naked I came from my mother's womb, and naked shall I return there; the LORD gave, and the LORD has taken away; blessed be the name of the LORD' (v 21).

Scenes 4 and 5 (2:1–6,7–10)

The fourth and fifth scenes in the prologue alternate between heaven and earth. Satan is given permission by God to intensify Job's suffering. Job is then depicted diseased, covered with sores, sitting among the ashes. Even his wife is scathing. But Job remains steadfast!

Scene 6 (2:11–13)

Job's friends arrive – Eliphaz, Bildad and Zophar. They have come a long distance to support and comfort Job. The genuineness of their sympathy is shown by the fact that they sit with Job in the ashes in silence for seven days. The phrase 'Job's comforters' is often used in a negative way! But the author takes care to depict them as righteous and God-fearing men, who are truly sympathetic and anxious to help. The dialogue which follows could be described as an extended cross-examination of Job. Satan disappears into the background, and Job's own friends are now his courtroom adversaries.

Irony is in fact an important feature of the book. Dramatic irony is where the audience knows things which are not known by the characters on stage. We know what has happened to cause Job's predicament, but this can never be known either to Job or to his friends.

READ ACT 2: DIALOGUE OF WITNESSES (CHAPTERS 3–31)

Act 2 can also be divided up into six scenes:

- Scene 1 (chapter 3)　　　Job's opening statement
- Scene 2 (chapters 4–14)　The first debate
- Scene 3 (chapters 15–21)　The second debate
- Scene 4 (chapters 22–27)　The third debate
- Scene 5 (chapter 28)　　　Interlude: A hymn in praise of wisdom
- Scene 6 (chapters 29–31)　Job's final statement

If time does not permit for you to read the whole of Act 2 in one sitting, then you may want to read scenes 1 and 2 (chapters 3–14) and then scenes 5 and 6 (chapters 28–31). This will give you a significant flavour of the debate as a whole and you can read the remainder at a later time.

There are three rounds of debate between Job and his friends. In the first two rounds, each of the friends makes a speech, followed by an answering speech by Job. In the third debate, there is no speech by Zophar, and it is not always absolutely clear who is speaking at some points. The disjointed nature of the third round of debate conveys the increasing frustration of the speakers.

The gist of the whole debate can be summed up something like this. For Job's friends, who are pious God-fearing men, there are only two possible explanations for Job's extreme suffering. Either Job has committed some grievous sin long ago, of which he has not repented, and for which God is now punishing him. Or God is treating Job most unjustly. Since their pious beliefs do not permit them even to countenance the second possibility, the friends insist that Job must have sinned in some terrible way in time past. They call on him to repent and to seek God's forgiveness for whatever it is that he has done.

in the second Act Job has put God on trial!

Job protests his innocence. He has done nothing which deserves such suffering. There seems to be no justice in God's universe. He speaks repeatedly of his despair – cursing the day he was born! His despair, however, alternates with great high points of faith – such as the well-known words in 19:25: 'For I know that my Redeemer lives, and that at the last he will stand upon the earth.' The word translated *redeemer* is a courtroom term. The *Good News Bible* translates the verse like this: 'But I know that here is someone in heaven who will at last come to my defence'.

Satan has put the prosecution case against Job and Job is convinced that God himself will come to his defence! Of course, these words find their ultimate fulfilment far beyond Job's immediate predicament in Jesus Christ, God's ultimate *redeemer,* who pleads the cause of all his people before God's throne.

Though he comes near to it on several occasions, Job refuses to 'curse God'. He remains faithful, as God had said he would. Satan's wager is lost!

The three rounds of debate finish at the end of chapter 27. There then follows a hymn in praise of wisdom (chapter 28). This hymn is a pause for the audience to reflect before Job begins his final summing up (chapters 29–31). Job's final speech is a powerful demonstration of courtroom oratory, in which Job questions the justice of the heavenly court. The speech comes to an abrupt end as Job makes a final denial of whatever charges have been laid against him.

The prologue has put Job on trial, but in the second Act Job has put God on trial!

READ ACT 3: THE 'SUMMING UP' BY ELIHU (CHAPTERS 32–37)

The third Act begins with these words:

> So these three men ceased to answer Job, because he was righteous
> in his own eyes. Then Elihu ... became angry. He was angry with
> Job because he justified himself rather than God; he was angry also
> with Job's three friends because they had found no answer, though
> they had declared Job to be in the wrong[13].

Elihu seems to appear out of nowhere. We are told that he was the
youngest person present. The Good News translation refers to him as
a 'bystander'. In a modern production, he might jump up out of the
audience on to the stage. He is the typical 'angry young man', full of
ideals and strong views which he cannot keep to himself – though he
does have the courtesy to wait until his elders have finished speaking
before interjecting his own contribution to the debate. Elihu adds
little that is new but he offers us a critical summary of the debate so
far, which heightens the tension as we await God's final verdict.

READ ACT 4: THE VERDICT (CHAPTERS 38–42:6)

Scene 1 (38:1–40:6)   Yahweh's first speech and Job's reply

Scene 2 (40:7–42:6)   Yahweh's second speech and Job's reply.

At last we hear the voice of God, speaking awesomely out of thunder
and storm. God's verdict is surprising in several respects. He makes
two speeches, in both of which it is Job who is roundly rebuked.

In the first speech, Job is rebuked for daring to question the
wisdom of the Almighty. In the second speech, he is rebuked for
questioning God's justice. Job is forcefully reminded that
there are many things in heaven and earth that he can **there is no**
ever hope to understand. He has no right to turn things **explanation**
round by putting God on trial! At the end of God's first **given to Job**
speech, Job gives only a brief answer, acknowledging the **for his**
foolishness of what he had said earlier. After God's second **suffering**
speech, he makes a fuller confession and speaks of his
shame and repentance.

It is sometimes said that God has browbeaten Job into submission. Who is going to argue when face-to-face with the Almighty?
God has not in fact answered any of the questions which Job had
raised. There is no explanation given to Job for his suffering. After all,

Job had remained loyal. He had not cursed God and God had been vindicated in his wager with the Satan. However, in Job's final answer to God he says: 'In the past I only knew what others had told me, but now I have seen you with my own eyes' (42:5 GNB).

Job has now met God and heard God speak. He has had a privilege which few mortals receive in this life. God is no longer a stranger to him, remote and inaccessible. In this very encounter, Job has been rewarded for his loyalty and faithfulness. Now that he has actually met God face-to-face, Job no longer doubts either God's wisdom or his justice. His specific questions have not been answered, but he is prepared at accept that all things do ultimately work together for good for those who trust God[14] – even though there are so many things in heaven and on earth that he can never hope to understand. Despite God's rebuke, in the end Job is vindicated. He is now restored to his former position of wealth, respect, and family – indeed he is even more blessed than he had been before (42: 2).

READ THE EPILOGUE (CHAPTER 42:7–15)

Job's friends are the ones who are finally convicted by God's verdict: 'The LORD said to Eliphaz the Temanite: "My wrath is kindled against you and against your two friends; for you have not spoken of me what is right, as my servant Job has"' (42:7). Their narrow-minded religiosity was in the end more culpable than Job's doubt and questioning.

This is a profound warning against a narrow dogmatism (like that of the New Testament Pharisees). For Job to question God's wisdom and justice was an affront for which he was rebuked. But it was even more of an affront for the friends to imagine that they could sum God up in a few sentences of orthodox doctrine! It is one of the striking ironies of the book that Job's friends are only spared when Job offers a sacrifice on their behalf.

The closing paragraph of the book contains an interesting footnote. In the description of Job's new family, his sons are not named but his daughters are! This is the reverse of so many lists of descendants in the Old Testament, where sons are named while daughters are not. And we are told that Job's daughters inherited equally with their brothers – quite a revolutionary concept even for modern times. In all the wisdom books women are often given value and esteem in marked contrast to the prevailing culture of the ancient world.

Audience response

What would the overall message of Job have been to an original audience? What thoughts would have been uppermost in their minds as they walked home? What thoughts should be uppermost in our minds after reading the book through?

The book offers no glib answers to questions about suffering though it does remind us that there are things in heaven and earth that we can never hope to understand. It is reassuring to know that even God's hero found himself questioning God's justice and that God understands that there are times when even the most faithful will feel anger against him. The challenge for us is to believe that God's wisdom is wiser than human logic and that justice will prevail in the end.

God sometimes calls on his people to suffer as part of furthering his purpose. Jesus called on his followers to deny self and to take up a cross[15]. A similar thought is contained in Paul's words to Timothy: 'Share in suffering like a good soldier of Christ Jesus' (2 Tim 2:3). Willingness to suffer in God's cause is part of our worship and service to God.

These are all important issues. However, the most important question asked in the book is perhaps Satan's question in the opening chapter: 'Does Job fear God for nothing?' (1:9). Or as the Good News Bible puts it: 'Would Job worship God if he got nothing out of it?'

The first Act of this drama had put Job on trial. The second Act put God on trial. But the final outcome of the book is to put you and me, the audience, on trial. Satan's question could be asked of any of us. Why do *we* serve God? Do we serve God only because we hope for a reward? Do we avoid wrongdoing *only* for fear of punishment? Goodness is not real goodness if it is done only for the sake of a reward. Loyalty and faithfulness are not true loyalty and faithfulness if they are motivated *solely* by a self-centred desire for blessing.

The New Testament makes clear that we can never put ourselves in the right with God by our own efforts. Just as we cannot lift ourselves by our own bootlaces, so we can never do enough good works to make us good enough for God. Not even Job was good enough for that and he was as righteous as any man could be. He required a redeemer!

The book of Job paves the way for the gospel message that justification can only be grace through faith, not by good works or by religion. Suffering may sometimes seem undeserved. But the real marvel is God's forgiveness which is undeserved even by the best of us! And God's forgiveness is the result of the *totally* undeserved suffering of Jesus Christ, the heavenly redeemer whom Job foresaw!

5.4 ECCLESIASTES 'VANITY OF VANITIES, SAYS THE TEACHER... ALL IS VANITY'

Whenever I read the book of Ecclesiastes, I am reminded of a man I once knew called Paddy, who worked on a farm belonging to friends of mine. He was what country people call a 'simple soul' but he was an invaluable worker on the farm. One day Paddy was listening to some farmers heatedly discussing the price of land. Paddy turned to me and said, 'I don't know why they are so concerned about the price of land. For one bit, six feet by two, will do each of them in the end!' Paddy was often the one who had the most wisdom. The writer of the book of Ecclesiastes would have approved of Paddy!

Ecclesiastes is one of the most puzzling books in the whole of the Old Testament. On first reading it can seem totally pessimistic. It sometimes seems contradictory. A Jewish rabbi, puzzled by this book, once suggested that King Solomon wrote Song of Songs in his virility, Proverbs in his maturity, and Ecclesiastes in his senility!

Like the book of Job, the book of Ecclesiastes is best understood as a form of drama. However, it is not a *dialogue* among different characters. Rather Ecclesiastes is a *monologue*, a one-character drama in which the writer debates with himself.

As with Job, we have to be very wary of taking one verse out of the middle of the book and using it as a proof-text. The writer puts up ideas to probe, to question, and sometimes to reject them. It could be quite misleading to take a verse out of context. For example: 'Do not be too righteous, and do not act too wise; why should you destroy yourself?' (7:16) This is not the final conclusion of the book!

The writer describes himself by a Hebrew word which in the NRSV is translated 'the Teacher'. Other translations use different words, such as 'the Preacher' or 'the Philosopher'. The title verse of the book says: 'The words of the Teacher, the son of David, king in Jerusalem.' This has traditionally been understood to mean that the author of the book was Solomon – though Solomon is not actually named. However, there are passages in the book which speak *about* the king in a way which would be odd if the king were the speaker. Some have suggested that this title verse refers only to the first two chapters as written by Solomon, the rest of the book being a later reflection and commentary on Solomon's words. Some have suggested that a woman may have written it.

A possibility is that the speaker in the book plays the part of the king asking the question, 'How would you see life if you were a rich and all-powerful king in Jerusalem?' At other places in the book, the Teacher plays other parts, the rich man and then the wise man. From whatever perspective you view life, rich or poor, wise or simple, royal or commoner, the conclusion is the same! 'Vanity of vanities, says the Teacher. Vanity of vanities! All is vanity'.

This refrain runs through the whole book from the first chapter onwards. The Hebrew literally means 'wind' or 'vapour' – usually understood as a metaphor for 'nothingness' or 'uselessness'. *The Good News Bible* puts it this way: 'It is useless, said the philosopher. Life is useless, all useless.' A better approach is to understand the metaphor as meaning *fleeting* or *hard-to-grasp*. On this interpretation, the book points to the fleeting, transitory nature of life – not to worthlessness or uselessness. The Teacher is reminding the audience how quickly death comes, and how pleasures and opportunities have to be grasped now or never.

READ THE BOOK OF ECCLESIASTES

The overall thrust of the book is to describe as *vanity* most of the things that people base their ambitions on. Wealth, prestige, power, fame, book-learning, even religion are all dismissed as of no lasting value in themselves. The things which ambitious people devote themselves to are like 'chasing after the wind' (1:14)! Death comes to everyone in the end – and what can we take with us?

The Teacher also notes the apparent lack of justice in the world. Hard workers do not always reap the benefits they deserve. The good often suffer and the wicked often prosper. 'Enjoy life when you can, appreciate and enjoy the good things God has given you each day and don't sacrifice today for a tomorrow that may never come' would sum up much of the book's message.

Ecclesiastes is very relevant to our frenetic modern western world. God meant life to be enjoyed. Hard work is fulfilling; but there are strident warnings in the book against the workaholic lifestyle that many church people fall into (myself included).

The words of the Teacher seem to finish at verse 8 of the last chapter repeating our opening words, 'Vanity of vanities ...'. It is a common practice for Old Testament writers to use a key phrase to mark the beginning and ending of a book or major section. There then follows a short epilogue, perhaps by a later editor, challenging the audience to take to heart issues raised by the Teacher in the earlier discussion.

In verse 11 of this epilogue, there are two interesting metaphors which sum up what wisdom is all about. The *Good News Bible* puts this verse well: 'The sayings of wise men are like the sharp sticks that shepherds use to guide sheep, and collected proverbs are as lasting as firmly driven nails. They have been given by God, the one Shepherd of us all'. The sharp sticks (or goads) are to provoke, stimulate and make us think. The nails provide firm secure reference points.

The reference to God as the Shepherd points forward to Jesus as the good Shepherd[16]. Much of the teaching of Jesus is reminiscent of Ecclesiastes. This is especially so of the Sermon on the Mount[17]. Look, for example, at Matthew 6:25–34, which ends with the words: 'So do not worry about tomorrow, for tomorrow will bring worries of its own. Today's trouble is enough for today'.

Like Job, Ecclesiastes paves the way for the gospel message. Human wisdom, religion, good works, none of these things is of permanent value, still less can they make us right with God. We cannot achieve salvation by our own efforts. It only comes as the gift of God's free grace in Jesus Christ.

The book finishes with these words: 'The end of the matter; all has been heard. Fear God, and keep his commandments; for that is the whole duty of everyone. For God will bring every deed into judgment, including every secret thing, whether good or evil'. This is the only satisfactory philosophy of life: fear God, keep his commandments, and enjoy each day as it comes. Don't sacrifice the ordinary pleasures of today for wealth, power, fame, or anything else that may be as elusive as grasping the wind.

Ecclesiastes can meet people amid doubts, uncertainties, and disappointments. The book acknowledges that there are no easy answers to many of life's problems. There are many people today who have questions very similar to those discussed by the Teacher. Ecclesiastes may well be a good place to begin in reaching such people for God. The book meets people where they are and does not demand dogmatic certainties they are not ready for. Some people may well be prepared to read a 'philosophical' book like Ecclesiastes who would not easily be drawn to other parts of the Bible. Perhaps we need to be more imaginative and resourceful in the way we use different Bible books in reaching different kinds of people for God!

Endnotes

1   Proverbs 22:17–23:11
2   Romans 1:20
3   See 2 Samuel 14:2
4   Luke 9: 23–24
5   Proverbs 3:2
6   Proverbs 5:22–23 (GNB)
7   Proverbs 19:16
8   See 1 Kings 3 for an account of Solomon's famed wisdom.
9   1 Corinthians 2:26
10 1 Corinthians 1:25
11 Proverbs 2:16–22 and at more length in chapters 5 and 7.
12 Wisdom speaks in 1:20–33
13 Job 32:1–3
14 See Romans 8:28
15 Mark 8:34
16 John 10:11
17 Matthew 5–7

Part Six

The preaching of God's spokesmen: Isaiah to Malachi

6.1 WHO WERE THE PROPHETS?

A prophet was Yahweh's *ambassador* on earth. The British ambassado in Washington speaks on behalf of Britain to the US government. H or she also conveys back to Britain messages from the US govern ment. The prophets spoke on behalf of Yahweh to the earthly kin and people. Sometimes the prophet's role was to plead with Yahwe on behalf of the people.

We have already noticed in Exodus how a prophet was regarded a God's mouthpiece (4:16). You will also remember how Abraham (th first person to be called a prophet) pleaded with Yahweh on behalf o Sodom and Gomorrah. Samuel, as Yahweh's representative anointe the first two kings and drew up the constitution for the monarchy Throughout the period of the monarchy, the prophets continued t speak on Yahweh's behalf to both king and people.

Only the prophets had authority to utter the awe-inspiring word 'thus says Yahweh'. Sometimes their message was one of encourage ment and hope[2]. More often the prophetic word took the form o rebuke to a disobedient king[3].

The historical books are full of stories of false prophets – such a those who claimed to be prophets of Yahweh but gave wrong advic to King Ahab before battle with the Syrians[4]. There were als prophets associated with the various Baal cults – such as th prophets of Jezebel's Baal religion whom Elijah defeated in th contest on Mount Carmel[5].

The prophetic books

The careers of the great prophets were remembered and writte down by their followers. Embedded within the books of Kings, fo example, we have the record of the life and work of Elijah and o Elisha. Later on books emerged which were named after individua prophets, recording their ministry and teaching. These prophets ar known as the *canonical prophets*– because they have canonical book named after them.

The prophetic books are arranged in the Old Testament in orde of length rather than in order of date. So first come the four majo prophets: Isaiah, Jeremiah, Ezekiel and Daniel. Then follow th

welve minor prophets, from Hosea through to Malachi. We do not
have much information about how the prophetic books came to be
written down. Isaiah had a band of disciples whom he instructed to
write down and to preserve his words. Jeremiah had a scribe called
Baruch who kept the record of his master's preaching.

Most of the prophetic books contain third-person descriptions of
the prophet's life and work which suggests that they were compiled
by disciples or followers rather than written by the prophet himself.
However, the prophetic books do also record the actual preaching of
the prophets themselves.

Some of the prophetic books are chronological in their arrange-
ment. In others, the individual prophecies are linked together by
theme rather than by date. This makes the prophetic books much
harder to read and follow than the narrative books – though it will be
much easier to follow the thread of the book if you already have a
good knowledge of the historical background.

Historical and religious back- ground

You will remember that there were three distinct
streams of Yahwism during the period of the
monarchy.

First, there was the royal cult of Jerusalem,
focused on Yahweh's covenant with King David,
and on Yahweh's eternal choice of Zion. There
had developed in Jerusalem a belief that Yahweh
would never allow his chosen city to be destroyed.
The Mosaic traditions were largely neglected.

> there had devel- oped in Jerusalem a belief that Yahweh would never allow his chosen city to be destroyed

Secondly, there was the official cult of the northern kingdom,
focused on the sanctuary at Bethel, with its notorious bull-image. It
was supposedly the worship of Yahweh, but in fact it was highly
syncretistic.

The third main stream of Yahwism was of a quite different kind. It
was not an official national religion but a *movement* among ordinary
people in both Israel and Judah. In rural communities there was a
strong memory of the exodus story and of the ancient covenant Law
of Israel. Many local sanctuaries and religious centres preserved these
traditions such as Anathoth, the home of Jeremiah. We know of this
popular allegiance to traditional Mosaic Yahwism through the
ministry of the prophets. They struggled to keep the ancient faith of

Israel alive even at times when it was threatened with near extinction (such as during the reign of Ahab and Jezebel).

Fore-tellers or forth-tellers

The word *prophet* in English usually implies predicting the future. The Old Testament prophets did, of course, foretell the future and there are many references in the New Testament to the fulfilment of prophecy. However, the main role of a prophet was to speak as Yahweh's ambassador to their own contemporary situation. The prophets were primarily *forth*-tellers of the word of Yahweh rather than *fore*-tellers of the future. It was only occasionally that they looked to the far future.

the main role of a prophet was to speak as Yahweh's ambassador

I am writing this chapter in Newcastle in County Down, looking out at the mountains of Mourne. Earlier in the summer, the children and I climbed Slieve Donard, the highest mountain in Northern Ireland. The view from the top is breathtaking. If you were to try and describe the scene in words, you might look first to one side and mention the bay in the foreground and then the Manx shore on the horizon. Moving round, you might refer to the town in the foreground, the forest and farmland in the middle distance, and then the distant silhouette of the Belfast shipyards. Turning yet again to describe the rest of the mountain range, it might be difficult to distinguish those peaks which are nearer and smaller from those which are distant but larger. As you look at a scene like that foreground and distance all merge into one great panorama.

In a similar way, the future stretched in front of the prophet like a great panorama – in which near, far and distant events were all part of one great scene. In describing this scene, the prophet might first mention events of his own time in the foreground, then speak about the immediate future, then lift his eyes further and speak of things to be fulfilled in the coming of Jesus – all merged as part of one prophetic vision. An example of this would be the well-known passage from Isaiah 9:1–7. The prophet begins by looking back to a period of humiliation and suffering for the northern tribes (v 1). The next two verses speak of the joy that comes with Yahweh's salvation. This is followed by a description of vindication in battle in the prophet's own time. The prophet then lifts his eyes towards the distant scene; and in verses 6 and 7 he looks forward to the birth of Jesus.

Like the other books of the Old Testament, the prophetic books should be read right through as books. They are not so easy to follow as the narrative books, but it is worth making the effort so as to grasp the overall message. Many doubtful interpretations and heresies have arisen by taking individual items of prophecy out of context!

6.2 Prophets of Israel and Judah Amos, Hosea and Micah.

Amos

We all know the expression, 'the calm before the storm'. Amos belonged to a period of calm in the history of northern Israel; the last period of peace and prosperity before the destruction of Samaria by the Assyrians in 722 BC. Amos is the earliest of the canonical prophets. He came from a small town in the southern kingdom of Judah. However, his preaching was at Bethel, the royal sanctuary of the northern kingdom. Those of us who live in Northern Ireland can readily imagine the resentment that must have arisen against someone from the south coming to preach a message of judgement in the north[6]!

Amos was a sheep-breeder; and his visits to Bethel were for the purpose of selling his sheep for the busy sacrificial cult at the Bethel sanctuary. He was keen to emphasise that he was not a 'professional' prophet, but someone whom God had called to deliver a specific message to Israel.

Amos' message is dated very precisely in the opening verse. It was two years before an earthquake; an event that everyone would have remembered. It took place during the reign of King Jeroboam II of Israel (who reigned from 783–743 BC). It was a time of unparalleled prosperity in Israel. There was more wealth in the country than there had been for years. The sanctuary at Bethel was thronging with worshippers. The people believed that their national prosperity was because Yahweh was pleased with them. They were God's chosen people and surely he would always bless them.

However, the new prosperity was concentrated in the hands of the elite few. There was more wealth in the country than before but there was also more poverty and deprivation. The sanctuary was booming but Amos makes clear that sacrificial ritual could be no substitute for obeying God's Law. Far from being pleased with the people, God would bring a terrible judgement on them. Amos never mentions the word *covenant*; but he judges the people by the standards of Yahweh's covenant Law, in particular, their failure to do the right thing by the poor, the widow and the orphan.

READ THE BOOK OF AMOS

Imagine Amos standing in the forecourt of the shrine in Bethel. There was probably a 'speakers' corner' in the sanctuary where Yahweh's prophets were allowed to proclaim their messages. Picture the scene in your mind's eye.

Amos begins to preach to the crowd. His opening words depict Yahweh thundering in judgement from Jerusalem. He pronounces words of judgement on Israel's traditional enemies. First he condemns Syria, then Philistia, then Tyre, and we can imagine murmurings of approval from the crowd. Next he castigates Edom, Ammon and Moab – these days the crowd might be shouting, 'Amen! Preach it man!' A crowd will always respond well to words of judgement on their enemies!

Then in chapter 2 Amos takes the crowd by surprise: he pronounces judgement on Judah. There was not always much love lost between north and south, but they were kindred people. To hear the prophet speak of the destruction of Judah must have been a sobering thought. Having now got the crowd's full attention, Amos finally rounds on them with a scathing condemnation of the northern kingdom of Israel itself. His condemnation focuses on the lack of social justice in Israel. The people have failed to provide for the poor. Immorality is also rife and there is even drunkenness in the sanctuary. The people have attempted to silence true prophecy. As a result, a terrible judgement will come.

We might imagine a heckler interrupting from the crowd. 'How can this be?' he shouts. 'Are we not Yahweh's chosen people?' 'But that makes it worse not better,' replies Amos! Because of all he has done for Israel, Yahweh regards their sins as more culpable than those of the other nations!

In chapter 3, we are given a vivid picture of the wealth of the leading citizens of Israel – which stood in such stark contrast to the plight of the poor. This time the hecklers are the well-heeled women from Samaria. Amos' reply to them is scathing. He calls them 'well-fed cows of Bashan' (4:1 GNB), condemns their decadent lifestyle, and promises no mercy for them when the invasion comes. Yahweh is not impressed by crowds flocking to places of worship. Without justice, worship means nothing.

Chapter 5 is a call to repentance. If the people repent, change their ways, and put Yahweh's Law into practice, then there is hope that Yahweh may relent. Yahweh wants true repentance – not more religion. In fact Yahweh goes so far as to say:

> I hate, I despise your festivals, and I take no delight in your solemn assemblies. Even though you offer me your burnt offerings and grain offerings, I will not accept them.

Those words of Amos sum up what God wanted of the people: 'Let justice roll down like waters, and righteousness like an ever-flowing stream (Amos 5:24).

The people were looking forward to 'the day of Yahweh' (5:18), when they hoped Yahweh would restore them to a position of greatness among the nations. Amos turns this idea on its head. The day of Yahweh when it comes will not be a day of rejoicing. It will instead be a day of judgement and disaster.

Amos relates four visions which God had given him (chapters 7 and 8). After the visions of the locusts and of fire, Amos pleads with God on behalf of the people and Yahweh relents, for the judgements threatened in these two visions would have hit the poor as hard as the rich. After the visions of the plumb line and the fruit basket, however, there is no prospect of God changing his mind. Doom will come; and it will fall primarily on the rich. The religious authorities at Bethel are outraged by Amos' preaching and he is rebuked by Amaziah, the priest in charge. Amos is banned from the sanctuary! To Amaziah, Amos' message was treason against the northern kingdom.

The same themes of judgement continue almost to the end of the book. Amos is often described as the prophet of doom. There are few expressions of hope, although chapter 5 does offer some hope for those who repent. For the nation as a whole, however, doom is an inevitability which cannot be avoided.

The closing five verses of the book do offer hope for the distant future – hope of a restored and reunited Israel under the Davidic dynasty. Indeed, in these closing verses, the prophet gives a glimpse of the new heaven and new earth that will one day be ushered in by the ultimate descendant of David, Jesus Christ.

Summary of the message of Amos

The primary message of the book of Amos is God's demand for social justice. It was no excuse for the rich in Israel to say that poverty and deprivation was not their fault. Nor was religion and sacrifice a remedy.

We live in a world where poverty and deprivation are widespread. God will judge us by the same plumb line that was used in Amos' vision all those years ago.

Hosea

The book of Hosea is an intensely personal book. Yahweh's distress at the faithlessness of Israel is compared to the pain of someone deserted by a spouse and then to the anguish of the parent of a prodigal child.

Hosea belonged to a slightly later period than Amos. The Assyrian threat was now looming large on the horizon. Hosea's message was also for the northern kingdom, but, unlike Amos, Hosea himself belonged to the north. His preaching extended over a longer period stretching into the turbulent years after the death of Jeroboam II, leading up to the final destruction of Samaria in 722 BC.

Hosea proclaims a final military defeat for Israel

READ HOSEA 1–3

Chapter 1: Gomer and her children

The first chapter begins with the astonishing command from Yahweh that Hosea should marry an adulterous woman[7]! Hosea then marries Gomer, who bears him three children. As these children grew up their names would be a constant reminder to the people of Hosea's message.

The first child was called Jezreel. Jezreel had been the scene of the notorious murder of Naboth by Queen Jezebel[8]. Jehu had later carried out a bloody purge at Jezreel. Jezreel (says Hosea) will now be remembered for the crimes of Jehu rather than for those of Jezebel! The dynasty founded by Jehu was still on the throne of Israel in Hosea's time so his message was a devastating judgment on the ruling regime. Jehu and his successors had so neglected Yahweh's Law that there was now more poverty, oppression, and injustice in Israel than ever before. Hosea proclaims a final military defeat for Israel in that very Valley of Jezreel.

The names of the prophet's other two children, 'Not-loved' and 'Not-my-people', imply the cancellation of Yahweh's covenant with Israel. How it must have horrified Hosea's original audience that he should even suggest that Yahweh might cancel his covenant!

In the closing verses of chapter 1, Hosea moves from doom to hope. This alternation between doom and hope is a pattern throughout Hosea. A reunited Judah and Israel will one day be restored. When that time comes, the name Jezreel will again come to mean prosperity and blessing; and the judgement implied in the names of the other two children will be reversed. Once again the people will be God's people and once again he will love them.

Chapters 2,3: faithless Israel

In the second chapter, the prophet draws a direct parallel between his own experience of an unfaithful wife and the faithlessness of Israel as Yahweh's 'bride'. Just as a faithless wife runs off with lovers who she thinks will give her wealth and favours, so Israel has gone after other gods in pursuit of wealth and luxury.

Yahweh, therefore, has rejected his faithless 'bride'. But towards the end of the chapter, the prophet looks forward to a time when the relationship between Yahweh and Israel will be restored. The prophet's hope for the future of Israel is summed up in a moving poem 2:19–23.

In chapter 3, the prophet is again told to marry an adulterous woman. The most common interpretation is that Hosea is told to seek out his original wife, Gomer, who has now been abandoned by her other lovers and sold as a slave. He is to buy her back, and take her again as his wife after a period of chastening. If Hosea loved Gomer so much that he was willing forgive her unfaithfulness, then surely Yahweh must love Israel enough to redeem and restore her to her former glory[9].

READ HOSEA 4–14

The rest of the book is constructed as a catalogue of Yahweh's charges against Israel and of the judgement he has pronounced against them. Yahweh's main complaint is not against the people as a whole, but against the priests, false prophets, and rulers who have led them astray.

Whereas Amos' preaching was largely to do with social justice, most of Hosea's condemnation is directed against idolatry and false religion. However, the two are closely inter-linked. True faithfulness to Yahweh would always involve social justice. Baal religion, by contrast, was always associated with exploitation and injustice. The prophet weeps not just at the wickedness but at the folly of the people. Yahweh's words are scathing:

> Wine, both old and new, is robbing my people of their senses. They ask for revelations from a piece of wood! A stick tells them what to do. ... Like a woman who becomes a prostitute they have given themselves to other gods (Hosea 4:11,12 GNB).

The people presumptuously imagine that Yahweh will always forgive them – whatever the circumstances. They have refused to listen to true prophecy, indeed they have sneered at it (9:7–9). They depend on sacrifices and offerings to save them. Yahweh proclaims through the prophet: 'I desire steadfast love and not sacrifice, the knowledge of God rather than burnt offerings' (6:6) [10].

The Hebrew for *steadfast-love* in this quotation is *hesed* – a key Old Testament term. It denotes love, loyalty, and commitment in a relationship. *Hesed* involves doing the right thing by others, and especially by the poor and the underprivileged [11]. *Knowing* God is another key theme. To *know* Yahweh is to have a right relationship with him. Knowledge of God and *hesed* are closely connected.

Perhaps the most moving passage in the whole of the book is the poem uttered by Yahweh in chapter 11. Yahweh is pictured as a loving parent who had nurtured Israel from the earliest days. He has suffered the heartbreak of a parent whose child has disowned him. But Yahweh's love for Israel is so great that he cannot let them go for ever: 'How can I give you up, Israel? How can I abandon you? ... My heart will not let me do it! My love for you is too strong' (11:8).

In chapter 12, the prophet reminds the people of their ancient faith – stretching back through Moses and the exodus to the ancestral figure of Jacob. Several times the punishment that Israel faces is portrayed as a return to Egypt – though, of course, it is to slavery in Assyria and not literally to Egypt that they will be taken.

Summary of the message of Hosea

God does not want mere religious observance from his people. He wants *hesed* – which could be defined as 'true love which shows itself in action'. Hosea's message is also a powerful testimony to the intensely personal nature of God's love for his people. We are also reminded that love and judgement are two inseparable sides of God's character.

There is an alternation in the book between despair and hope. God's love can never fail. But can God keep on forgiving forever? This is the paradox that is not resolved until the Son of God hangs on a cross to satisfy both God's love and his judgement for a sinful world.

Micah

I am writing this chapter a few days after 11 November, the day of remembrance for those who died in the two world wars. Almost always at remembrance services, the prophet Micah's words are read:

> [The LORD] shall judge between many peoples, and shall arbitrate between strong nations far away; they shall beat their swords into ploughshares, and their spears into pruning hooks; nation shall not lift up sword against nation, neither shall they learn war any more (Micah 4:3).

These famous words look forward to Yahweh's universal reign of peace – a vision that we believe will find fulfilment after the Second Coming of Jesus.

The title verse dates Micah's ministry to the reigns of three Jerusalem kings, Jotham, Ahaz, and Hezekiah (740–687 BC). He was from the south, but from Judah, not Jerusalem. Indeed, much of his preaching is directed against the Jerusalem establishment for their neglect of social justice[12].

Micah dared to proclaim that Yahweh would one day destroy Jerusalem (3:12)[13]. His words of judgement are unrelenting. Yet Micah, much more than Amos, offers assurance of forgiveness and restoration. Yahweh is the God of constant love and mercy.

READ THE BOOK OF MICAH

Chapters 1–3

After the title verse, the opening poem depicts Yahweh's power and judgement. This is followed by a vivid prophecy of the destruction of

Samaria which took place during Micah's own lifetime. Some in Jerusalem may have believed that the destruction of Samaria was because of the north's rebellion against Yahweh's chosen king in Jerusalem. Micah quashes any such notion. Yahweh's anger is against both north and south. The same fate awaits Jerusalem as had befallen Samaria.

The second chapter closes with the moving picture of Yahweh, the shepherd, leading his people back from exile (vs 12,13). This kind of juxtaposition of doom and hope is a common feature in the prophetic books and is particularly characteristic of Micah.

In chapter 3, rulers, priests, and prophets in Jerusalem are all condemned. The destruction of Jerusalem will be total and complete (v 12).

Chapters 4–6

Chapter 4 begins with the poem which depicts Yahweh's eternal rule of peace. The latter part of the chapter speaks of eventual forgiveness and restoration for Jerusalem.

Chapter 5 begins with the well-known Bethlehem prophecy. We should not underestimate how remarkable it is that Micah should have foreseen the Bethlehem story from a distance of over seven hundred years! We would be totally amazed today if a prophecy were to come true after such a long period. Yet the words of Micah were preserved through the ups and downs of Israelite history, through conquest by Babylonians, Persians, Greeks and Romans until the scribes in Jerusalem were able to quote Micah's words to King Herod that the Messiah would be born in Bethlehem (Matt 2:5,6).

In chapter 6, the people are reminded of the exodus and of Yahweh's past care and protection – which should have prompted them to grateful obedience. Yahweh does not want more religion. Instead, says Micah: 'What does the LORD require of you but to do justice, and to love kindness, and to walk humbly with your God?' (6:8).

Chapter 7

The final chapter draws together the themes of the book. Judgement is inevitable, but Yahweh *will* come to the rescue of his people and

Jerusalem *will* be rebuilt. There will be a secure future for a penitent people. In the final section, Micah prays to Yahweh on behalf of the people. He expresses his confidence in Yahweh's forgiveness and mercy, as evidenced across history. Micah's closing words get to the very heart of his message:

> There is no other god like you, O LORD; you forgive the sins of your people who have survived. You do not stay angry for ever, but you take pleasure in showing us your constant love. You will be merciful to us once again. You will trample our sins underfoot and send them to the bottom of the sea! You will show your faithfulness and constant love to your people ... as you promised our ancestors long ago (Micah 7:18-20, GNB).

6.3 Isaiah: THE GREAT PROPHET OF JERUSALEM 'THE FIFTH GOSPEL'

Though written hundreds of years before the time of Jesus, the book of Isaiah has often been referred to as the *fifth gospel*. Isaiah is quoted in the New Testament more often than any other Old Testament prophet. The book contains many significant pointers to the gospel story, for example, words from chapter 9 are closely associated with the birth of Jesus:

> For a child has been born for us, a son given to us; authority rests upon his shoulders; and he is named Wonderful Counsellor, Mighty God, Everlasting Father, Prince of Peace[14].

Chapter 53 prefigures the crucifixion story:

> But he was wounded for our transgressions, crushed for our iniquities; upon him was the punishment that made us whole, and by his bruises we are healed[15].

When Jesus preached at the synagogue in Nazareth, he proclaimed the purpose of his ministry with these words from Isaiah 61:

> The spirit of the Lord GOD is upon me, because the LORD has anointed me; he has sent me to bring good news to the oppressed, to bind up the broken-hearted, to proclaim liberty to the captives, and release to the prisoners; to proclaim the year of the LORD's favour ...[16].

Chapter 11 foretells a future era of 'paradise restored', which belongs after the Second Coming of Jesus:

> The wolf shall live with the lamb, the leopard shall lie down with the kid, the calf and the lion and the fatling together, and a little child shall lead them ... for the earth will be full of the knowledge of the LORD as the waters cover the sea[17].

Isaiah the man

Often the prophets received little recognition in their own day. Sometimes they were faced with outright opposition or even violence. At other times they were dismissed as cranks or fanatics. For this reason, many of the prophets caught the attention of the people by doing things which seem to us outlandish or bizarre. At one point Isaiah wanted to draw attention to the folly of depending on Egyptian military help (instead of depending on Yahweh). He had warned the people that they would soon see Egyptian prisoners of war marching naked through Judah on their way to slavery in Assyria. To reinforce this point, Isaiah himself walked about Jerusalem naked! When his words came true, the people would not be able to deny that Isaiah had warned them! He had made his words unforgettable by his action. In a similar way the names of his children made them 'walking prophecies'.

Isaiah lived in Jerusalem during the reigns of Jotham, Ahaz, and Hezekiah which covers the period from 740–687 BC. Isaiah was the first canonical prophet to come from Jerusalem itself. He was contemporary with the prophet Micah from Judah.

Isaiah himself walked about Jerusalem naked!

You can read the awe-inspiring story of Isaiah's *call* to the prophetic office in chapter 6. Isaiah probably belonged to a priestly family. The book is steeped in the Jerusalem and Temple traditions; and in his preaching Isaiah conveys a profound sense of the awesomeness and holiness of Yahweh.

Isaiah makes very few direct references to the Mosaic and exodus traditions (traditions which you will remember were greatly neglected in Jerusalem). However, he was clearly familiar with the principles of Yahweh's Law and he judges Jerusalem by those standards. He seems to have been familiar with the book of Amos and he echoes Amos' call for social justice.

Isaiah had a band of disciples who were responsible for collecting and preserving the record of his life and teaching (8:16). For much of his ministry he received little attention or respect from either king or people. He did, however, enjoy the confidence of the godly King Hezekiah – especially during the crisis of the Assyrian siege of Jerusalem. However, this was to change when Hezekiah's son Manasseh came to the throne. There is even a legend that Isaiah was martyred by Manasseh.

Historical background to Isaiah's ministry

Throughout his ministry, Isaiah had a close involvement with the ups and downs of national affairs. Whether his message was heeded or not, he fulfilled his prophetic role as God's spokesman.

One of the most tragic events of Israelite history took place early in Isaiah's career. In 722 BC, the Assyrians destroyed Samaria and the northern kingdom of Israel was wiped off the map for ever. Some years before the fall of the northern kingdom, Jotham, king of Judah, had refused to join a defensive coalition against the Assyrian threat. This coalition had been organised by Pekah, king of Israel, along with the king of Syria. Israel and Syria then invaded Judah in an attempt to force Judah to join the coalition. In the middle of the crisis Jotham died and was succeeded by his son Ahaz.

Isaiah's first intervention in national affairs came during this crisis. You can read about it in chapter 7. Isaiah assured Ahaz that Yahweh would protect him if he remained steadfast in his faith. However, Isaiah took with him to the meeting his ominously named son 'A-remnant-will-return' (v 3). This name represented both doom and hope; doom because only a remnant of the people would be left; hope because that remnant would be allowed to return and make a fresh beginning for God's people.

This was the occasion when Isaiah gave the sign of the child named *Immanuel* (*God-with-us*). This prophecy had a contemporary meaning and fulfilment for Ahaz. A prince would be born in the royal house. Before the child would be weaned, the two kings threatening Ahaz would be no more. Of course, as we look back, we realise that Isaiah's words found their final fulfilment with the ultimate *Immanuel* child – Jesus Christ himself.

Assyrian gods were worshipped inside the Temple itself!

Ahaz did not take Isaiah's advice that he should depend on Yahweh alone. Instead he appealed to the Assyrian emperor for help, with the result that Judah and Jerusalem voluntarily became part of the Assyrian Empire. Ahaz remained loyal to Assyria throughout his reign. He even imported Assyrian religious practices into Jerusalem and Assyrian gods were worshipped inside the Temple itself!

Ahaz's son, Hezekiah, was a man of a very different stamp. During his reign, he sponsored a major religious reformation in Jerusalem. This involved not just the cleansing of the Temple of all pagan practices, but also a reintroduction into Jerusalem of the Mosaic tradition. The historical books make no explicit reference to social reform by Hezekiah, but he could scarcely have enjoyed the support which he received from Isaiah had he not paid heed to Isaiah's strident demands for social justice.

Hezekiah's expulsion of Assyrian religion from Jerusalem was effectively a declaration of independence from the Assyrian Empire. This resulted in the invasion of Judah by the Assyrian emperor,

Sennacherib. You can read the story of Sennacherib's siege of Jerusalem in Isaiah chapters 36 and 37. With Isaiah's support and encouragement, King Hezekiah trusted in Yahweh – and miraculously the city was delivered.

Throughout the reigns of Ahaz and Hezekiah, Isaiah's message was consistent. The king and people should depend on Yahweh alone. They should not depend on armed forces or on alliances with foreign powers (such as Egypt). Nor should they take up arms to rebel against Assyria. They should wait for Yahweh's moment to save them. If only the people would trust Yahweh and obey his Law, then they would be spared.

Sadly, it seems that the miraculous delivery of Jerusalem from Sennacherib's siege reinforced the false belief among Zionists that Yahweh would *always* intervene in some such miraculous way. What had been a last-chance warning from Yahweh was misinterpreted as a guarantee of permanent security.

The book of Isaiah

The book of Isaiah has engendered much debate as to its authorship and unity. Since this has been a major issue in the world of scholarship, it is worth summarising the main points here.

The first thirty-nine chapters of the book are addressed to the people of the prophet's own day (from around 740 BC onwards). However, the middle section (chapters 40–55) addresses a much later period, when the Jews were in exile in Babylon. The remaining chapters seem to belong to an even later period, after the return of the Jews to Jerusalem and the re-building of the city and temple.

Could Isaiah of Jerusalem have written about events so long after his own time? Scholars have always been sceptical about prophetic prediction of the future. In particular it is said that Isaiah could not possibly have known the name of Cyrus, the Persian emperor, who lived a 150 years or so after Isaiah[18]. Consequently, the theory has developed that the later sections of the book (often referred to as second and third Isaiah) could not have come from Isaiah himself but were added by one or more later writers. This view has achieved widespread acceptance among scholars.

However, it is not just a matter of unwillingness to believe that a prophet could foretell future events. The later chapters are quite different in style from the earlier part of the book. They are mostly poetic while the earlier chapters are largely in prose. The middle section speaks of the destruction of Jerusalem as a past event. The third section also refers to the return from exile as a past event – and it reads as if written by someone living in the rebuilt Jerusalem. This all suggests that chapters 40–66 are the work of later writers.

On the other hand, the whole book is clearly a unified composition. Key themes run right through all sections of the book in a structured way. It is certainly not impossible that Isaiah wrote down a God-given message that was to be preserved and read to people of later generations. Furthermore, Jesus seems to refer to the later chapters of the book as written by Isaiah[19].

In all of these discussions it should not be forgotten that the book itself does not claim to have been written by Isaiah himself! There are quite a number of passages in the earlier part of the book which are in the *third* person; that is, they are written *about* Isaiah not *by* him (though, of course, the book does also contain the actual words of Isaiah's preaching). Even the first thirty-nine chapters of the book do seem to have been collected, arranged, and put together by one of Isaiah's disciples.

Could it not therefore be that the later chapters of the book were written by a later generation of disciples? This would be remarkably similar to the way the New Testament was produced. The New Testament begins with the four Gospels, written not by Jesus himself but by disciples. After Jesus' death, Paul and others wrote the later New Testament books, expounding and applying the message of Jesus for their own day and for future generations.

Something similar could have taken place with Isaiah. The first thirty-nine chapters may consist of a record of the prophet's life and ministry, put together by his disciples. As the generations passed, later disciples who had preserved their master's teaching may have re-applied his teaching for their own day, adding new material, and carefully structuring the unified book as we now have it. If some parts of the book were written later, this does not make them any less the Word of God. The whole book has a message for future generations, including ourselves. Sometimes scholars get so bogged down in debating who wrote the book that they neglect its message for today!

Before you read through Isaiah, you should first read through 2 Kings 16–21 so that you have an understanding of the historical background to the prophet's preaching. Remember that the book is not arranged chronologically but by themes – and this sometimes makes it hard to follow. Before reading the later chapters (from chapter 40), you may want to familiarise yourself with the history of the Jews after the destruction of Jerusalem, perhaps by reading through Ezra and Nehemiah.

READ ISAIAH 1–5: SUMMARY OF THE PROPHET'S MESSAGE

The first five chapters of Isaiah are like a roller-coaster ride – from depths of despair at the coming judgement to heights of hope for Yahweh's everlasting reign of peace. Up and down, back and forward, the prophet alternates between judgement and hope, destruction and restoration, punishment and salvation. The story of Isaiah's call to prophetic ministry does not come until chapter 6. The first five chapters provide an introductory summary of his message. The rest of the book then gives a more detailed account of the prophet's preaching.

From the very beginning, the prophet's condemnation of the people is scathing. Their neglect of the orphan and the widow, their ignoring of Yahweh's Law on land tenure and debt, their drunkenness even at worship, the corrupt rule of their leaders, and their idolatry; these are all part of the picture of a people who have turned their back on the Holy One of Israel. These words are particularly scathing:

> You are doomed! Heroes of the wine bottle! Brave and fearless – when it comes to mixing drinks! But for just a bribe you let the guilty men go free, and you prevent the innocent from getting justice (5:22,23, GNB).

Like Amos, Isaiah has harsh words not just for the men but also for the decadence of the women:

> Look how proud the women of Jerusalem are! They walk along with their noses in the air. They are always flirting. They take dainty little steps, and the bracelets on their ankles jingle. But I will punish them ... (3:16,17, GNB).

Immediate judgement is going to come in the form of an Assyrian invasion, but the prophet also alludes to even more terrible judgement at the hands of the Babylonians. Interspersed with this message of doom and despair, the prophet also soars to heights of forgiveness and hope. Yahweh says: 'You are stained red with sin, but I will wash you clean as snow. Although your stains are deep red, you will be white as wool' (1:18, GNB).

In the midst of it all, Isaiah lifts his eyes to the far future and quotes the hymn (also quoted by Micah) which speaks of everlasting peace for a new Jerusalem under Yahweh's rule: when 'men shall beat their swords into ploughshares ...' (2:4).

READ ISAIAH 6–12: JUDGEMENT AND PROMISE

Chapter 6: Isaiah's call

Few people have been able to say, 'My eyes have seen the King, Yahweh Almighty'! What a sense of Yahweh's overwhelming holiness must have been experienced by Isaiah as the angels proclaimed: 'Holy, holy, holy is the LORD of hosts; the whole earth is full of his glory' (v 3). The angel touches Isaiah's lips with a coal from the altar as a symbol that his sins are forgiven. Then comes the voice of Yahweh himself, 'Whom shall I send, and who will go for us?' and Isaiah's reply, 'Here am I; send me!' (v 8).

This vision took place at the end of the tragic reign of King Uzziah[20] when the people were full of hopes for a brighter future. However, it was not to be. Things were to go from bad to worse. The commission which Yahweh gives to Isaiah is a heavy burden. He will preach to the people but they will not hear or understand. His preaching will dull their ears and harden their hearts. And there is to be no prospect of any change of heart until the destruction comes.

Chapters 7–12: the messianic hope

Juxtaposed with Isaiah's unrelenting message of judgement is the promise of a future messianic age. The promises of Yahweh to David had not found fulfilment in David's successors – many of whom had been unfaithful to God. As the years and centuries went by, faithful people longed for a descendant of David in whom Yahweh's promises of blessing would become a reality. And so the word *messiah* came to denote the hope of a future king who would be even greater than David.

As each new king came to the throne, the people would have hoped that this would be the *Messiah* they had been waiting for. King Hezekiah's reformation and his attempt to reunite north and south[21] under one king may have appeared to be the first stages of a *messianic era*. In this period, Isaiah proclaimed a messianic figure who would indeed be a descendant of David but who would be no ordinary human being.

The famous poem in chapter 9 may have started out as a poem to mark the birth of a new king (possibly Hezekiah); and it offers short-term hope for both northern and southern tribes. But Isaiah lifts his eyes beyond the immediate future to speak of a king who will be no mere human monarch:

> He is named Wonderful Counsellor, Mighty God, Everlasting Father, Prince of Peace. His authority shall grow continually, and there shall be endless peace for the throne of David and his kingdom. He will establish and uphold it with justice and with righteousness from this time onwards and for evermore. The zeal of the LORD of hosts will do this (9:6,7).

This future messianic hope is further developed in the poems of chapter 11 and 12 which look forward to the messianic age that we associate with the Second Coming of Jesus.

READ CHAPTERS 13–23: PROPHECIES AGAINST OTHER NATIONS

Many in Jerusalem believed that the gods of the other nations were a reality – and a powerful force to be reckoned with. If the Assyrians had subjugated Judah, did this not mean that the Assyrian gods were more powerful than Yahweh? Isaiah's prophecies against the nations proclaim that Yahweh alone is God of *all* nations. He is the one who controls the destiny even of the world's greatest empires.

In several of these prophecies Isaiah looks well beyond his own day. This is especially so with regard to Babylon. Yahweh would one day use Babylon to bring judgement on Judah and Jerusalem; but Babylon herself would not escape devastating punishment for her cruelty and arrogance[22]. The macabre picture in chapter 14 of the king of Babylon's arrival in the world of the dead[23] is a chilling reminder that even the most powerful of rulers must face death and judgement!

READ CHAPTERS 24–27: THE ISAIAH APOCALYPSE

Isaiah now moves from the stage of world history to speak of events of *cosmic* significance. These chapters are sometimes called the *Isaiah Apocalypse*. They are an excellent example of the way the prophet looks into the future and sees the whole of time stretching out in front of him in one great panoramic view. In these chapters, he speaks of the coming judgement on Jerusalem and of the return from exile and rebuilding of the city. He also looks right forward to the new Jerusalem of the messianic age. In chapter 24 the nations of the world will tremble under a cloud of darkness. In chapter 25 the nations gather for a banquet in the new Jerusalem where even death will be destroyed for ever[24].

There are only a few places in the Old Testament where there is explicit reference to the resurrection of the faithful. The words of Isaiah 26:19 are clear:

> Your dead shall live, their corpses shall rise. O dwellers in the dust, awake and sing for joy! For your dew is a radiant dew, and the earth will give birth to those long dead.

READ CHAPTERS 28–39: FURTHER WARNINGS AND PROMISES

Chapters 28 –35 further develop the same alternation between judgement and hope, and the same intertwining of the near and distant future in the prophetic vision. The first main section of the book then concludes with a narrative account of Isaiah's interaction with Hezekiah at the time of the Assyrian siege of Jerusalem. These four chapters are virtually identical with the corresponding account in 2 Kings 18–20.

READ ISAIAH 40–55: 'COMFORT MY PEOPLE'

I will never forget the headline in the Belfast morning newspaper the day after the Good Friday agreement was signed: 'IT'S OVER!' Twenty-five years of trauma for the people of Northern Ireland were at an end – or so it was hoped. Older people in Britain will have similar recollections of the headlines on VE day and VJ day at the end of the second world war.

The opening words of Isaiah 40 are a declaration to a long-suffering people that it's over:

> Comfort, O comfort my people, says your God. Speak tenderly to Jerusalem, and cry to her that she has served her term, that her penalty is paid, that she has received from the LORD's hand double for all her sins (Isa 40:1,2).

It is at this point that the ethos of the book changes dramatically. The emphasis has been on the coming judgement for Judah and Jerusalem. Now the message is addressed to the generation who had already suffered the destruction of Jerusalem and the trauma of exile. The accent is now on hope, comfort and forgiveness. These chapters are not terse prophecies of judgement as before but a collection of moving poems which develop the themes of restoration and joy.

There is an emphasis on the power and sovereignty of Yahweh as controller of the destiny of nations and empires. The gods of the nations are not gods at all. It is hard for us to comprehend the boldness of this claim; that the God of a tiny vanquished nation is in fact the one true all-powerful God! He is not just the God of Israel, but the creator and sustainer of the universe, the one who shapes the future.

Israelite faith must have been shaken to the core by the destruction of Jerusalem and by the humiliation of exile. Did it mean that Yahweh had not been powerful enough to save them? Or did it mean that Yahweh had abandoned them and would take some other nation as his chosen people? How hard it must have been even for the most faithful to cling to the belief that Yahweh was indeed sovereign over all nations, that he had not abandoned Israel, and that the hoped-for restoration would come.

the God of a tiny vanquished nation is in fact the creator and sustainer of the universe

These prophecies were part of the means by which God rebuilt the faith of the people and enabled them to cling to their belief in Yahweh's power in the face of ridicule from the Babylonians. Across the centuries, Isaiah's words have brought comfort to countless suffering peoples who have placed their faith in Yahweh, the God of the Hebrew slaves, the God of the Babylonian exiles, the all-powerful God of hope and comfort.

The ridicule of the Babylonians against the faith of the Jews is turned on its head by the prophet's scathing condemnation of idol worship and false religion. For the Israelites to believe that their God was the Sovereign of the universe might seem an absurdity to outsiders, but it was nothing to the absurdity of the idolatry of the Babylonians! Look, for example, at 44:9–20 where the makers of idols are ridiculed.

Cyrus, the Persian emperor, eventually overthrew the Babylonian Empire in 539 BC. The Babylonians had ruled by a regime of terror and coercion; but it was the policy of the Persian emperor to encourage the loyalty and affection of conquered peoples by a liberal regime. Almost immediately Cyrus issued a decree allowing the Jews to go home; and he even provided for the rebuilding of the Temple out of the imperial exchequer. Isaiah declares that Cyrus, the great emperor, is acting as Yahweh's servant, Yahweh's agent[25]! Again, it is hard for us to comprehend the magnitude of Isaiah's claim that the ruler of the world's most powerful empire was no more than a puppet in Yahweh's hands!

The servant songs

Among the best known passages in Isaiah is chapter 53 which speaks of the servant of Yahweh who will suffer for the sins of others. This passage found its ultimate fulfilment in the sufferings and death of Jesus Christ. There are many expressions and phrases in this chapter which point us to the crucifixion scene.

This passage is one of several poems which speak of Yahweh's suffering servant[26]. Sometimes the suffering servant represents Israel as a nation. Sometimes the servant is the faithful remnant of Israel. Sometimes the servant is an individual, perhaps even the prophet himself.

The point is, that whoever is the servant of Yahweh can expect to suffer for the sake of others. At times Israel as a whole had suffered as part of the outworking of Yahweh's purposes for the nations. At times it was the faithful remnant within Israel who had suffered along with the guilty. The faithful prophet would find rejection, abuse, or even martyrdom. In chapter 53, the prophet develops this theme to its logical conclusion – the ultimate servant of Yahweh will suffer ultimately – and will do so for the sins of others.

The Jews did not equate the suffering servant of Isaiah 53 with the Messiah, for they expected the Messiah to be a powerful, reigning king. It was Jesus himself who took the role of a *suffering* Messiah and interpreted his sufferings and death as the fulfilment of Isaiah's words[27].

READ ISAIAH 56–66: 'SOON MY SALVATION WILL COME'

The scene has changed again. We are back in Jerusalem. The exile is over. The small band of Jews who have returned are struggling to re-build their nation and their faith.

Chapter 56 opens with a reminder that the community of Yahweh's people is not confined to Israelites alone. Right from the time when the 'mixed rabble' left Egypt, it has always been possible for foreigners to be adopted into the community of God's people. But Isaiah now takes this further – for the new Temple in Jerusalem will be called a 'house of prayer for all peoples' (v 7). Sadly, we find in these verses that the people have slipped back into their old ways. Idolatry is widespread and social justice is neglected. As so often in the Old Testament story, the people are allowed a fresh start, a new beginning, but they cannot, by their own efforts, make themselves worthy of a holy God.

Sabbath is mentioned several times in these chapters. In the exile period, sabbath had become one of the marks which distinguished the Jews from other peoples in the empire. Keeping the sabbath was a means of demonstrating allegiance to Yahweh. Sabbath, of course, should not be seen in isolation. Jesus was later to be scathing of a legalistic sabbath with no real love for God or for neighbour. Similarly Isaiah says of fasting:

> Is not this the fast that I choose:
>   to loose the bonds of injustice,
>   to undo the thongs of the yoke,
> to let the oppressed go free,
>   and to break every yoke?
> Is it not to share your bread with the hungry,
>   and bring the homeless poor into your house;
> when you see the naked, to cover them? (58:6,7)[28]

There is a similar emphasis in chapter 61 – the words which Jesus proclaimed as the purpose of his ministry in the synagogue of Nazareth:

> The spirit of the Lord GOD is upon me,
>   because the LORD has anointed me;
> he has sent me to bring good news to the oppressed,
>   to bind up the broken-hearted,
> to proclaim liberty to the captives,
>   and release to the prisoners;
> to proclaim the year of the LORD's favour ... (61:1,2)[29] .

In these chapters, the prophet often lifts his eyes beyond the immediate horizon to speak of the ultimate fulfilment of his message. In chapter 65 he speaks of a new heaven and a new earth, with a new Jerusalem where there will be no sadness or weeping – words taken up and developed in Revelation 21.

Summary of the main themes in Isaiah

Above all else the book of Isaiah speaks of the holiness and sovereignty of Yahweh. He is proclaimed as controller of the destiny of all nations and as the one who holds the future of the whole world.

From God's holiness flows his concern for social justice and his judgement on Judah and Jerusalem for their neglect of his Law. But God is also the God of forgiveness and mercy, the God who will allow a fresh start, a new beginning. Isaiah has a clear vision of Israel's role in bringing God's blessing to *all* the nations.

More than any other Old Testament book Isaiah looks forward to the messianic age – to the birth and death of Jesus, to the new Jerusalem, and to Yahweh's kingly rule of peace and justice. Isaiah proclaims a messianic king who is also the suffering servant, 'wounded for our transgressions'.

It has rightly been said that all the main themes of the Bible, Old Testament and New Testament alike, are to be found in this great book.

6.4 THE REMAINING PROPHETIC BOOKS

Only a brief survey of the other prophetic books can be given here, but I hope you will find the opportunity to read through these books also.

Jeremiah

Jeremiah is the most emotional of all the prophetic books. He speaks movingly of the suffering he personally endured because of his calling as a prophet. He deeply loved his people and he hated the task of pronouncing judgement on them. However, the word of Yahweh was like a fire deep within him: he could not keep it back.

Jeremiah was born in the town of Anathoth, the home of the descendants of Abiathar, the priest, who had been expelled from Jerusalem by Solomon. Abiathar's ancestors had once been the guardians of the ark of the covenant. Jeremiah may himself have been a descendant of Abiathar. He was certainly steeped in the ancient covenant traditions of Israel. He was also familiar with the ministry of the northern prophet, Hosea.

Jeremiah's ministry belonged to the final years of the kingdom of Judah. He not only foretold but also witnessed and endured the destruction of Jerusalem in 586 BC. Because he proclaimed the Babylonian invasion as a judgement from God, he was denounced as a traitor to his own people. Indeed he would have been executed for treason had it not been pointed out that Micah had previously foretold doom for Jerusalem[30].

Unlike Isaiah, who came from within the Jerusalem 'establishment', Jeremiah's background was similar to that of Hosea, Amos and Micah, who had proclaimed the traditional Mosaic Yahwism still very much alive in Judah and Israel.

During Jeremiah's time, the godly King Josiah had found the book of the Law in the Temple. Josiah's reformation (like that of Hezekiah before him) was not just about abolishing foreign religion. It was about bringing together the Mosaic traditions, which had been preserved in Israel and Judah, and the Davidic traditions which had been the focus of Jerusalem and Temple. There were at times great tensions between these two streams of tradition; and, like many a bridge-builder, Jeremiah found himself under attack from both sides. The people of his home town in particular rejected him because of his support for Josiah's policy of centralising worship in Jerusalem.

Most of the book of Jeremiah is in the first person. It is the prophet's autobiography, in which he records the main events in his career, the main themes of his preaching, and his own personal feelings and reactions. Jeremiah had a disciple and secretary called Baruch to whom he dictated much of his message and who may have edited and arranged the book after his death. Before reading the book you will find it helpful to read 2 Kings 22–25, to become familiar with the historical background.

The introductory chapter of Jeremiah tells the story of the prophet's call. He was perhaps the most reluctant of all the prophets.

The first main section (chapters 2–25) gives a thematic (not chronological) summary of the prophet's preaching across the last half century of the kingdom of Judah. He ministered during the reign of King Josiah, through the apostate reign of Jehoiakim, and through the final crisis years leading up to the catastrophe in 586. Most of these prophecies are in poetic form.

The second main section of the book consists of chapters 26–45. It is a largely prose account of significant events across the prophet's career. Like Amos and Isaiah, Jeremiah proclaims prophecies against foreign nations (chapters 46–51). Chapter 52 recounts the destruction of Jerusalem.

Jeremiah reiterates the prophetic theme of judgement on the nation's lack of social justice. His message, however, is not only of judgement. He specifically promises that there will be a return from captivity after seventy years (25:11,12).

Perhaps the greatest flash of insight and inspiration which came to Jeremiah is recorded in chapter 31. Jeremiah despairs that the covenant of Yahweh with Israel could ever be made to work. God being God, how could he fail; man being man how could God succeed? Jeremiah proclaims that there will be a *new covenant*, which will be significantly different from the old:

> But this is the covenant that I will make with the house of Israel after those days, says the LORD: I will put my law within them, and I will write it on their hearts; and I will be their God, and they shall be my people. No longer shall they teach one another, or say to each other, 'Know the LORD,' for they shall all know me, from the least of them to the greatest, says the LORD; for I will forgive their iniquity, and remember their sin no more (31:33,34).

This new covenant is of course the New Testament gospel in Jesus Christ!

Ezekiel

If Jeremiah is the most emotional of the prophetic books, Ezekiel is undoubtedly the most puzzling. He has been described as a man of deep faith and vivid imagination. Much of his message is conveyed through symbolic visions and drama.

Ezekiel ministered during the period immediately before and after the destruction of Jerusalem in 586 BC. He probably was among the leading citizens of Jerusalem who had been transported to Babylon in 597 BC. His message was from the vantage point of Babylon and of exile. He was contemporary with Jeremiah, but the two may never have met.

Ezekiel emphasises the need for inner renewal of mind and spirit

The first three chapters of the book are devoted to the mysterious account of Ezekiel's call. This is followed by the first main section (chapters 4–24), which contains messages of judgement addressed back to the people of Jerusalem from Babylon. Next come Ezekiel's judgements on foreign nations (chapters 25–32).

From chapter 33 onwards, the dominant theme moves from judgement to promise. This section includes the well-known vision of the coming-to-life of the valley of dry bones (chapter 37); and also the apocalyptic vision of the defeat of the enemies of God's people (symbolised as Gog and Magog).

The final section of Ezekiel (chapters 40–48) gives a detailed description of the Temple which is to be rebuilt in Jerusalem. This passage not only represents Ezekiel's vision for a future earthly Jerusalem community, focused on the Temple, it also looks forward to the new Jerusalem hinted at by Isaiah and later foretold in Revelation.

Throughout the book, Ezekiel emphasises the need for inner renewal of mind and spirit. Individuals must take responsibility for the consequences of their own actions. As a man of priestly background, Ezekiel had a special interest in the Temple as symbolic of Yahweh's sovereignty and holiness. He proclaimed a vision and hope for the renewal of the nation, looking forward to the day when Jesus would come as the Shepherd of the sheep and then to the new Jerusalem of Jesus' Second Coming.

Daniel

Daniel has probably engendered more debate than any other Old Testament book! Scholars have long discussed questions of the date and authorship. Christians of all traditions have debated the meaning of the puzzling visions which occupy the second half of the book. Some of the most fantastic end-of-the-world predictions have arisen from the book of Daniel.

It is interesting that Daniel is not regarded by the Jews as one of the *prophetic* books, but as one of the later writings. It is certainly different from the other prophetic books; and is often described as *apocalyptic*.

The book is set in the period of the exile of the Jews, under the Babylonian and Persian empires. The stories of the first six chapters are well known and loved by people of all ages, including the fiery furnace and the lions' den. Daniel and his friends are vindicated by God for their stand against the false religion of the pagan empires. The book also testifies to the way in which Jews were able to reach high office in those empires and to be used by God in those positions.

The remaining chapters (7–12) contain Daniel's visions which symbolically predict the rise and fall of successive world empires, followed by the ultimate vindication of God's people. Scholars have disagreed over the exact identification of Daniel's vision with particular historical empires (such as Babylon, Persia, Greece and Rome) but the overall thrust is clear.

The best known passage from Daniel's prophetic visions is in chapter 7, where Daniel sees 'one like a Son of Man' coming on the clouds of heaven to be presented to the 'Ancient of Days'. This messianic passage links closely with Jesus' description of himself as the 'Son of Man' who will one day come to gather his people from all over the world[31].

The Book of the Twelve

The twelve books from Hosea to Malachi are traditionally known as the Book of the Twelve Minor Prophets. However, each of the books is complete in itself, and the books come from widely differing periods. We have already looked at **Hosea**, **Amos** and **Micah**; prophets who ministered in Israel and Judah during the monarchy years.

Zephaniah (like Isaiah) was from Jerusalem and he ministered i the early years of King Josiah. He may well have been one of thos who guided Josiah in his boyhood days (Josiah had become king a the age of eight); and he was seemingly influential in bringing abou Josiah's reformation. He would have been contemporary with th earlier years of Jeremiah.

Habakkuk was a contemporary of Jeremiah's later year preaching in the last days of Judah and Jerusalem, just before 586 B The people were complaining that it was unjust of God to allow th cruel Babylonians to conquer peoples who were less unrighteou than the Babylonians themselves! Habakkuk assures them that Go will work justice in the end. His words in 2:4 are another of the cle references in the Old Testament to life after death. The book enc with a psalm, which summarises Habakkuk's faith and vision for th future.

The short book of **Obadiah** may belong to the period of th northern monarchy – if it is to be associated with the Obadiah wh remained faithful in Jezebel's time[32]. However, the subject matter the book suggests a later prophet of the same name. He declar Yahweh's judgement on Edom, Israel's age-old enemy, to the sout east of Judah, after they had taken advantage of the destruction Jerusalem to loot the city and to aid and abet the invader.

The books of **Haggai** and **Zechariah** belong to a later perio after the Jews have been allowed to return to Jerusalem. It will helpful to read Ezra chapters 1–6 as background to these books. T small band of 'returnees' to Jerusalem had struggled to rebuild t city and to re-establish a community of faith in the face of hardsh and opposition. Morale was at low ebb, but with the encourageme of God's prophets a new beginning is made.

Haggai encourages the people to knuckle down and to get c with the job of rebuilding the Temple, which was still lying in rui twenty years or so after the return. Without this demonstration allegiance to Yahweh, the people cannot expect his blessing.

Zechariah gives similar words of exhortation to the people of l day; but he also looks to the far future. Like Isaiah he sees ti spread before him, stretching forward to the messianic age a indeed to the final judgement.

The book of **Jonah** is quite unlike any of the other prophe books. It is the story of Jonah's reluctance to preach God's messa to Nineveh, the capital of the Assyrian Empire – the empire whi had persecuted both Israel and Judah for generations and which w responsible for the destruction of the northern kingdom in 722 BC. The book proclaims Yahweh as God of all the nations who would prefer to save and forgive his enemies rather than punish and destroy them.

The stories of the shipwreck and the 'big fish' capture our imagination; but the events at the end of the story are the real punchline of this book. The repentance of the Ninevites was a far greater miracle than the big fish episode! It is always hard for people to contemplate that their traditional enemies might repent and find God's forgiveness and blessing.

In Jonah himself we have a fascinating insight into human nature, especially in the last chapter, in which this God-fearing man struggles to come to terms with God's will. In Jonah we may well see ourselves!

Some people believe the Jonah story to be more of a parable rather than a historical account; a 'what if' story to make readers think how they themselves might react if they were put in Jonah's shoes. Others believe strongly that the book should be understood as a factual story.

I for one have no problem in believing in the miracles which the book describes! However, one reason for regarding Jonah as a parable is that there is no hint elsewhere in the Old Testament of any repentance by the Ninevites; and the short prophetic book of **Nahum** celebrates the eventual destruction of Nineveh by the Babylonians around 605 BC, as God's punishment on a cruel and unrepentant nation.

The prophet **Joel** is hard to date. Most scholars believe it describes events in the Persian Empire period. The book describes a devastating invasion of locusts. In vivid poetic language the onward march of the locust army is portrayed. Try reading chapter 2 aloud and you will sense the power of the poetry!

Joel interprets this locust invasion as a warning of the Day of Yahweh, when God will intervene in judgement on the nation. However, God is also the God who saves and restores. Many Jews and Christians across the centuries, who have looked back on lost or wasted years in their lives, have found comfort and hope in the words of Joel: 'I will restore to you the years which the swarming locust has eaten ...' (2:25, RSV).

The book of **Malachi** is the final book of the Old Testament (as the books are arranged in our English Bibles). It also belongs to the Persian period, after the time of Ezra and Nehemiah, when affluence and corruption have again set in among the elite and undermined the faith of the people. They are even bringing lame and stolen animals for Temple sacrifices! Yet again God's covenant Law is being forgotten. So much has changed historically across the centuries since the events in Genesis at the beginning of the Old Testament story, and yet so little has changed: human nature is still the same as ever!

In chapters 3 and 4, Malachi brings the Old Testament to a close by proclaiming the future messenger, the second Elijah[33], who will pave the way for the new covenant in Jesus Christ. The New Testament points to the fulfilment of Malachi's prophecy in the person of John the Baptist[34].

The ultimate fulfilment of prophecy

Throughout all the prophetic books we find the parallel themes of judgement and promise. The prophets look forward to the coming of Jesus Christ as God's 'infinite' Messiah in whom both judgement and promise are resolved; in the new covenant, in the messianic age, in the New Jerusalem and in Yahweh's eternal rule of justice and peace.

Endnotes

1   1 Samuel 10:25-27

2   Such as the reassurance given to King Hezekiah by the prophet Isaiah during the siege of Jerusalem. See 2 Kings 19.

3   Such as Elijah's rebuke of King Ahab after the murder of Naboth. See 1 Kings 21:17-29.

4   1 Kings 22

5   1 Kings 18

6   See, for example, the words of Amaziah, the priest of Bethel, in Amos 7:12.

7   It is not clear whether this means that Hosea was to marry a woman who was already a prostitute or that the woman he was to marry would eventually become unfaithful to him.

8   See 1 Kings 21.

9   However, there are some problems with this interpretation. It would in fact have been illegal for Hosea to divorce his wife and then remarry her again – according to Deuteronomy 24:1-4. Some scholars therefore maintain that chapter 3 does not refer to a second marriage at all, but gives a first-person account, in Hosea's words, of the original marriage to Gomer already described by the narrator in chapter 1. Others take the alternative view that in chapter 3 Hosea is told to enter into a second marriage with a different woman, who will also be unfaithful.

0 Hosea 6:6. These words are are quoted twice by Jesus, in Matthew 9:13 and 12:7. They are reminiscent of Samuel's earlier words to Saul in 1 Samuel 15:22.

1 You will remember that in the book of Ruth *hesed* was a key word for the inter-personal relationships which Yahweh expects of his people.

2 In the opening verses of chapter 7, for example, Micah refers to the fact that the hungry cannot find any gleanings in the vineyards or fig groves – as the law required.

3 See Micah 3:12. Jeremiah was later nearly put to death for suggesting that Yahweh would destroy his chosen city; and he was spared only because someone remembered that Micah had already foretold such a disaster. See Jeremiah 26: 16–24.

4 Isaiah 9:6 (see also vs 2,7)

5 Isaiah 53:5

6 Isaiah 61:1,2, quoted by Jesus in Luke 4:16-20

7 Isaiah 11:6–9

8 See Isaiah 44:28 and 45:1,13

9 See, for example, Matthew 8:17

0 See his story in 2 Chronicles 26.

1 The Assyrians had, of course, destroyed the northern kingdom. But Hezekiah was later able to extend his rule over those who were left in the devastated northern territory.

2 Isaiah 13:17-22; 21:1-10

3 Isaiah 14:3–21

4 Isaiah 25: 8. Also Revelation 21.

5 See Isaiah 44:28–45:8.

6 Isaiah 49:1-6; 50:4-9; 52:13-15

7 See Mark 10:45 and Luke 22:37.

8 These words were surely in Jesus' mind when he told the parable of the sheep and the goats (Matt 25:31–46).

9 See Luke 4:18,19

0 See Jeremiah 26.

1 See Matthew 24:29–31

2 See 1 Kings 18.

3 Malachi 3:1; 4:5

4 See Luke 1:17; Matthew 11:10–15.

Part Seven

Old Testament Theology

Covenant

When an architect draws plans for a new building, he provides a number of 'cross sections', which make it possible to visualise the overall shape of the building from a number of angles.

Old Testament theology seeks to discover the *overall* message of the Old Testament and to relate the Old Testament to the New. One way of doing this is to take key themes, and trace them across the Bible as a whole.

One major theme is that of *covenant*. *Covenant* and *testament* have the same meaning, so covenant is clearly an important 'cross section' which can be traced through both Testaments.

The Old Testament story is built around a series of *covenants*. Yahweh first entered into a covenant with Noah and the whole human race, promising never again to destroy the world by means of a flood[1]. God would find an alternative way of dealing with the sinfulness of humankind. The stage was thus set for the whole process of 'salvation history'.

In the covenant with Abraham, God promised that Abraham would be the father of a great nation, which would occupy the Promised Land of Canaan. He also promised that through Abraham's 'seed' all the nations of the world would be blessed[2]. This was a clear pointer to the future Messiah. Next, came the covenant in the time of Moses. At Mount Sinai, God entered into a covenant with the people of Israel as a whole. They were to become his 'treasured possession out of all the peoples'[3].

The covenant with Abraham had been largely unconditional. However, the covenant at Mount Sinai introduced a major conditional element – the Ten Commandments and rest of the covenant **the Old Testament story is built around a series of covenants** Law. The people would enjoy God's blessing in the Promised Land but only so long as they kept his Law. This covenant Law was the basis of the tribal confederation of Israel, founded by Joshua[4]. It was to be the basis for a new egalitarian society, radically different from anything else in the Ancient Near East. Covenant Law was 'bottom up', with an emphasis on the rights of the poor and underprivileged, rather than the rich and powerful. However, Judges shows how quickly the nation degenerated; and there is little evidence of any serious attempt to implement covenant Law during the period of the monarchy.

The covenant with King David and his descendants was the next significant development. David was promised an everlasting dynasty on the throne in Jerusalem. The king in Jerusalem was even referred to as Yahweh's 'son'[5]. Out of this covenant developed the Messianic hope. Isaiah, for example, looked forward to a divine Messiah, descended from David, who would be the ultimate fulfilment of the covenant with David[6]. The Davidic covenant was not, of course, intended to replace the existing covenant established at Mount Sinai. The two were to be complementary. However, in Jerusalem there was a tendency for the Davidic covenant to dominate. Covenant Law was forgotten.

The Prophets, however, judged the nation (both north and south) by the standards of Covenant Law, castigating in particular the lack of social justice. They warned of Yahweh's judgement. Tragically, these warnings went unheeded. The northern kingdom was destroyed in 722 BC. In the south, the reformations of Hezekiah and Josiah were attempts to restore the covenant relationship between with Yahweh. But it was too little too late; and the destruction of Jerusalem in 586 BC had become inevitable.

Each of the individual covenants with Noah, Abraham, Moses, and David was a distinctive stage in the overarching covenant relationship between Yahweh and his people. It was Jeremiah who was the first to speak of a *new* covenant. As he contemplated the fate of Jerusalem, he realised that the old covenant could never succeed because of the inevitability of human sinfulness. And so he declared:

> The days are surely coming, says the LORD, when I will make a new covenant with the house of Israel and the house of Judah. It will not be like the covenant that I made with their ancestors when I took them by the hand to bring them out of the land of Egypt. ... But this is the covenant that I will make with the house of Israel after those days, says the LORD: I will put my law within them, and I will write it on their hearts; and I will be their God, and they shall be my people (Jeremiah 31:31–33).

The new covenant which Jeremiah foretold was, of course, the New Testament gospel. Other prophets also looked forward to this new era, for example, the well known prophecy of Joel, which was fulfilled on the day of Pentecost:

> 'Then afterwards I will pour out my spirit on all flesh; your sons and your daughters shall prophesy, your old men shall dream dreams, and your young men shall see visions. ... Then everyone who calls on the name of the LORD shall be saved' (Joel 2:28–32).

The New Testament, with its promise of eternal salvation, is in one sense fundamentally different from the old covenant. No longer are we looking for an earthly Promised Land. Yet the whole story of salvation history through both Testaments is nonetheless a unity. The story of redemption begins with Noah. Paul writes that as Christians we are spiritual descendants of Abraham and heirs to the promises made to Abraham[7]. In that same passage Paul also writes of the continuing relevance for Christians of the Law of the Sinai covenant. The promises made in the Davidic covenant find their fulfilment in Jesus, who was both Son of David and Son of God. The old covenant was essential preparation for the new. The New Testament is the fulfilment of the old. (Paul expands on this topic in Hebrews 8.)

Hesed – covenant love

The Hebrew word *hesed* is an important word in the context of covenant. It is translated 'steadfast love' or 'covenant loyalty' or 'faithfulness'. It implies love, commitment and a willingness to go the second mile in our relationships with one another. God does *hesed* in his faithfulness to his covenant promises, despite the unfaithfulness (or lack of *hesed*) of the people in return. Covenant people should do *hesed* by one another, an important theme in the book of Ruth. God's people should do *hesed* by the poor and disadvantaged, an important principle underlying the covenant Law. Much of the teaching in Jesus' Sermon on the Mount could be summed up by this Old Testament word.

Messiah

Another obvious theme to trace through both Testaments is *Messiah*. Several distinct strands of Old Testament teaching are woven together in the New Testament concept of the Messiah. There are allusions to the messianic theme right from the earliest chapters of Genesis. After the sin of Adam and Eve, God speaks of a descendant of Eve who will one day crush the serpent underfoot; a pointer to the final defeat of Satan by Jesus[8]. The 'seed' of Abraham through whom blessing will come to all the nations is interpreted in the New Testament as fulfilled by Jesus[9].

The actual Hebrew word 'messiah' is first used of Aaron and the Israelite priests. The word means 'anointed'. At the time of their consecration, the priests were anointed with oil as a sign that they were set apart by Yahweh for the sacred office. This was a pointer to the priestly role of Jesus who offered himself on the cross as a once-and-for all sacrifice for sin. You will remember also that the writer to the Hebrews perceived Jesus to be the ultimate fulfilment of the priesthood of Melchizedek (the ancient priest-king of Jerusalem)[10].

However, the most significant use of the word *messiah* in the Old Testament comes with the rise of the monarchy. The king was 'Yahweh's Messiah' which means 'Yahweh's anointed'. Even Saul was described as 'Yahweh's anointed'[11]. However, the phrase acquired a fuller significance in the covenant with David. David was promised an *everlasting* dynasty; and (as we have seen) the king in Jerusalem was even referred to as Yahweh's son. The phrase *Yahweh's anointed* became a customary way of referring to the king (almost like the expression 'His Majesty' in English). This usage is common in the psalms[12].

The promises to David, however, were not completely fulfilled in David's descendants, many of whom strayed far from faithfulness to Yahweh's covenant. And so there gradually developed the hope of a future Messiah; that one day God would send one greater than David in whom the promises would be truly fulfilled. Isaiah looked forward to a divine descendant of David who would be far greater than any earthly king[13]. This hope is found in the Psalms as well as in the Prophets. In New Testament times, the Jews were still expecting a messiah, descended from David, who would be a powerful ruler and make them a great nation once again[14].

> the king was 'Yahweh's Messiah' which means 'Yahweh's anointed'

There are other themes in the Old Testament in which the actual word *messiah* is not used, but which the New Testament nonetheless interprets as belonging to the messianic hope. One such theme is the 'suffering servant' of Isaiah 53. The 'king on a cross' was a fulfilment of the hope of a *kingly* messiah, descended from David, combined with Isaiah's prophecy of the *suffering* servant.

Another Old Testament theme which the New Testament combines with the messianic concept is the mysterious figure of the 'one like a Son of Man' in Daniel 7. Jesus referred to himself both as Son of Man and as Son of God. The Daniel prophecy especially looks forward to the Second Coming of Jesus:

> To him was given dominion
>   and glory and kingship,
> that all peoples, nations and languages
>   should serve him.

> His dominion is an everlasting dominion
> that shall not pass away,
> and his kingship is one
> that shall never be destroyed (Daniel 7:14)[15].

Another theme which can be interwoven into this broad messianic concept is the 'redeemer' figure of Job's great cry of faith[16]. The personification of Wisdom in the book of Proverbs is another pointer to Jesus as the living Word of God through whom all things were created[17]. The picture in Revelation of the church as the bride of Christ draws on the imagery of the Song of Songs[18]. In fact, Jesus is seen as being the ultimate fulfilment of all of the main Old Testament roles. He is the 'second Adam'[19]. He gives a new interpretation of the Law of Moses. He is Prophet, Priest and King. He is the ultimate fulfilment of Old Testament wisdom.

When we speak of the Old Testament as fulfilled in Jesus, we do not *just* mean that Old Testament predictions have come true. A whole range of Old Testament themes and roles find their ultimate fulfilment in Jesus Christ.

The wisdom tradition

Many such themes can usefully be traced across the testaments. God's mighty acts in history, promise and fulfilment; judgement and forgiveness, creation and new creation, sin and redemption, and prophecy fulfilled are among the 'cross sections' which can illuminate the overall message of Scripture. Each one helps us to learn more of the overall message of the Bible.

The wisdom books are sometimes neglected in this process. By and large, they do not deal with covenant or salvation history or law or sacrifice. They are not primarily concerned with Yahweh's special choice of Israel, and in that sense they are 'universalist' in their outlook. They speak of the natural laws of the world which Yahweh has created, of the practicalities of daily living, and of the problems and suffering which we all must confront on the journey of life.

The wisdom books are as much a part of the Bible as any of the other Old Testament books, and we must take care not to neglect the wisdom themes in an overall summary of Old Testament theology. We have already noted that the *Messiah* cross section embraces Job's redeemer and the personification of wisdom in Proverbs.

We should not forget that the considerable extent to which the teaching of Jesus was anchored in the wisdom tradition. Matthew

6:25–34 could well be an exposition of Ecclesiastes. Much of the Jesus' teaching is proverb rather than law, and parables are a wisdom form of teaching. The undeserved suffering of Jesus is the ultimate answer to the undeserved suffering of Job. The universal nature of the wisdom literature is a reminder that God's blessing is ultimately for 'all the nations' and a pointer to the universal nature of the gospel. There are other books in the New Testament which owe much of their inspiration to Old Testament wisdom, especially the letter of James.

God's wisdom is very different from worldly wisdom. From the point of view of human wisdom, it makes no sense to go the second mile, to love your enemy, to give, to share, and to forgive seventy times seventy times. Yet Jesus taught that this was not only the *right* way to live but also the *best* way. Jesus expressed this in terms of the paradox: 'For those who want to save their life will lose it, and those who lose their life for my sake will save it' (Luke 9:24).

The kingship of God

The *kingship* or *sovereignty* of God is one of the most important themes which can be traced through the Old and New Testaments. From the beginning of Genesis, the sovereignty of Yahweh is proclaimed in creation, in judgement, and in blessing. The paradox of God's sovereignty and human free will is also brought out in those early chapters. God being God, how can he fail? Man being man how can God succeed? The whole long process of salvation history is the story of how the Sovereign God sought to deal with human sinfulness.

to speak of an earthly king at first seemed an affront

Israel was called to be a model nation of which Yahweh himself was King, to be a priestly kingdom and a holy nation[20]. The nation was to be governed by Yahweh's covenant Law. Every citizen was to be equal; and *hesed* was to be the underlying principle of all human relationships.

But how was the kingship of God actually to be implemented on earth? The days of the judges demonstrated the bizarre depths to which the people could sink without strong earthly leadership upholding Yahweh's Law. On the other hand, the book of Ruth was a demonstration of how it could be done when even women, widows, orphans and foreigners get their rights! Even to speak of an earthly king at first seemed an affront to the sovereignty of Yahweh; and the people's demand for a king 'like all the nations' was inevitably going to undermine their distinctiveness as the people of God.

Right from the time of the covenant with Abraham, Yahweh had foretold that kings would be descended from Abraham[21]; and the monarchy was, of course, the basis for the eventual messianic hope. Yet God is angry with the Israelites for their demand for a king, presumably because they are asking for an earthly monarchy for all the wrong reasons. Overall the monarchy was a failure despite the successes and achievements of individual kings. Having a king chosen by Yahweh did not result in the kingdom of God on earth.

much of the Old Testament is story, not concept

Jesus was the descendant of David, and the ultimate fulfilment of the promises made to the Davidic monarchy. Yet his was a very different kind of kingship from the military campaigns and the pomp and ceremony of the kings of old. The kingdom of God which Jesus proclaimed was a kingdom in which the greatest would be the servant of all[22].

The sovereignty of God is celebrated in the Psalms[23]. Job and Lamentations explore the question of how a sovereign God can allow suffering. Song of Songs can be understood as an allegory of the love of sovereign Yahweh for Israel.

There are few parts of the Old Testament message that cannot be related in some way to the theme of the kingship or sovereignty of Yahweh and the theme is one of the major bridges between the Testaments.

Old Testament theology is living and dynamic

Walter Brueggemann has recently published a new and radical approach to Old Testament theology[24]. Rather than tracing different themes through the Old Testament, Brueggemann likens the different biblical writers to *witnesses* in a courtroom. Each of them is giving *evidence* of their own particular experience of Yahweh's involvement in history and of his nature and purpose. Each Old Testament writer testifies to a different aspect of God's character and purpose. These many and varied witnesses together form the collective testimony of the people of God.

Many of the Old Testament characters, of course, were far from perfect in their behaviour or in their understanding of the will of God. Indeed, the Old Testament is full of the stories of men and women who were chosen and used by God despite their faults, not because of their virtues! Part of the task of the interpreter is therefore to *cross-examine* the witnesses.

We must probe and question Joshua and the early Israelites in their belief that God had called them to exterminate the Canaanites. We must cross-examine the psalmist who called for the babies of enemy nations to be smashed against a rock. We must challenge the kings in Jerusalem who departed so far from the implementation of Yahweh's covenant Law. We must cross-examine Job who comes so near to cursing God. There is something to be said for this approach – so long as the standard by which we cross-examine is the collective testimony of Scripture, and above all, the teaching of Jesus. Indeed often what we will be cross-examining is the traditional *interpretation* of Scripture rather than the biblical witness itself.

Brueggemann also emphasises the living and dynamic aspect of the Old Testament witness, and the often unpredictable nature of Yahweh's involvement in history. Yahweh often does the unexpected and often chooses and uses the most unlikely people for the fulfilment of his purposes.

The trouble with the cross-section approach is that it reduces the Old Testament to a collection of theological concepts (such as covenant, salvation, promise, redemption), when in fact so much of the Old Testament is *story*, not concept, and so much of the story is about Yahweh's dynamic interaction with individuals, with Israel, and indeed with all peoples.

The Old Testament witnesses speak out of personal encounter with Yahweh, who is the God of the Hebrews, the God of Israel, the God of Sinai, the God of all the nations. They write out of desperation and despair as well as out of joy and hope. They did not set out to produce a theological textbook but to bring us face-to-face with the living God.

The cross-section approach has tended to focus our attention on a narrow selection of passages and texts, which are often then considered out of their original context. That is perhaps why we tend not to read the Old Testament books as books – but only to know a text here and a story there.

By plotting cross-sections through the Old Testament, we can all too easily by-pass the problems, difficulties and challenges of much of the Old Testament witness. There are many passages which are hardly ever read, perhaps because they puzzle or even shock us. But this inevitably distorts our understanding of the books of which those passages form part, and undermines the challenge of the Old Testament message as a whole.

A cross section is only one way of looking at a building. Tracing key themes through the Bible undoubtedly contributes to our understanding the overall message of Scripture and I do not wish to underestimate the value of that approach. But it is not the only approach; and we should not neglect the vast array of other issues raised in the Old Testament which are still very much of practical relevance to us as Christians. That is why in this present book I have so strongly encouraged you to read the Old Testament books as books – right through from beginning to end.

We need to allow the Old Testament to engage with the issues which we actually face in the world of today, issues of social justice; of racism and sectarianism; of women's rights and gender roles; of poverty, oppression and undeserved suffering; of practical politics and of environmental and economic issues; of personal morality and of the suffering we may face if we belong to God's people. We are not always given the answers directly; but the Bible, by stirring our emotions as well as by informing our minds, can challenge and provoke us into thinking through such questions under the guidance of the Holy Spirit.

Do not misunderstand me. I am not seeking to undermine the fundamentals of the Gospel message, or to substitute a social gospel for the gospel of salvation and eternal life, which is the ultimate message of the whole of the Bible, Old and New Testaments alike. But those of us who are saved by the grace of Christ, and who form part of the community of faith, are called to do Christ's work in the world. The church is called to speak from God's word with a prophetic voice to governments and nations. There is much in the Old Testament to help us with this task.

The Old Testament is not *just* a repository of theological themes, it is a dynamic collection of living books through which Yahweh speaks into the situations and issues we face as Christians, both as individuals and as communities.

Endnotes

1   Genesis 6:18 and 9:9–17
2   Genesis 15:18 and 17:1–21
3   Exodus 19:5

4   See Joshua 24

5   2 Samuel 7:14. See also Psalm 2:7

6   See especially Isaiah 9:2,6,7

7   Galatians 3:29

8   Genesis 3:15

9   See Acts 3:25–26

10 See Genesis 14:18; Hebrews 5:7

11 See, for example, 1 Samuel 24:6.

12 Psalms 2:2; 18:50; 20:6; 28:8; 45:7; 84:9; 89:38; 132:10

13 Isaiah 9:2,6,7

14 In John 6:15, the people try to take Jesus and make him king.

15 See Matthew 24:30 and Revelation 11:15.

16 Job 19:25

17 Proverbs 8. See John 1:1–5.

18 See, for example, Revelation 19:7–9 and 21:9

19 See Hebrews 15:45–49

20 Exodus 19:6

21 See Genesis 17:6

22 See, for example, Matthew 20:25–28 and 23:11

23 See, for example, Psalms 10, 24, 29, 47, 93, 95, 96, 97, 98, and 99

24 Walter Brueggemann, *Theology of the Old Testament* (Fortress 1997).

Appendix
Old Testament Maps

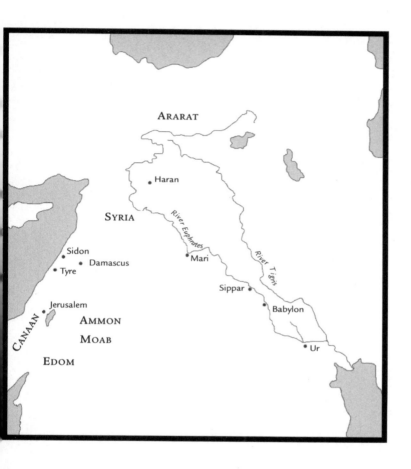

The ancient near east

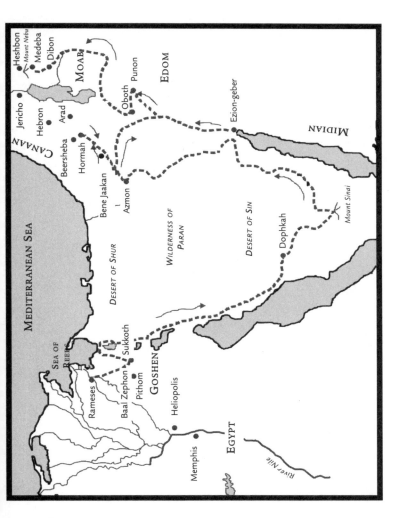

Possible
route of
the
Exodus

The Twelve Tribes of Israel

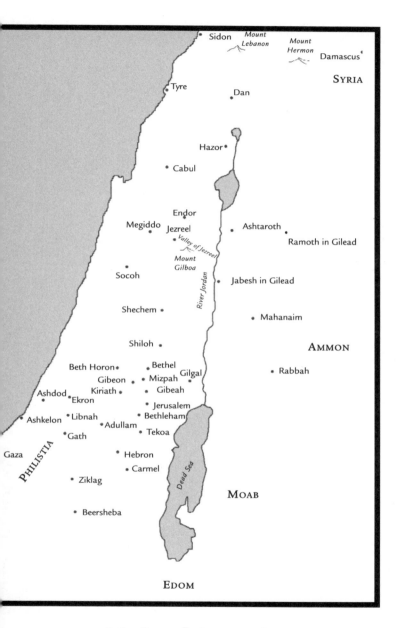

United Israel

Divided Israel